C000016304

SIX FOOT TWO
EYES OF BLUE

COLIN LESLIE

EMPIRE PUBLICATIONS
1 Newton Street, Manchester M1 1HW
© Colin Leslie 2019

ISBN: 978-1-909360-63-1

Front cover photo: Copyright Colorsport
Back cover: *Danny McGrain celebrating with John Blackley (No 14) as an exhausted Jim Holton peels off his Scottish jersey following a 2-0 win over England at Hampden in May 1974.* © *Eric McCowat*

CONTENTS

For Neal, Sally, Jay and Harrison

ACKNOWLEDGEMENTS

THIS BOOK WOULD never have been written without the permission and backing of the Holton family. From the moment of initial contact, Jan Holton has been supportive, enthusiastic and helpful. It has been a pleasure to meet the family – Jan, Neal, Rachael, Harrison, Sally and Jay – and I thank them all for their encouragement.

Special mention to all at Empire Publications for recognising the merit in sharing Jim's story and having such faith in the project – to mangle Feargal Sharkey's words, a good publisher these days is hard to find! Thanks to Jan Williamson for all the endless transcribing, and to renowned Manchester United fan and author Iain McCartney – one of the original fans of Big Jim who has not only been a font of Manchester United knowledge, but a huge source of help and encouragement.

Thanks also to all the people who have helped secure interviews or provided me with information, including Kevin Owen at Bangor City FC, Matt Maher at the *Express & Star*, Sean Mulligan at North Shields FC, Ed Fryatt, Ian Whitfield at Shrewsbury Town FC, Jim Brown and Dean Nelson of Coventry City Former Players Association, Jack Davidson, Lance Hardy for his Sunderland input, Plymstock School for putting me in touch with the Holtons; Roger Faulkner, Sue Jones, Terry Christian, Eamonn Holmes and all the Manchester United fans who have helped me via Twitter, Oliver Milne, Geoff Snape from West Bromwich Albion Former Players Association, Stephen Halliday, Alan Pattullo, Donald Walker and Graham Bean at *The Scotsman* newspaper, Daniel Nardiello and Greg Edmonds. Thanks to Ian Williamson for his proof-reading and Jim Divine for his creative input.

And a huge debt of gratitude to the interviewees, who spoke with such fondness about their memories of Jim: John Blackley, Andy Blair, Laurie Brown, Martin Buchan, Gary Campbell, Len

Cantello, Paddy Crerand, Tommy Docherty, Alex Forsyth, Gary Gillespie, Joe Jordan, John Hannah, Asa Hartford, John Hillan, Tommy Hutchison, Mike Jones, Denis Law, Lou Macari, Mick Martin, Jim McCalliog, Iain McCartney, Sammy McIlroy, Gordon McQueen, David Meek, Gordon Milne, Willie Morgan, Dr Greg Myers, Donato Nardiello, Bill Nuttall, Ally Robertson, Arnie Sidebottom, Alex Stepney, Garry Thompson, Ian Wallace, Ruth Williams Paul Cannell, Jimmy Rimmer and Dave Bradley.

THE GREATEST GUY I NEVER KNEW

"Six Foot Two, Eyes of Blue, big Jim Holton's after you."

THERE COULD BE only one title for this book. Every person interviewed – some, like Harry Gregg and Tommy Docherty well into their 80s when I talked to them - has either quoted or sung the words to me, proving it is one of the best known terrace anthems of all time.

West Ham fans used to sing their own version about Billy Bonds and Fulham did so in tribute to Ernie Howe but had it been copyrighted it would be the fans of Manchester United and Scotland who would be first in the queue to collect any royalties. The fact that big Jim had brown eyes is neither here nor there.

Some will even dispute that he stood six foot two but on a football pitch he was a giant, with a presence to match. It is especially cruel when someone larger than life is cut down in their prime, and so it proved for the much-loved Jim Holton. An undetected heart problem struck suddenly and fatally and robbed a wife of her husband and two teenage children of their father on 4 October, 1993. Jim was aged just 42.

I first heard Jim Holton's name in the school playground. I had never seen him play, didn't know who he was, but damn that song was catchy. I was born just a little too late to appreciate his folk hero status as a footballer. My obsession with Scotland and World Cups (yes, we did used to qualify for them on a regular basis) would start a few years later when Ally's Tartan Army carried then buried the hopes of a nation in Argentina in 1978.

A year after that cataclysmic experience, I would see Jim play in the flesh for the one and only time. It was Hibernian v Coventry City at Easter Road in the Skol Festival Trophy – a 'festival' it was not! In front of a few thousand bored supporters seeking a fix of football to get them through the summer, the teams ground out a 0-0 draw. My abiding memory is being mesmerised by Coventry

City's notorious chocolate brown away kit, although the scoreline suggests that defensively Holton was as impenetrable as ever.

So why write a book on Jim? As mentioned, my fascination with Scotland and the World Cup runs deep, a historic interest now sadly akin to a geologist poking around fossils. A previous biography I worked on focused on the fascinating life and career of another member of Scotland's 1974 squad, Erich Schaedler, who also died tragically young. It was during my research that the old playground song zapped back into my mind, and I made a mental note to discover whatever had happened to big Jim Holton of "Six Foot Two, Eyes of Blue" fame.

To learn that he had died so suddenly 25 years ago was a shock. The peaks and troughs of his career were also startling. The peaks saw him swept into the epicentre of the Tommy Docherty revolution at Manchester United, excel as a central figure in arguably Scotland's most gifted national team, and play in the company of Pele and Franz Beckenbauer in the North American Soccer League. The troughs saw him rejected from his first professional club West Brom, break his leg twice while at United, and eventually forced into retirement by tree trunk legs ravaged by thousands of thunderous tackles.

Away from the football pitch, people only have good words for Jim. Soon I would learn just how adored he was. How could a man so fearsome and fearless on the field be such a gentle giant and genial fellow as soon as his work was done? His family, friends, team-mates and admirers have been kind enough to tell me how, and I hope you agree by the end of the book that their testaments combine to deliver an intimate story of a wonderful character.

The old cliché that 'behind every great man lies a great woman' has never been truer in the case of the Holtons. Jan Holton has been a dream to work with for this author and I am delighted I can now call her a friend. The final chapter contains her heartbreaking account of the day Jim died. I don't mind admitting that I had tears streaming down my face when she shared with me her personal account of that day in 1993. I know myself that grief stays with you forever when you lose a loved one in such tragic circumstances, but so too do the feelings and memories you hold. I can assure you that a donation in Jim's memory will be made to the British Heart Foundation from the proceeds of this book.

Also, please spare a thought for many of Jim's peers, who have been living with dementia or Alzheimer's. I was shocked to discover just how many of Jim's former team-mates or opponents are affected by this condition, and – not meaning to sound too political – I hope in future we see more support offered to the growing number of footballers and their families who are struggling to cope.

It has been my privilege to write Jim's life story, and I am indebted to the Holton family for trusting me to do so. My only regret is that I never met the Big Man – the greatest guy I never knew.

A copy of this book will be placed by Jim Holton's final resting place at Canley Garden Cemetery, Coventry. I hope it raises one of those big, toothless smiles up there.

Colin Leslie

FOREWORD

By Jan Holton

SOME FAMOUS NAMES have contributed to this book, and I know all of them would have gladly written a foreword about Jim, so as his wife I am delighted to have the honour.

Those of you who remember Jim Holton will remember him as the rough, tough player on the pitch, who would tackle his own granny if he was asked. He was a Manchester United legend and a Scotland icon. He was loved too by fans of Shrewsbury Town, Sunderland and Coventry City. And of course, he had his very own song which followed him from pillar to post: Six foot two, eyes of blue, big Jim Holton's after you. The irony that he had twinkling brown eyes only made it better.

Supporters and team-mates have many wonderful memories of Jim's thundering tackles, occasional naughty red cards, and unforgettable goals. They remember his dressing room banter, his penchant for removing his false teeth and leaving them in inappropriate places, his mischievous sense of humour. They salute him as a dedicated and loyal footballer – the consummate professional.

At home though, he was simply Jim, my husband. To our two children Neal and Sally, he was just Dad.

Our lives were turned upside down when Jim was taken from us, suddenly and shockingly on 4 October, 1993. How could such a fit, strong man with such a zest for life be taken from us at the age of 42? It was a question that haunted me in the early days. But the reality is the ischaemic heart disease that caused Jim's heart attack, could have struck him down at any time. He could have died at the age of 6, 16 or 60. As much as I will always miss him, I am eternally grateful for the time that we did have together.

And what a character he was! From the moment he tumbled, a little worse for wear, at my feet in a Birmingham nightclub, me and this big, beautiful lump of a man from Lesmahagow were destined to be together. That night, I had no idea he was a footballer. He was just Jim.

We were only starry-eyed teenagers then, and we had no idea of the adventures that were ahead of us, but believe me it was quite a journey.

He picked himself up from the disappointment of being freed by his first professional club West Bromwich Albion to learn his craft under Harry Gregg, a lovely man, at Shrewsbury Town. We were married during his time there and had not long moved into our first home when his career suddenly went into overdrive. I knew there were clubs interested in him, but when he walked through the door and told me "I'm signing for Manchester United", I knew he was going to make it big.

And so he did. He was quickly adopted as the darling of Old Trafford, playing alongside Bobby Charlton, George Best and his childhood hero Denis Law. He became an international himself and starred for Scotland at the World Cup. He was a household name. And the greatest thing about it was that his personality didn't change one bit, he was still just Jim.

He was what you would call a real 'man's man'. What made me laugh was that if you put him in a room with more than two women at a time he would go all shy and fly into panic mode, and yet he could run out on to the pitch in front of 60,000 people and never think twice about it. When I pulled his leg about it he would shrug and say: "Och, you just blank it out. It's only noise!"

Stardom never went to Jim's head – how could it when he came from a humble place like Lesmahagow? I'm proud that throughout his career, whatever happened, he remained the same beautiful person. Not that everyone saw him that way. He got called some downright nasty names about his style of play, especially in his early days with Manchester United. People would say he would take out the man if he could not get the ball. But that was not the man that I knew and was married to. At home, he was the gentlest, softest man you could wish to meet.

He was also a good father and always provided for his children.

The kids didn't realise what he did, or who he was at the time – they were too young really. By the time his career was over they were still too young to appreciate how big a name he had been in football. He was just Dad.

Jim was immensely proud of his career, and rightly so. He had his share of knocks, including two broken legs, but he wasn't one for holding grudges. Journalists admired his dignity, honesty and humility and he never had a bad word to say about anyone. Unless it was a centre forward he was marking of course!

So often footballers struggle to fill the void when age or injuries force them to retire, but Jim was happy and content running our pubs in Coventry alongside me. We were quite the Jack & Vera of our day!

His time at Coventry City made him a hugely popular and respected figure locally and whenever Manchester United came to town bus-loads of fans would stop in to say hello to pay their respects and sing a few choruses of "Six Foot Two" for old times' sake.

Jim was the ultimate people person, as you will quickly discover reading the many stories and memories in this book. As well as his football achievements, there is a lot of content about his life with me and the kids, and I hope this will give you the whole picture of the man he was. It is clear he left an impression on people and lived his life true to his mantra: "It's nice to be nice."

One of the last memories I have of Jim is that a friend of ours, who had just had a little girl, dropped into the pub to visit. The baby was only around eight months old and big Jim Holton – the so-called scary giant who terrified so many centre forwards - did nothing but walk around with her in his arms for two hours, just talking away to her and making her laugh. He was such a big softy! I know he would have made a wonderful Grandad.

When my Grandson Jay recently went on a trip to Old Trafford there was a placard of his Grandad on the wall of the Stretford End – a striking portrait of Jim at the peak of his powers. We Holtons are close and, as a family, we are proud of everything Jim achieved at United, his other clubs, and in the dark blue of his beloved

Colin Leslie

Scotland. But mostly we celebrate and remember him as just Jim.
Enjoy the book, and if you don't know the song by now…

1: THE 'NOBODY WHO BECAME AN IDOL'

*"My spell with Manchester United was short-lived but it was good while
it lasted and I'll never forget those big-hearted supporters"*

Jim Holton

CRACK! It's the noise every footballer dreads hearing.
The victim sprawled on the turf is Jim Holton, unlikely
Manchester United hero and, until that moment,
seemingly indestructible. The date is 7th December, 1974, the time
a little after 3.15, the opponents are Sheffield Wednesday, the venue
is Hillsborough, and the atmosphere is foreboding.

As Sheffield Wednesday's combative midfielder Eric McMordie
protests his innocence, and United physio Laurie Brown and
trainer Tommy Cavanagh scramble on to the pitch to assess the
stricken Holton, United's Red Army – who have spent the past
four months tearing their way around the grim staging posts of the
Second Division – turn increasingly violent.

Until that moment, a routine win appears on the cards for
Tommy Docherty's top-of-the-table United. They lead 1-0, and
the Jim Holton-Martin Buchan axis looks as solid and dependable
as ever. But as Holton leaves the field on a stretcher, chaos descends
on and off the pitch.

With Holton gone and United's defence plunged into disarray,
Wednesday take full advantage and surge into a 3-1 half-time lead.
To rub salt into the wounds, the first two goals come from tame
set-plays sent speculatively into a penalty area the absent No 5
would have otherwise been patrolling with ease.

In the second half, United summon up some of the Jim Holton
spirit and the game eventually ends in a breathless 4-4 draw. The
headlines, however, are dominated by more sinister events. Scores
of pitch invaders, mounted police charges, a snooker ball and beer
bottle hurled at the home goalkeeper, 106 arrests and 51 people

hospitalised – 52 if you count Holton, a forlorn figure amid the convoy of injured bodies being transported to Sheffield Infirmary.

The Red Army don't know it yet, but the sight of a grimacing Holton stretchered from the field and disappearing up the tunnel, would be the last time their chosen favourite would wear a United shirt in a meaningful game. Never again in unison would thousands of Stretford Enders belt out the daddy of all terrace chants: "Six foot two, eyes of blue, big Jim Holton's after you."

Football is full of turning points, and in the extraordinary career of Jim Holton, this was huge.

Prior to that grey December afternoon in South Yorkshire, United manager Docherty was hailing the imposing defender he had plucked from obscurity as the finest central defender in the land. "Jim is the rock forwards perish on," he said, waxing lyrical about his giant stopper. "When he's around forwards can't even get into the penalty box. He is terrific both in the air and on the ground."

Under 'The Doc', Holton's confidence had soared to the same statuesque levels as his impressive physical frame. Just like the human body, however, confidence can take some punishing knocks.

Docherty was a manager who lived by the harsh doctrine that a player is only as good as his last game, and an injured player is no good at all. With his shattered right leg encased in plaster of Paris from toe to hip, Holton would find out that previous endeavours counted for little in his manager's ruthless quest to return United to the pinnacle of English football.

Holton's achievements until that point had been considerable. In a spectacular two-year trajectory of rapid ascent, he had gone from untested Third Division novice at Shrewsbury Town to valued team-mate of Manchester United's Holy Trinity of George Best, Bobby Charlton and Denis Law. All three would be gone within a year of Jim's arrival, for different reasons, but a vacuum had been left for United supporters to find a new icon, and Holton was the man who filled it.

Lifelong United supporter Iain McCartney, the author of many books on the club, explains why supporters took Holton to their hearts and kept him there.

"It wasn't just his size that made him stand out," says McCartney, "I think for me and countless others in the Stretford End, Scoreboard Paddock or whatever section of Old Trafford you stood in, it was Jim's wholehearted, take no prisoners attitude to the game. He was one of us. He wanted United to win every game no matter what.

"This was a United you have to remember, that had gone downhill rapidly since winning the European Cup on that memorable night at Wembley back in 1968. By 1973, United were liable to lose more games than they would win, so we needed someone of Jim's stature at the back. Someone who would get stuck in and let the opposition know he was there."

It was certainly a bedraggled, topsy-turvy period in the club's history. Despite the arrival of Docherty, and the wave of reinforcements he quickly brought in, United danced dangerously close to the relegation precipice during the 1972-73 season. The malaise had already set in before The Doc strode through the door, and even his considerable ability as a manager wasn't enough to arrest the slide. The writing was on the wall, and the next season United succumbed to gravity, Docherty unable to prevent this proudest of institutions free-falling into the Second Division.

Paradoxically, throughout this pain and turmoil, Holton's popularity rocketed. Supporters saw something of themselves in the hard, honest grafter willing to strain every sinew for the cause each time he pulled on the red No 5 jersey, particularly as he was willing to smash any opponent who got in his way. United were in decline and they knew it. They had to take a step back before they could go forward. The glory of 1968 had been and gone, and fans were in a state of alarm about how quickly fortunes were unravelling.

The great Sir Matt Busby – who, as manager, had secured the holy grail of the European Cup in 1968, a decade after the Munich Air Disaster - had been succeeded first by Wilf McGuinness and then disastrously by Frank O'Farrell. In a next throw of the dice Sir Matt, from his new position 'upstairs', had been instrumental

3

in bringing the dynamic Docherty to Old Trafford in December 1972. The new manager's brief was simple: restore pride and build a new side. But there was to be no quick-fix – the past, present and future collided and sparks flew. A major rebuilding job was needed and the rebirth of the club was unquestionably a medium to long-term project. Supporters steeled themselves for the reality of relegation to the Second Division, and loyally put their trust in The Doc to deliver them back to the Promised Land.

Showing togetherness in adversity was the only way United could meaningfully regroup and regenerate, and the club's vast Red Army were up for the fight – sometimes quite literally, as they travelled in their thousands the length and breadth of the country to support the team and ensure their exile to the Second Division was as brief as it possibly could be.

Rather than look back on that chastening Second Division experience with embarrassment, fans who embarked on those raucous trips to Blackpool, Cardiff, Orient and Millwall, instead look back on those expeditions with a great sense of sentiment and nostalgia. Yes, it was humbling for a club of United's reputation, but it was also a time when the supporters re-engaged with the players and got right behind the team. Docherty restored excitement, endeavour and a winning mentality, and while United attacked with all their might at one end of the pitch, Jim Holton – standing tall, his broad chest puffed out - embodied those qualities at the other end.

Holton had been the overwhelming choice for Player of the Year in the relegation season, a beacon in a blackout. He had the fastest-growing Fan Club at Old Trafford. He had earned 15 full Scotland caps. He had played and impressed in front of a global audience at the World Cup finals. He had just signed the longest contract in United's history. He had the world at his feet. And then he heard his right leg crack at Hillsborough.

Of course, football is a game full of ups and downs, and it hadn't all been praise and plaudits for Big Jim at United. There had been notoriety and a flurry of red cards, cautions and brushes with the Football Association's disciplinary committee. There had been distaste and sometimes downright hostility towards his aggressive style of play from the Press Box and from opponents and rival managers. He, like all those around him, had also been powerless to stop United suffering the ignominy of relegation.

But Holton stepped off the team bus at Hillsborough that day with a spring in his step. United were determined to right a wrong, sitting top of the league and bang on track to bounce back to the First Division with fresh purpose. Jim also boasted the proud personal record of never having played in a losing side that season. He loved the club and the fans, and like them he had placed his unwavering faith in Docherty.

The Doc would eventually steer United back on the path to glory, starting with the Second Division Championship title less than five months after that fateful 4-4 draw at Sheffield Wednesday. But as unthinkable as it was at the time – Hillsborough was the last time the manager would scribble the name 'Holton' on his team-sheet for a competitive match.

Far from being the beginning of the end for Jim Holton, it was more like the end of the beginning. A man as hard and resilient as Jim wasn't done with football, far from it, but his resolve was thoroughly examined. After Holton was scraped off the turf at Hillsborough, he then had to suffer nearly two years of setbacks and frustration, including a second leg break and a "million to one" freak knee ligament injury. Some setbacks were self-inflicted, however. Holton's recovery certainly wasn't helped when he tried to move his car with his entire leg in plaster, demolishing his garage and killing an unsuspecting pet hamster in the process. When he had his head screwed on and concentrated on more conventional methods of rehabilitation, he would return to full fitness and eventually find contentment again at Coventry City, via the extremes of Miami and Wearside.

But in club football it is Manchester United, undoubtedly, with whom Holton is synonymous. Reds of a certain age become animated when they hear his name and get sentimental when they hark back to that raw, rough and ready period in the club's history more than 40 years ago typified by Big Jim's playing style.

A poem written by United supporter Anne Williams, published in the Jim Holton Fan Club newsletter in 1975, typifies the esteem in which he was held. The final verse is particularly poignant and has stood the test of time. She wrote...

In the middle he stands quite renown
£80,000 from Shrewsbury Town
His name is known from Brazil to Bolton
It is of course our own Jim Holton

There he stands in his bright red shirt
Many a forward bites the dirt
Opposing attackers are heard to cackle
Shirking in fear of a Holton tackle

Of the great centre halves he's one of the band
Whether for United or his native Scotland
Jim Holton is big and strong
With his fans he can't go wrong

Manchester United will always thrive
As long as big Jim's at number five
Sometimes he abandons his defensive role
Goes up for a corner and heads a goal

All praises to you Jim, we will sing
Because to us you are our king
When your career is over and you have gone
The memory of you will still linger on.

Dovetailing with heroic displays in Willie Ormond's celebrated Scotland side, Holton's spell at Old Trafford represented the zenith of his football career. The speed with which he rose to prominence was startling, the way he remains fabled in the club's folklore equally so.

The man himself would happily have stayed with United his entire career, had Docherty not decreed otherwise, but when he had hung up his boots he reflected: "I had a fair old share of setbacks but I don't look back with any bitterness. I prefer to think about the great moments. My spell with United was short-lived but it was good while it lasted and I'll never forget those big-hearted supporters."

Iain McCartney sums up his enduring appeal. "Jim is perhaps not one of the United all-time greats in many people's eyes. Many who go to Old Trafford today will not even know of him. But to me he is an unforgettable figure in United's history. Once seen never forgotten, that was Jim Holton."

Physically, Holton was certainly an unmistakable figure. With thick shoulder-length dark hair, square chin, broad shoulders and a powerful torso, he would have made the perfect William Wallace, before a vertically-challenged Australian came along to claim the part in Braveheart years later. His thighs were like twin oaks, and he joked that his thinner calf muscles were built that way for maximum speed. With his dentures removed, he looked even more imposing, although referees would occasionally associate his wild appearance with villainy.

The Premier League is now packed with athletic players who are 6ft 2 plus, but in the 1970s Holton literally stood head and shoulders above many of his peers. The sheer power and size of the man is obvious when sifting through footage of matches he played in the 1970s.

Holton's style of play was uncomplicated rather than basic. He had skill in his armoury, but first and foremost he had a very specific job to do. Win the ball was his mantra. When he came out of a challenge with the ball at his feet, he had the nous to pass to one of the more creative players in the side – be it Willie Morgan or Sammy McIlroy at United – or Tommy Hutchison or Ian Wallace at Coventry. Rarely was he caught out of position. He was a manager's dream: a player who could absorb instructions and follow them to the letter. It was an added bonus that he had the heart of a lion and a fierce will to win.

Besides Manchester United, Holton was also held in the highest regard and with the greatest affection by fans of his other clubs, Shrewsbury Town, Sunderland and particularly Coventry City. His status as a *bona fide* Scotland legend is assured too – courtesy of those blood and thunder tackles that became his trademark and the headed Hampden goal which helped take the country to their first

World Cup in a generation.

Holton made the most of that once-in-a-lifetime opportunity, taking the 1974 World Cup by storm with exemplary performances against Zaire, Brazil and Yugoslavia. The Fates may have conspired to limit Scotland to an all-too-brief role in the group stages, but the Tartan Army elevated Jim to hero status in the same way United fans already had.

An article filed from the 1974 World Cup by Alan Hoby for the *Sunday Express* provides a perfect snapshot of his popularity at that moment in time.

"Everywhere the Scots have gone here, it has rung out… in the streets, on the trains, at the games, in the bars and strip clubs of Frankfurt's notorious neon-splashed Kaiserstrasse district… Six foot two, eyes of blue, big Jim Holton is after you. Why? Why has Holton – a defender who has never played any serious football in Scotland – become such a folk hero? Why with such stars as Peter Lorimer, David Hay, Denis Law, David Harvey and Billy Bremner, has Holton aroused such fervour and rampant nationalism among his countrymen? To an outsider like myself it is a phenomenon, a mystery. For how can a centre half who a year ago was not even rated as a class First Division player, let alone at world level, trigger such tribal emotions?

"The answer lies in human chemistry. There is the Jim Holton who appeals to the Scots because of his sheer size and strength. And there is Jim Holton who commands their idolatry because he is warm, friendly and has a big beaming smile for everyone.

"'It is because he is big. He knocks them down,' said one. 'He is like a lion. His aggression and determination on the field typify the new nationalism, the whole spirit of modern Scotland. He is one of us and plays for us.' 'Aye,' said another, 'he's just one of the boys. He has no side. He's always got that happy grin and he always gives the fans a wave whether he is on the coach or running on to the field.' [At this World Cup] the saga of Jim Holton is, I think, the most moving and remarkable. He is the nobody who almost overnight became a national idol."

He was an idol then and an idol he remains. Along the route

This picture, taken by fan Sue Jones,
should settle any debates on whether Jim was 6ft 2!

of the Leeds and Liverpool canal, there is a wall that still bears the slogan 'Jim Holton MUFC' in large white lettering. Incredible, given that the last time he played for Manchester United was 44 years ago! The way he played, centre forwards would no doubt swear that Jim and that brick wall were made of pretty much the same stuff.

"Jim was a big lovable gorilla," says his great friend and team-mate Mick Martin, signed by United in the same month as Holton, January 1973. "On the pitch he'd hound you, he'd kick you, he'd push you, he could bite you – you'd never know what he'd do to you because that's what centre halves had to be like in those days. But there's no doubting Jim was a gentleman off the pitch. He was a great character, great company and he is sadly missed."

2: SIX POUNDS TWO, EYES OF BLUE

"Jim had a heart the size of Ben Nevis"

Childhood friend John Hannah

JUDGING BY THE height and breadth of his adult frame, the infant Jim Holton probably weighed considerably more than 6lb 2oz when the head that nodded one of Hampden Park's most famous goals appeared for the first time on 11 April, 1951. But why let the facts get in the way of a good chapter title, eh?

James Allan Holton was the fourth child of parents John – known as 'Jock' – and Mary, joining big brother John and sisters Annie and Mary (known as May), in their terraced home at 26 Woodpark in the South Lanarkshire village of Lesmahagow, situated 25 miles from Glasgow and 35 from Edinburgh.

Jock, like the majority of working men in the village, was a miner, and he came from a brood of 12 boys and a girl. Strong and powerful, rather than tall, Jock had a baritone voice people took notice of and he was respected as a hard-worker and popular figure in the village. He would supplement his wages from the mine by working shifts behind the bar at the Black Bull Inn in Abbeygreen and split his social time between there and Lesmahagow Miners Welfare Club.

The wider Holton family was well dispersed around the area, but Jock's youngest son was destined to become the most famous of the clan. Jim Holton would put Lesmahagow on the map, even if he seemed to spend half his life explaining to people exactly where it was.

When fame came his way Jim would get so exasperated trying to explain and spell the name of his home village, he would eventually just shrug and fib: "I'm from Hamilton!" A well-developed sense of mischief would lead him to tell others that he was from a quaint little place called Wogahamsel (think about it!).

The main road between Glasgow and Carlisle passed through Lesmahagow when Jim was a boy, but the terminal decline of the coal mining industry coupled with the construction of the M74 motorway left the village literally by-passed. Its fortunes and vibrancy have since suffered as a result, and the landscape has changed dramatically over the years, but a strong sense of community prevails in the 'Gow'.

Jim's oldest friend was John Hillan, who lives in the village to this day. The pair remained the very best of mates from toddlers through to Holton's untimely death. They shared a lifetime of memories – a bond that was never compromised by stardom or geography. You could even say John owed his life to Jim, his pal having pulled him to safety during a childhood misadventure when he got into difficulties swimming in the River Nethan.

"He pulled me out when I was young otherwise I would have drowned," says Hillan. "There was a part of the river where we went swimming, even though it was dangerous and we were told not to. The river had a man-made dam and I slid down it. If Jim hadn't pulled me out I would have been swept away. I couldn't tell my ma and da or I would have got murdered for being there in the first place!

"We made our own adventures back then. Sometimes we would get the boxing gloves in the back garden and have play fights. I can't recall where the boxing gloves came from, but we used to fight a family from the next close, and Jim would put them to good use! Mostly we played football, although most of us never owned a ball. The older boys used to play all day Sunday up the park, and they'd let Jim play because he was bigger. He was good at everything in an athletic sense – sprinting, running, tennis, football, you name it. Jim wouldn't let anyone mess him around but he wasn't loud or threatening. He was a peaceful lad.

"Even from the early days at the primary school, Jim was naturally big and strong. He would win all the races he entered at the school sports day and Highland Games. Once a year, all the schools in the area would race against each other and Jim would be racing against guys who were two or three years older and beat them."

Another of Jim's friends, Gary Campbell, remembers his first childhood encounter with Holton. "I was 12 and Jim was 9," says Gary. "He and a couple of other lads were out catching tadpoles just up the road from where I lived. Five of us went over to investigate and Jim, who was a big kid for 9, was standing in the water with a jam jar looking up at us on the embankment. I could see he had a newt in the jar and I asked him innocently what it was called. Without batting an eyelid he said: 'Ah've never met it afore, how am I supposed tae know its name?' After a few seconds of silence, we all burst out laughing. That was our first introduction to his dry sense of humour and he had employed it to defuse a tense situation of being surrounded by hostile older kids."

John Hillan and Jim both started school at Milton Primary, a 30-minute walk for five-year-olds, which involved crossing the old A74 road. However, when the old Milton building was closed down within months of them starting, they switched to Woodpark Primary where the pair would spend the remainder of their junior years. The friends parted ways – in the classroom at least - when it was time to go to High School. "I was classed as 'brainy' and Jim wasn't so academic, so I went to Larkhall Academy and Jim went to Lesmahagow High," says Hillan, who went on to qualify as an engineer.

Jim was already starting to show promise as a footballer at primary school, although games were infrequent and there was no organised league back then. As hard as it is to imagine, his first position was as a winger. "I don't really know why I played on the wing," Jim would later recall, "back then I was only slightly above average height for my age. It wasn't until after I left school that I really began to shoot up in height."

John Hillan remembers that if Jim had overstepped the mark at school and needed disciplining, the teachers found the most effective way to punish him was dropping him from the school team. Holton would also drive the teachers mad with another problem. "Jim could never, ever remember his date of birth," laughs

Hillan. "I can tell you his date of birth no problem - the 11th of April - but he never could. The headmaster and the janitor used to run the football teams, but when they asked Jim for his date of birth so they could fill out the team-sheet, he would be scratching his head and I would have to step in to help him!"

One of the teachers at Lesmahagow High was the first to recognise that the growing Holton had all the natural attributes to stand out at centre half, and the move paid off when Jim − then 14 - helped his school win the Lanarkshire Cup.

Holton, whose family had moved on to Eastwood Drive then to a new home at Briar Bank in the village, found the classroom far more challenging than the football pitch and before his 15th birthday he jumped at the first chance he got to leave school.

His first taste of employment, as an apprentice brick-layer, lasted only six weeks, and a spell working for a machine tool company was similarly short-lived. "My next job was in a steel works as a general dogsbody, but I found that interfered with my playing football so that didn't last too long either," said Jim.

Jim − now standing at six-foot plus - had been turning out for the Lesmahagow Miners Club side, when he was invited to play for a successful local youth side Fairholm, based in Larkhall and run by Jim McCartney. Fellow Lesmahagow boys John Hannah and Alan Gates had already been recruited by Fairholm, and it was on Hannah's recommendation that McCartney gave the strapping 15-year-old Holton a trial.

"I went to Larkhall Academy and Jim went to Lesmahagow High, but we were good pals and I knew how good he was," says Hannah. "You knew when he came up for corners we were always in with a chance of a goal. Even though Lesmahagow was only small, there were a few good players from the village around that time. We always had matches between the 'top scheme' and our side, the 'bottom scheme', and over the years the honours were probably about even-stevens.

"We played most of our home games at Bryce's Park in Larkhall," says Hannah. "It was an ash pitch and it wasn't great. I remember Jim going in for a tackle and the next thing it was as if his mouth had been transplanted on to his knee. This huge gash opened up and there was blood everywhere. I can't remember how many stitches he must have got in that injury, but that typified Jim' style, even back then – he was totally committed. Before he had even became a professional he suffered a broken ankle and a number of other injuries. I always admired his grit and determination in coming back from them."

Also in the Fairholm ranks were future Motherwell, Dundee and Hearts full-back Stewart McLaren, Mark Cowan, who would play for Airdrie, and Dougie Telfer, son of Willie Telfer the former Rangers and Scotland centre half who went on to manage Albion Rovers.

Celtic scouts soon had Holton on their radar and the Glasgow giants invited him to train with their youth side. "Jim was made up when Celtic invited him to come and train with them," says Hillan. "It was a dream come true. By that time he had left school and he would go straight from the steelworks to go and train with them at Parkhead on Tuesdays and Thursdays."

Competitively Jim continued to play for Fairholm, who looked serious contenders for the coveted Under-16 Scottish Youth Cup. They swiftly progressed into the quarter-finals and were drawn at home to face St Bernard's of Edinburgh. "There was a big noisy crowd and, as usual for Larkhall, a fair bit of drink involved," says John Hannah. "It was a very close game and towards the end we got a penalty. I was the penalty taker and Jim came up to me and, as if I wasn't nervous enough, said to me 'You better fucking stick this away!' The look he gave me was all the persuasion I needed. But I didn't even get the chance to take the penalty because the crowd erupted and the game had to be abandoned. I remember saying to Jim afterwards 'Thank fuck for that!' I had been shitting myself in case I missed.

"We played them back at their place in Edinburgh on a beautifully manicured pitch. We were used to playing on ash pitches and had never seen anything like this. We had a really good side, Jim was a rock at the back and we fancied our chances, but we lost 3-2. It was the worst bus ride home ever. If we had won we would have played Glasgow United in the semi-final, who had Kenny Dalglish in their side."

Fairholm may have fallen short in the Scottish Cup, but their talent had not got unnoticed and they were quickly scouted by England's big-name sides. West Bromwich Albion, in particular, had strong links with the club – even wearing their famous navy and white vertical stripes – and as part of the arrangement Albion invited the whole team down to play against their youth side in 1967.

"The game was played on the Saturday evening after West Brom played Spurs in the afternoon. It rained the whole day and by the time we started to play at 7pm the pitch was six inches deep in mud," says Hannah. "Asa Hartford played for West Brom that night and we spent the whole game trying to get his white shorts dirty. Needless to say we never got near him. He left the field as clean as he came on it - a great player."

On another occasion Fairholm were invited down to Lancashire to play against Bury, who had Kenny Dalglish playing as a trialist for them that day. "We actually beat them 4-2 and I remember Jim going over and talking to Kenny afterwards. They knew each other fairly well, as they were both training with Celtic at the time. Jim was training at Celtic and I was training with Rangers, which I think was a real feather in the cap of Lesmahagow – both of us training with the two top clubs in Scotland.

"Lesmahagow in those days was steeped in religion, Protestant and Catholic. In fact if you were Catholic you had to go to the next village to go to church as there were no Catholic Chapels in Lesmahagow. Jim had a great sense of humour and he was always trying to get me to support Celtic. Bless him, but he had no chance!"

Jim's love affair with Celtic began as a teenager when he started to go to matches on a local supporters' bus. "Jim loved playing and he was dead keen, but whenever Celtic got to a cup final or had a big game, he would be posted missing from the Fairholm games," John Hillan recalls. "We were both Celtic fans. It didn't come from our dads. My old man was a Motherwell fan and the first ever game

I saw was Motherwell v Third Lanark. A double-decker bus for Celtic supporters stopped in Lesmahagow, went down to the next village Kirkmuirhill, then on to Hamilton and Burnbank. Because of that Jim just started going to the Celtic games.

"I remember me, Jim and another lad went down from Hamilton on a bus to see Celtic play at Liverpool. I'd lied to my parents that I had a ticket to get in, just so they would let me go. None of us had tickets of course, so when we got to Liverpool, Jim went into a pub to try and buy us tickets while we waited outside. He was the only one who looked old enough and I would never have got through the door – I looked like a paper boy! After a while, he came out all excited, saying 'Ah've got a ticket'. When we asked if he'd got one for us too, he said 'Aw naw, I forgot' and he headed back into the pub to get them for us."

Jim's dream of wearing the famous hoops of Celtic was short-lived, however. With a queue of clubs showing interest in Kenny Dalglish, Jock Stein quickly realised the vast potential of the youngster and quickly snapped him up for Celtic. But in Jim's case they deliberated too long, and West Bromwich Albion showed no such hesitation and moved in.

Albion's manager Alan Ashman travelled up to Scotland to watch Jim and another couple of potential signings and, satisfied with what he had seen, offered Jim terms as an apprentice professional. "It came as a great surprise at the time," Jim recalled later, "and I really had no intentions of joining Albion because I still had my heart set on Celtic. But after talks with Jock Stein it appeared they were not prepared to take me on."

However, John Hillan reveals that Celtic made one last-gasp effort to stop Holton from signing for West Brom. "Someone from Celtic sat in his house till 12 o'clock on a Friday night. They had obviously got word that West Brom were offering him terms, but Jim was away at the dancing, with boys that were a lot older than him. Because of his size, he was an absolute monster physically, so he could pass for a lot older. The man from Celtic must have given up waiting for him to get in and gone home and Jim ended up signing for West Brom."

Gary Campbell was one of the older boys Jim was regularly socialising with, and he recalls another occasion a thirsty young Holton tagged along with him for an underage pint.

"One Saturday night I was on my way down into the village all dressed up in the suit and tie, as was the style in the Sixties, and I saw Jim walking towards me. He was also wearing a suit and tie, but he was only 15 years old. He asked me if I'd go to Hamilton on the bus with him as he'd heard that former Rangers and Scotland international great Eric Caldow had not long opened a bar in Hamilton and he wanted to go there for a pint.

"I was 18, the legal drinking age, but I warned him I would get strung up for taking a 15-year-old to a pub. 'Aw naw', he insisted, 'I can pass for 18 no problem'. True enough he was at least 6ft 2in and built like a tank, so I gave him the benefit of the doubt. When we got to Hamilton and walked into Eric Caldow's bar, the man himself was serving, all healthy and sun-tanned and looking like he could still play 90 minutes for Rangers. I ordered two pints of heavy and Eric asked us if we were both 18. There were no ID cards in those days so I told him I was of legal age. He then looked Jim up and down and before he could utter another word Jim piped up 'I'm 18 today day Eric, it's my birthday and I just came in to celebrate'. Eric bought it, hook, line and sinker. 'Happy birthday big man', he said, then poured the pints and only charged me for one - the other one for Jim was on the house! Back then I had no idea Jim was a Celtic fan and I only assumed he wanted to go to Hamilton that night to meet a retired Rangers star."

When Jim was thrust into his new life in the Midlands as an apprentice with West Brom, it wasn't long before his new pals would hitch lifts on long-distance lorries to go and visit him.

"We were invited by Asa Hartford and Jim to watch them training at The Hawthorns," remembers Campbell. "After it was finished Jim met us at one of the exit gates where there were a huge crowd of young lads waiting for autographs. Jim was signing away and John and I were getting autograph books shoved in our face. John asked Jim what we should do and Jim just shrugged his shoulders and shouted 'Just sign them!' so we did. Later that night we went to a night club named The Rum Runner in Birmingham where there was a queue of people waiting to get in. As we neared the door the bouncers shouted 'Jim Holton, West Brom' and we were whisked in and seated right away. We felt ten feet tall. It was a different world to Lesmahagow.

"I emigrated to Canada a month later and returned on holidays three years later to watch Jim on the TV at the Black Bull Inn in Lesmahagow playing for Scotland in the 1974 World Cup. It was a proud moment indeed."

Although Gary was three years older than Jim and the two Johns – Hillan and Hannah – the quartet formed a strong bond and it continues to this day, involving emails, Facebook and Skype calls, across three continents. Campbell lives in Canada, Hannah in South Africa, with Hillan holding the fort in Lesmahagow. Jim, of course, is there with them all in spirit.

The trio all treasure some great memories of Jim. At the time when Jim was turning out regularly for Scotland, Gary Campbell remembers visiting John Hillan's parents and being met at the front gate by his mother Ada, who excitedly ushered him to the garden where she had a surprise waiting for him. "She had washed all the Scotland team's football strips and had them hanging out on the line in the back green. The washing line was surrounded by a crowd of neighbourhood kids and I could hear their wee voices saying 'There's Bremner, Johnstone, McGrain, Holton, Jardine' as they read out the Scottish national team displayed before their eyes on a washing line."

Like Campbell, John Hannah moved overseas, and he too is cheered by the moments they spent together. "I live in South Africa now, but I first emigrated to New Zealand and when Jim signed for Manchester United I was over the moon for him," says John.

"United came to New Zealand on tour in 1975. I met him at the airport and the first thing he said to me was that he was a dad – his wife Jan had just had a baby. It was great to be able to celebrate that with him. I spent lots of time with him at the hotel and out and about with his team-mates. What a fantastic experience it was. You had stars like Lou Macari, Martin Buchan and Steve Coppell walking around - it felt like I was in Disneyland.

"After one of the Scotland games Jim came back to Lesmahagow and came to see my mother and gave her the strip Kenny Dalglish had played in that day. He asked her if she could post it on to me. That was typical of Jim – he had a heart the size of Ben Nevis. The sad fact is that I never received it because it got lost in transit. I remember him asking me 'Did you get the jersey John?' 'Aye Jim, fantastic, it's up on my wall' I lied. There was no way I was going to tell him I never got it!"

While United were in New Zealand, they faced an Auckland Select side and co-incidentally the club John Hannah was playing for, Eden FC, were hosting a function for the touring team after the game. "Jim gave me his bag to put in my car as I was giving them a lift to my club," laughs Hannah, "but Tommy Docherty stopped me and in his own gruff manner said to me 'Where the fuck are you going with that?' I was trying to explain to him it was Jim Holton's bag and I was his friend, when Jim appeared and said 'It's okay boss, he's with me'. Then as I was making my way to the car with the bag some fans must have thought I was a player because they were running after me asking for my autograph. Thanks to Jim I had my wee moment of fame.

"After the game we went back to my club for the function. My car was an old Skoda and I had Jim, Alex Stepney and Stewart Houston in the back and me and my mate in front. The rain was lashing down and the Skoda didn't have a petrol cap, so I stuck a rag in it so the rain wouldn't get in. I can't believe now that I had all these famous players in the back and I'm driving them in an old Skoda with an old rag in the petrol cap, worrying that I'm going to get there in one piece. Jim was pissing himself laughing. Needless to say we had a great time at the function."

John – now living in Cape Town - also remembers asking Jim what stuck in his mind about playing for Scotland in West Germany at the 1974 World Cup. Instead of regaling his pal with tales of rubbing shoulders with the superstars of Brazil, Jim said the thing that had really stuck in his mind was the number of buses he had seen in Germany that were supplied by the Scottish bus firm,

Park's of Hamilton. "Of all the wonderful things he must have seen in West Germany, the thing that impressed him most was seeing Park's buses – he was something else!

"I remember when he died and my sister Rachel in Scotland phoned to tell me, I practically dropped the phone. I cried a few tears I can tell you."

3: COMING OF AGE

*"I was standing minding my own business when all of a sudden this
body came crashing down the stairs and landed at my feet"*

When Jan met Jim

WHEN JIM HOLTON joined West Bromwich Albion
in 1968 the club was riding the crest of a wave, having
won the FA Cup for the first time in their history that
May. Wembley match-winner Jeff Astle was perhaps the main man
at the club, but he was surrounded by many good professionals,
including a clutch of Scots - Eddie Colquhoun, Duggie Fraser,
Bobby Hope and Ray Wilson.

Albion operated a prolific scouting network north of the
Border and compatriots Alastair Robertson, Asa Hartford and
Hugh Maclean all featured alongside Jim in a promising West
Bromwich side who were tipped to do well in the 1968-69 FA
Youth Cup.

"At that time there must have been about 12 Scottish lads at
West Brom, which was incredible," remembers Robertson, who
would himself go on to become an Albion legend. "There was
never any danger of losing your accent because everybody in there
was speaking 'Scottish'. Jim and I used to give each other a bit of
stick, because he was a Celtic fan and I supported Rangers, but it
was always good natured and we hit it off right away. You could get
a little homesick, but because you were there with a lot of other
Scottish lads it made it a lot easier to settle in."

Jim – an easy-going character - had no problem forging
friendships and settled in well to his new base in the Black Country,
and although he missed his friends and family in Lesmahagow, he
would take any available opportunity to return home on spare
weekends, sometimes sharing a train north with his team-mate

Robertson.

The club billeted Jim in digs run by an elderly landlady, Mrs Wigley, and comforted by a surfeit of home cooking and his host's mothering tendencies, Jim bonded quickly with the other apprentices staying under the same roof, particularly Len Cantello – another player destined for a long and distinguished career with West Brom.

"Jim was a top lad and we had some great times together," says Cantello. "We shared digs together and he was always winding up Mrs Wigley. He was a very funny lad, full of mischief. He liked a laugh and he was always standing in front of the mirror, admiring himself. Mrs Wigley must have been 80-something, and as she was sat in her old chair Jim would be standing there in front of her with just his string underpants on, combing his hair in the mirror before a night out. What a sight!"

Nights out were a luxury, and the young apprentices were expected to knuckle down and work hard when they reported for duty at the Hawthorns, usually put through their paces by trainers Albert McPherson and Jimmy Dunn – both well-respected coaches, credited with bringing a succession of top youngsters through the ranks.

"Both of them knew football inside out and we were in good hands," says Cantello. "Jimmy Dunn was known as 'Little Jim'. He was only small, but he had been a very good footballer and had won the FA Cup with Wolves as a player. Training was very basic then, it was nothing like it is today. You'd go in in the morning, do a few jobs then you'd hear the noise of the trainers coming into the hall-way shouting at you to either put on your boots or your running shoes. Monday was always a running day. Whether you'd had a good weekend or not you knew you were going to run on the track on a Monday. But we got plenty of time with the ball too. Little Jim had us playing five-a-sides a lot, no doubt because he liked to join in himself."

Robertson says the club was a special place to be at that time. "We all lived in each other's pockets, but the dressing room was a fantastic place to be. The laughs and the giggles we had were something else," he says, "Everyone took the mickey from start to finish but it was a great club. The staff were great, the first team were playing well and setting us a good example, we had a good reserve side and a good youth team. You would never want to miss a day's training. There was a buzz right through the club, from top to bottom."

Holton applied himself to training, but could be a little reluctant to embrace the menial tasks expected of ground-staff. "Jim used to get away without doing a lot and it would drive the kit-man Dave Mathews crazy," recalls Cantello. "Jim would do anything to get out of doing the chores. He would clean the odd pair of boots, but he wasn't one for doing the toilets or sweeping the stands or anything like that. It didn't go down well with Dave, but I think Jim was probably about twice the size of Dave so he wasn't pulled up on it."

Holton may have only been 17, and averse to getting his hands dirty, but his sunny disposition, allied to his physique and power on the field quickly earned him the respect of his peers and the coaching staff. "For a young kid he was a unit," says Cantello. "He didn't mess about. He was physical, good in the air, and he loved a tackle."

Asa Hartford, another friend of Holton's and fellow apprentice at West Brom, agrees: "As a centre back, being able to head the ball is crucial, and aerial prowess was definitely Jim's biggest asset. In those days you had to be able to handle yourself on the pitch, and he had no problems there. You would whack people in the tackle. We were all at it and things weren't as they are nowadays. Jim wasn't shy in coming forward in that department!

"For a big fella he didn't have a lot of power in his legs, though. Looking at him, I used to think he had thin calf muscles. He also had a big heid, which I used to tease him about endlessly. He bought himself a wee Spitfire sports car, a two-seater, and when he sat in it he looked like Humpty Dumpty with that big head of his sticking out!"

Cantello chuckles at the mention of Jim's first car. "The car is one of the funniest things I remember about Jim," he says, "he was only 17 at the time and he came into the digs all excited, telling me 'You want to come outside and look at it Len, it's a belter'. I went outside and saw that he'd bought a Triumph Spitfire. He was bigger than the car, I'm not joking! It was a convertible and it was so low down that I told him, 'Jim, you'll never fit into that!' I'm not being funny but he had a big head and it was just comical to see him trying to squeeze into this compact little car. Sports cars must have been a thing with the Scottish lads because Asa had a Triumph Vitesse convertible, although to be fair to Asa he was on the little side. But for big Jim it was a ridiculous sight."

Jim was coming of age, but a tragic event forced him to grow up even faster when his father Jock died suddenly in 1968 at the age of 62. Holton senior had been waiting to catch a bus near the Miners' Club in Lesmahagow when a friend stopped and offered him a lift. Moments into the journey Jock suffered a brain haemorrhage and died instantly.

Jim, wracked with grief and concern for his widowed mother Mary, thought seriously about leaving West Bromwich and returning home for good. "When Jim lost his dad, he told me he wasn't going to go back to England," says his friend John Hillan. "I don't know how he eventually reached his decision, but he changed his mind and went back south."

At the age of 15, Jim had lied to Eric Caldow that he was marking his 18th birthday to avoid being thrown out his pub in Hamilton, but on 11 April 1969, Jim turned 18 for real. To add to the new car, he soon also had a new girlfriend. More than a girlfriend as it turned out – the future Mrs Holton no less – and their romance had unusual beginnings when Jim literally fell at Jan's feet. "It was a different way of meeting, very different," laughs Jan. "I had gone with some friends to Birmingham city centre and we were at a nightclub. He was with a crowd of players from West Brom, not that I even knew he was a footballer at the time. I had no interest in football at all. I was standing minding my own business when all of a sudden this big body came crashing down the stairs and landed at my feet. I look down, said 'Hello!' and then we started chatting and later exchanged numbers.

"I used to spend hours in a telephone kiosk outside my work talking to him, because we weren't allowed to use the landlines. When we first met, we weren't even courting. I used to see him maybe once a month. Then it progressed and it was twice a month, then twice a week. It was a gradual progression into courtship."

Jan lived in Quinton, four miles away from Jim's digs in West Bromwich. Thankfully her parents immediately took to the young Scotsman their daughter had fallen for, even if Jan's mother could barely understand a word he was saying. The language barrier presented itself frequently. "I can remember the very first time I went to Scotland," says Jan. "Jim invited me up to meet his mum Mary, who was widowed by then, and the rest of his family. We went to her flat and Jim said, 'Mum, this is Jan. Jan, this is Mum' and then he disappeared for about three hours! He must have been away to meet his pals for a pint. He just left me with this lady I had never met before, making polite conversation. She went through into her bedroom and shouted through, 'Jan, can you get my message bag out the press?' I was a Sassenach and was left wondering what on earth did she mean? I soon found out that a press was a cupboard, and a message bag was a shopping bag. I was on a very steep learning curve.

"But there were never any problems with me being English. In fact, it was him that got roasted for saying 'yes' rather than 'aye' when he went back to Scotland. They accepted me and always made me feel very welcome, although it could be a bit intimidating when I was the only English person in Lesmahagow Miners' Club, especially when I used to have little men coming up to me and singing to me. It could be a bit embarrassing, but it all added to the colour of the place!"

Like his blossoming romance with Jan, Jim's relationship with West Brom was also showing great promise. The club had a good reputation for blooding young players and giving them a chance to shine, and Asa Hartford had already made his first team debut by the time West Brom embarked on their 1969 Youth Cup campaign.

Given the depth and talent of their squad, Albion were being talked about as contenders for the trophy and they underlined their credibility as potential winners by surging through the early rounds without conceding a goal. They thrashed Aston Villa away, then saw off Stoke and Coventry to set up a quarter-final at Chelsea, which they edged 2-1. In a two-legged semi-final, West Brom took the scalp of Manchester United home and away to book their place in the final against Sunderland, winners of the prestigious trophy two years earlier.

More than 15,000 turned out on a Monday night to watch the first leg of the final at the Hawthorns and saw Albion seize a commanding but flattering 3-0 advantage. "I thought we were a bit fortunate and thinking to myself Christ, how did that happen?" admits Asa Hartford.

Buses were hastily arranged to transfer Albion fans up to Wearside for the second-leg at Roker Park five days later, where they confidently expected to see their young team lift the trophy. It was, however, to provide a match of infamy — both Jim and Asa were sent off as West Brom succumbed to a chastening 6-0 thrashing. One of the scorers in the second leg, Colin Beesley, revealed in an interview recently that there was never any doubt in the Sunderland ranks that they could turn the tie around. "Apart from the scoreline we were still fairly happy with the way things had gone at West Brom. We knew they'd had a bit of luck," he said. His team mate Richie Pitt agreed: "We had just had an off day at West Brom. Our manager Billy Elliott told us there was no way we were out of it, to score first and to apply ourselves like we could."

Their cause was helped considerably by the transgressions of Holton and Hartford. "We may have had a few Scottish lads in the team that day, but there weren't many left by the end of the game," laughs Len Cantello. "The pitch was a bit of a bog and after we had two men sent off it all went rapidly downhill."

Holton was the first to go. "As I remember it, Jim nutted one of their players," chuckles Ally Robertson, who had a reputation as a hard player himself. "All I heard was a whack and their centre half was lying on the floor. After Jim had been sent off we should have had a penalty when one of their lads handled the ball. When Asa complained to the referee he got sent off too. We had to play the whole second half with nine men, so the 6–0 scoreline wasn't too surprising."

Hartford recalls: "Jim only lasted about 20 minutes and I got sent off 15 minutes later. I think Jim stuck the napper on someone. You wouldn't want that because he had a big head! As Jim was sitting in the dressing room feeling sorry for himself, he heard the pitter-patter of someone's studs clacking on the tiles of the corridor and when I opened the dressing room door, he looked up and said to me 'I knew it would be you wee man, even before the door opened!'"

The pair might have engaged in a bit of gallows humour as they sat together in the dressing room, but their red cards were no laughing matter, and soon they would be forced to face the music. When asked for a comment after the match, embarrassed West Brom manager Alan Ashman did not even attempt to defend the indefensible. "I would not say the referee wasn't right," he said.

"It was shocking losing 6–0, and we felt pretty sheepish that we had let the lads and the club down," admits Hartford. "The next day the chairman Jim Gaunt had us in to his office and gave us such a rollicking for shaming the club."

Despite their humbling defeat against Sunderland, the club could at least console themselves with the knowledge that they had a production line of emerging talent at their disposal. "Even if you were young, you were given a good chance back then at West Brom. They were a club that threw youngsters in," says Cantello. "It was a club that didn't go out and buy for the sake of it and were instead prepared to develop their own young players. We had four dressing rooms – one each for the A and B teams, the reserves and the first team. It was a case of trying to get from the B dressing room to the A then one step up to the reserves, and that's how you progressed, by dressing rooms."

The majority of the Youth Cup final squad would go on to make significant contributions to the first team. Unfortunately, Jim wasn't one of them

Competition for places in defence was especially fierce and with Albion over-stocked in central defenders at that particular time he would soon be on his way elsewhere. "Jim wanted to prove that he was as good as the guys that were in the first team at West Brom, but it was hard for him to break through," says Hartford. "There were a lot of established players in the squad and others coming through."

Like Hartford and Robertson, Len Cantello was sad to see his pal leave. "Unfortunately, when decision time came they decided not to offer him a professional contract, for whatever reason. It can be pot luck, it's not always the right decision and sometimes it's left to the coach to say yes or no. Unfortunately for Jim it was a no."

4: SHREW BEGINNINGS

"When I first met Jim he was a big, raw boy with a skinhead haircut –
and a big mouth. But the potential was most certainly there"

Harry Gregg

"YOU'RE going to make it right to the top, son - to the First Division and the Scotland international team too." This was Harry Gregg's cast-iron promise to Jim Holton, who was still without a single senior game to his name, as he prepared to take the plunge into the Third Division with Shrewsbury Town.

Gregg's words, lavished on the 20-year-old Holton in the summer of 1971, could easily have been dismissed as fanciful, but within a couple of years his bold prediction would be proved emphatically true – it was just another feather in the cap of the remarkable Northern Irishman.

Gregg was Manchester United's goalkeeper in the fabled team of Busby's Babes, and helped pull survivors from the wreckage of the 1958 Munich Air disaster which claimed the lives of 23 people, eight of them team-mates. Extraordinarily, the Coleraine man was back playing within 13 days of the devastating crash and was then named the best goalkeeper at the 1958 World Cup in Sweden where he excelled with Northern Ireland. To this day, the tag of hero doesn't sit easily with him. In the year of the 60th anniversary of Munich, he insisted: "What I did was what I did, it wasn't heroic."

Leaving the terrible events of that fateful February night to one side, he was and remains a shining example to many. George Best called him 'my hero' when he supplied the foreword for Gregg's autobiography in 2002, and Jim Holton saw him in much the same light, describing him as his mentor and the biggest influence on his career.

In 1971, Gregg was three years into his first job in management at Shrewsbury. He was desperate to improve finishes of 17th, 15th and 13th in the division and in a bid to eke out some progress in his side, he was scouring the transfer market for young, hungry players of good character to join him at Gay Meadow. Gregg first caught a glimpse of Holton playing for West Brom reserves and liked what he saw, but before he made his move he wanted to be certain the powerfully built youngster had the right temperament to join his squad.

Knowing that Jim hailed from an area of Scotland where religious beliefs ran deep, Gregg – who abhorred sectarian bigotry – decided to grill the youngster on his views before signing him.

"I was looking for a centre half and knew of this young lad that had been at West Brom and had never had a break. I also knew that he had been at Celtic as a kid, and being Irish I've always been wary about people's outlook on religion, because I would have nothing to do with that sort of thing. I would always be wary of any Scottish man with strong views on religion: someone who wouldn't think twice about asking if you if you were Orange or green – that kind of thing. Fortunately big Jim didn't have that in his character at all. I found him to be a big, open, easy-going kid. He would do for me."

Jim himself had other offers, but Gregg's pull was magnetic and something about Shrewsbury felt right for Holton. "When I was released by West Brom I was heartened by the fact that about ten clubs showed interest in signing me," said Jim, "that meant, I felt, that they had seen something about me which they felt could be groomed for a career in professional football. I wasn't quite on the scrapheap. But which club to join? That was another matter altogether. I didn't want to make a mistake, and I thought hard and long. Fortunately for me, I came to the right decision.

"Harry talked straight to me, and I felt that here was a manager who meant everything he said. The most important thing he said was that if I joined Shrewsbury Town he believed he could make me into a centre-half fit for First Division football. What's more, it wasn't just a pie-in-the-sky sort of promise. He reckoned I could become a First Division player in two years, so I decided to take him at his word and work at my game, and hope that his forecast was proved correct."

On and off the pitch, Jim was still wet behind the ears. When Gregg invited him down from West Bromwich to his home to discuss terms, the young Holton naively assumed he was visiting a bought-and-paid-for club house, and that he would be entitled to something similarly salubrious. He couldn't sign quickly enough on the dotted line. By the time the penny had dropped, Holton had been installed in humble digs more in line with his pay grade.

Shrewsbury Town used the Abbey Gardens Hotel in Whitehall Street to accommodate their young players and Jim roomed with winger Alan Groves. By a sad coincidence, Groves − like Jim − would die of heart failure at an all-too-early age. After his time at Shrewsbury, the mercurial Groves went on to Bournemouth where Harry Redknapp rated him one of the most gifted talents he has ever played alongside. Groves then become a fans' favourite at Oldham Athletic and had started to forge a similar reputation at Blackpool when he took ill at home in June 1978 and tragically died of heart failure aged just 29.

The Abbey Gardens Hotel was run by the remarkable Ruth Williams, a Shrewsbury Town fanatic, who looked after hundreds of players over nearly 40 years as landlady at the 24-bedroom hotel, along with her husband Jack.

Ruth was nearing her 87th birthday when I spoke to her, and neither the marching of the years nor three encounters with cancer had dimmed her passion for watching and talking about Shrewsbury Town, having missed fewer than a dozen matches, home or away, since 1960. She doesn't hesitate in nominating Jim as one of her favourites as a player, person and boarder. "He was wonderful, you couldn't have met a nicer person," says Mrs Williams. "He always had time for you - he'd always stop and have a chat."

"I would be looking after him during the week then watching him on a Saturday and he was an excellent player for Shrewsbury. He was wonderful with his head and won everything in the air. He scored the odd goal or two, but was even better at heading the ball in for somebody else to put away, usually Alf Wood."

Other Scots staying at the Abbey Gardens included Glasgow pair Sammy Irvine and Jake King, a future manager of the club, but Jim's best pal at the club in those days was Groves. "I remember scaring the life out of Jim one night when he was with Alan," laughs Mrs Williams. "We had a hatchway between the kitchen and dining room and he and Alan came into the kitchen to make themselves a drink before they went to bed. Jim put his hand through the hatch to get a teaspoon out of the tray, but he hadn't seen me in the dining room and when I grabbed his hand, he practically passed out! You don't expect somebody 6 foot 2 to almost collapse in a heap."

Broadcaster and author Mike Jones, a supporter since 1948 and self-confessed "walking encyclopaedia of Shropshire sport", wrote the official history of Shrewsbury Town FC 'Breathe on 'em Salop' and he too remembers Jim with affection. "I remember he couldn't get into the West Brom first team because John Wile was keeping him out, and that's when he became available on a free transfer. Jim was still very raw when he came to Shrewsbury and that was obviously why West Brom hadn't considered him ready to play in the top-flight of English football.

"Basically, Jim was signed by Harry Gregg to take over from Alf Wood as centre half. The season before, we had really struggled to score goals and Harry's masterplan was that he wanted to convert Alf to a centre forward. It was a very successful move because Alf scored 36 goals and actually tied with Ted MacDougall for the leading goal scorer in the Third Division that year, before he was sold to Millwall."

For Gregg it was a calculated gamble. In Holton, he felt he had a promising replacement for Wood at centre back, and the shrewd Northern Irishman also had the football know-how to recognise the potential in switching his prize asset from defence to attack. "When I first met [Jim] he was a big, raw boy with a skinhead haircut – and a big mouth. But the potential was most certainly there," says Gregg. "I did a piece in the local paper in Shrewsbury at the time saying that I was going to move Alf Wood up front and bring this untried youngster in at centre half. I went to the pre-season shareholders' meeting and one of the leading shareholders stood up and said it was the most ridiculous statement he had ever read. The chairman – a lovely man, Tim Yates – ducked under the table, for want of a better expression. But I stood my ground. All I could do was say 'Judge me at the end of the season rather than before a ball has been kicked'. At the end of the season, Alfie Wood had scored more than 40 goals and broke all records and Big Jim had become a local hero."

Chairman Tim Yates, a popular local farmer and coal merchant, ran the Shrews efficiently and kept the books neatly balanced. However, resources were limited even by modest Third Division standards and Gregg knew from the moment he walked through the door in 1968 that he was operating at a club who would always be willing to sell their best players. Harry knuckled down to the task in hand from day one, recognising that he had to quickly win over supporters who were still coming to terms with losing his predecessor in the dug-out, club legend Arthur Rowley, who had been lured to Sheffield United.

Rowley, nicknamed 'The Gunner', had been a phenomenal goalscorer for the club, and thanks to his exploits, mainly with Shrewsbury and Leicester City, he still holds the record for the most league goals in the history of English football – a staggering 434 from 619 games. Rowley's popularity had transferred seamlessly from his role as player to player-manager and then manager, and in his ten years at the helm at Gay Meadow he got the team promoted from the Fourth Division and twice came close to taking the club into the Second Division, finishing third the season before he passed the reins to Gregg. He was a particularly hard act to follow.

"In truth, we were a bit of a mediocre side when Harry came," says Jones, who still reports on Shrewsbury matches for Sky Sports' Soccer Saturday programme. "Harry was so frightened of losing that he turned us into a very physical side that really got stuck in. All Harry's clubs that he managed – Shrewsbury, Swansea and Crewe – were brought before the Football League to explain their disciplinary records. In a way, Jim was part of that; he was a proper no-nonsense centre half basically. He quickly learned his trade under Harry at Shrewsbury, no doubt about it.

"We signed Jim during the close season in the summer of 1971. He made his debut in the first game of the season against Bournemouth and he only missed four games in the 18 months he was at Shrewsbury. He was always on the team sheet if he was available. Of the four games he missed, I imagine a couple of them might have been one-match suspensions. Shall we say he was wholehearted!

"He quickly established himself as a fans' favourite. I wouldn't swear to it – and plenty of Man U fans would say otherwise - but I'm pretty sure that the song '6 foot 2, eyes of blue, big Jim Holton's after you' started at Shrewsbury!"

Jim's rapid improvement was plain for all to see, including his team-mates, with Alf Wood recalling some years later: "He drove us mad, trying to catch the ball on his chest and stroke it around our box. But he's an intelligent boy and soon learned better."

For Jim's part he just remembered, "I went straight into the first team and became a regular. I clocked up match after match and all the time Harry Gregg kept on building my confidence, pointing out my good points, working on my weaknesses. He really took a personal interest in me."

Holton's progress was a product of the extra sessions he was putting in on the training ground in the afternoon under the watchful eye of Gregg, who taught him to forget trying to play silky football and focus on his more obvious strengths. "Harry told me I'd never be the kind of player I'd hoped and started working on my true assets - strength, heading and aggression," said Jim. "Harry signed me and set me on the right track. It was because he believed in me that I began to believe in myself. I'll never cease to be grateful to him for the football education which he gave me."

But the ever-modest Gregg insists, "I didn't teach, I just helped him develop. I don't like this idea that coaches make players, to my mind coaches destroy players these days by over-complicating things. The only thing I said to Jim was, 'There is only one ball on the pitch, son. I don't want you to mark anybody, mark the ball. Don't mark a man, don't go and stand over a fella the same height as yourself, just go for every ball.' I played people for what they had to offer, not what I would like them to offer. I picked them for what they had and if they didn't have it, they shouldn't have been in the bloody team. I said to big Jim in the kindest possible way 'Basically, you're the hammer thrower; the only thing that matters to you is the ball. If you don't get it, the other guy definitely won't get it either because it will drop to one of your colleagues behind you.' All he wanted to do was learn.

"He was very committed in training. I expected the same thing from my players in training as I did on the Saturday. I mean a 50-50 in a five-a-side is still a 50-50, same as a Saturday. You didn't take prisoners. If you took prisoners during the week, you were no good to me on the Saturday; and that was Jim's outlook too."

One particular game where Jim was at his competitive best was the January 1972 FA Cup tie against Derby County at the Baseball Ground, when Shrewsbury gave Brian Clough's table-topping side a huge fright before succumbing to two late goals from Kevin Hector.

"It was one hell of a game and Jim's defensive qualities were a major factor in that," remembers Mike Jones. "Hugh Johns annoyed many Shrewsbury supporters with his commentary by saying, 'Holton keeps kicking the ball the way he is facing.' What else was he going to do? The ground at Derby was a total quagmire, there was not a blade of grass on it and it was just deep mud. Jim was playing against what proved to be the best side in the country that year with a top-class forward line and basically, kicking it the way he was facing was a bloody sensible thing to do! Hugh Johns got a bit of stick among Shrewsbury fans for that because they knew how well Jim had played."

Holton's first season in Shropshire saw The Shrews finish 12th – an improvement of just one place on the previous campaign – but it was at least a move in the right direction into the top half of the table. On the plus side, there had been plenty of clean sheets and stirring performances as well, including an Alf Wood-inspired

7-1 win over Blackburn Rovers, yet inconsistency had restricted them to mid-table.

Wood's conversion to centre forward by Gregg had been nothing short of a masterstroke and he and Holton brought out the best in one another with some memorable jousts on the training ground. "Those two were great competitors, kicking lumps out of each other," laughs Gregg. "I used to love to see Jim in training because he terrified people and yet he was such a nice fella. He didn't go out to terrify people, but he was such a huge man.

"Jim was a quiet lad in the dressing room, believe it or not. It was a great bunch of lads, and there was mutual respect throughout the club. Woody was the shop steward and when the players had meetings I used to walk in and say, 'Alf, have you something to say?' He would say, 'Why do you always pick on me gaffer?' And I would tell him, 'If you haven't said it before I came in you're going to say it after I go out, so you might as well say it to my face now!' But Woody was a great guy to have around - he still wanted to be the best centre half as well as the best centre forward."

Before the 1972-73 season got under way, Jim was preparing for perhaps the biggest match of his life – his wedding to Jan – and in typical Holton style it did not pass without incident.

The couple tied the knot in Quinton on 17 June, 1972 – Jan having chosen the date because she wanted to get as close to her mum and dad's wedding anniversary, which fell on the 19th. After the ceremony the wedding party made the seven-mile trip to a function suite at Dudley Zoo for the reception, and that's where the 'fun' really began!

"We had a long gap in between the wedding meal and the evening reception starting," says Jan, "and during that time Jim and his best man John Hillan disappeared. I should have known there and then what I'd married! Where had they gone? I had no idea!

"The pair of them eventually rocked up about three hours later by which time I was threatening divorce. It turned out that they decided to go and pick up some supplies, booze or whatever, from West Bromwich. They had a car which had a gear change on the steering wheel column. Holton being Holton had never driven a column-change before and when he went to change gear he pulled the gear stick clean off! They ended up having to track down somebody who could repair his car so they could get back to Dudley.

"Even before that, we'd had a hysterical scenario where John had ended up losing all the cards and messages he was supposed to have read out at his best man's speech. The minute he got out the car when we arrived at the venue the wind took them and they all disappeared into the air. They were blowing underneath cars in the car park, so John ended up on his hands and knees for the next 20 minutes in his best suit trying to get all these cards back together into some kind of order. It was one disaster after another really! It was a portent of things to come, but it certainly wasn't dull and it all made for good fun."

John Hillan winces with embarrassment at mention of the wedding. "I've never been as nervous in my life. I think that was my first ever run-in with stress," he says. "And, because of my Scottish accent, I'm pretty well sure 95 per cent of the people in there didn't have a clue what I was saying! Harry Gregg was sitting next to me, and did his best to try and keep me relaxed. He noticed I was a bit agitated and kept saying 'Don't worry about it, have another drink!' I had a pile of cards that I had to read out during the speech and even though I was hungry I couldn't eat anything at the meal. I was a nervous wreck."

At the end of the eventful bash, the newly-weds jumped in to Jim's Triumph Spitfire and headed not for some romantic island paradise, but instead to his digs at the Abbey Gardens Hotel in Shrewsbury. This was 1972 after all! "We were allowed a whole two days of a honeymoon," says Jan. "We were given the Sunday and Monday and then on the Tuesday morning there was a bang on the door and it was his trainer at Shrewsbury. He basically said, 'Right Holton, get your kit on, you're training' and that was it!"

The next day, Jim and Jan moved into their new marital home in Bayston Hill, a three-bedroom semi which had cost them

£3,000. "We had hardly any furniture for the new house," says Jan. "I'd got a second-hand dining room suite, a second hand washing machine that was supposed to have been bolted to the floor, but wasn't because I didn't want to damage the floor. So when it went on to the spin programme, I used to have to sit on top of it because it would vibrate across the kitchen and end up jamming the back door. We had no carpets which proved quite funny because we had a new three-piece suite with castors. The minute Jim used to sit in the armchair it would slide across the lounge because it was on vinyl flooring. We were just a typical newly married couple!"

On the pitch, Jim was rock-steady. Shrewsbury started the new 1972-73 season with plenty of defensive steel, but shorn of their star striker Wood, who had been transferred to Millwall. His absence had an immediate impact on the team's firepower, and their first three league home games all finished 0-0.

It was around this time that Gregg put the name Jim Holton on Tommy Docherty's radar, when The Doc was in charge of Scotland, urging the international manager to try out his young defender at Under-23 level. "He was playing so well I simply had to let The Doc know, since Jim looked like great Under-23 material. I phoned the SFA for five days in a row before I could contact Tommy."

Under-23 honours would arrive after Jim had moved on from Shrewsbury, but Gregg had at least paved the way for the call-up. In the short term, he took great satisfaction from seeing Holton visibly growing in confidence and stature. He was, however, always sure to keep his young charge grounded, and wasn't averse to instilling some discipline from time to time.

"In those days you could talk to professional footballers in ways you cannot talk to them now," chuckles Gregg. "Jim had long hair at the time so I told him to get a haircut. This was on a Friday and he said, 'Aw c'mon gaffer, I've got to go to Asa Hartford's wedding.' I said, 'Get a bloody haircut, or I'm fining you!' He went to Asa Hartford's wedding on the Monday. I said, 'That'll be £15 for Friday, £15 for Saturday, £15 for Sunday and I'll let you off with today. Now get a bloody haircut'!

Gregg left Shrewsbury for Swansea in November 1972, to be replaced by existing coach Maurice Evans, and within days of his mentor's departure Jim had tabled a transfer request. "Shrewsbury was my first job in management and it was tough," says Gregg. "Players were being sold and I had no say. The crowd were shouting and calling names. I was getting the blame and it was time to move on."

Holton was placed on the transfer list along with team-mate John Moore, who followed Gregg to the Vetch Field. Even from his remote outpost in South Wales, the wily Gregg was able to pull enough strings in the background to help engineer Holton's dream move to Old Trafford, which was signed and sealed in January 1973. By then, Jim had played 67 times for Shrewsbury and scored four goals.

"The big rumour in Shrewsbury at the time was that it was on Harry Gregg's say-so that Jim had signed for Manchester United. And nobody from United had even watched him!" recalls Mike Jones. "But they needed a centre half and obviously with Harry's connections at United, Docherty listened and as they say, the rest is history. He grabbed his opportunity with both hands and became a very good player. At the '74 World Cup he looked cultured rather than the raw boned youth he was at Shrewsbury."

Gregg confirms that he helped make the move to Old Trafford happen. "I was working away behind the scenes. I told him to sit tight and wait for the offer I knew was coming. 'I know where you're going', I told him. 'You're going to the top, son'."

Their time working together may have been over, but Gregg would remain a major influence on Jim's career, making himself available at any time to chat on the telephone about opponents' strengths and weaknesses and aspects of his own game. "It's nice to talk about a beautiful human being," says a sentimental Gregg. "The nice thing about it is that Jim always remained the same fella, he was never a big-head. He still remained a big, easy-going lad off the pitch. He was a fine handsome fella, 6 foot 2, eyes of blue – and yet he had the brownest eyes any man had ever had!"

5: MACCHESTER UNITED

"If Jim was playing now he would be worth a fortune. The Jim Holtons of this world are hard to come by these days"

Alex Forsyth

THE DOOR OF the Auld Hoose bar in Hamilton swings open and in breezes former Manchester United and Scotland full-back Alex Forsyth, owner and manager here since the 1980s. On the day of our meeting he is looking fit and well – and so he should be, having just weeks before retired from the pub game, a letter from Sir Alex Ferguson among the many messages he has received from well-wishers. We are not here to talk about the end of an era, however, rather the start of one – the Tommy Doc Era.

Following the wretched 18-month reign of Frank O'Farrell at Old Trafford, Tommy Docherty was prised away from Scotland's national team by Sir Matt Busby and appointed Manchester United's new manager on 22 December 1972. A frenzied month of transfer activity followed, and when the dust settled - Forsyth, Holton, George Graham and Lou Macari were paraded as United's new signings. It was no coincidence that all of these recruits were Scots.

Fittingly, Forsyth has travelled the short distance to meet me from Holton's home village of Lesmahagow, where he now lives with his wife, an old class-mate of Jim's at Woodpark Primary. He has scribbled down a few of her memories on the page of a notebook to share with me – namely that he was already known back then as 'Big Holton' and that he would routinely be given extra helpings by the school dinner ladies, particularly ones who followed Celtic as he did.

"Jim was a smashing big fella, an absolute gem of a guy," says

Forsyth, who stayed with United until joining his own boyhood heroes Rangers in 1978. "He was a great player, a hardy bugger. Anything up in the air or on the ground, he was there – that was his game. If Jim was playing now he would be worth a fortune because, for me, there are no old-fashioned centre halves like that. They all want to play out from the back. They are not interested in 50-50s, winning the ball the hard way, they see themselves as ball-players and some are more interested in taking free-kicks than getting wired in. The Jim Holtons of this world are hard to come by these days.

"Jim was a true professional, a good trainer, worked hard at his game and the fans absolutely loved him, as the Six Foot Two song showed. They used to sing it all the time because he was such a big, honest player. He was a legend down there.

"I was never the best of defenders, but I think people liked you if you were genuine, honest and gave your best. The Stretford End loved Jim. Every week they were singing the song. We would wind him up about it on the pitch, telling him 'Go on then, wave to them' and he would just grin back with that big toothless grin! He was a working class guy and he shared that background with the fans. A lot of players now forget where they come from but Jim had been brought up to work hard and that showed in his football."

Forsyth beckons me to follow him to the other side of the pub where a framed black and white picture of Manchester United, circa 1973, takes pride of place on the wall. "There's me, big Jim, wee Lou, Willie Morgan, Martin Buchan," he points out, "we had loads of Scots back then. They even used to call us MacChester United. I was one of the Doc's first signings. He signed me, Lou Macari and George Graham all in one week and then big Jim quickly followed from Shrewsbury."

United were in dire straits before Docherty walked through the door. A humiliating 5-0 defeat at Crystal Palace on 16 December, 1972 left United bottom of the league, with only five wins and 16 points from their first 22 matches. It proved to be the final straw for the club's beleaguered board who were left with little option but to wield the axe, dismissing O'Farrell and his assistants

Malcolm Musgrove and John Aston. That same day they told a disillusioned George Best, who had walked out on the club in November, that he would never play for the club again, although another 'final chance' would be granted to their maverick star the following season.

Within days Docherty had been appointed. He met his players for the first time at Mottram Hall in Cheshire on 23 December, as they prepared to face Leeds, and although Paddy Crerand and Bill Foulkes took the team that day, The Doc was presented to the crowd before the match. He took his seat in the stand to watch a 1-1 draw, his mind no doubt busily formulating his immediate signing plans. A 3-1 defeat at Derby on Boxing Day underlined that he had little time to waste.

New players were a priority, but Docherty also moved quickly to assemble his back-room team. His old Preston North End team-mate Tommy Cavanagh was appointed trainer and, effectively, assumed the role as his right-hand man. Old Trafford legend Crerand was manoeuvred into the role of assistant manager, but the pair would have a fractious relationship.

Docherty had been authorised by the Old Trafford board, headed by chairman Louis Edwards, to spend big. Sir Matt, a director and by far the biggest influence at the club, acted as a sounding board as The Doc set about approaching his targets. "Matt ran the show," said Docherty, "the other board members didn't know a centre half from a mince pie."

In the final days of 1972, Docherty swooped to sign Graham from Arsenal for £125,000 and Forsyth from Partick Thistle for £100,000. The Forsyth deal, in particular, happened at breakneck speed, the defender racing south from Glasgow to sign with 35 minutes to spare before the Scottish transfer deadline.

Drama also surrounded the capture of Lou Macari. Docherty snatched the Celtic man, literally, from under the noses of Liverpool, cosying up to him in the stand at Anfield and offering him better terms as the in-demand forward sat watching his prospective team-mates play. Afterwards, as Docherty spirited Macari away from Parkhead, the pair were lucky to escape serious injury when the manager's new Mercedes was rammed from behind by a lorry in thick fog near Gretna.

Two days after the unscathed Macari signed for a club record £200,000, big Jim joined the new-look United – putting pen to paper on 10 January, 1973. It is a matter of debate whether Docherty had even seen Holton in action, but he had heard glowing reports and desperately needed a dominating figure to play alongside Martin Buchan at the heart of the United defence.

When Shrewsbury put Jim Holton on the transfer list towards the end of 1972, United had quickly been alerted to his availability by Harry Gregg. Other clubs, including Coventry City, were circling, but Gregg – now in charge of Swansea, advised his former charge to stay non-committal, disregard all offers, and wait for United to make their move.

Intrigued, United decided to act on Gregg's tip-off and sent Crerand to go and watch Shrewsbury. Crerand recalls: "Harry Gregg was the one that phoned us up and told us about Jim. I had no idea who he was. I went down and watched him play. I thought, 'God almighty I wouldn't want to play against him!' He was big, strong in the air, good on the ground and couldn't half tackle – all the qualities of a top-class centre half. How he hadn't been snapped up by somebody else before then I don't know. I didn't even know then that he was Scottish, that's how much I knew about him! I reported back to Tommy Docherty and we signed him."

Docherty insists he didn't have think twice about making the move for Holton. "The club had him watched repeatedly and there were reports on him from all our scouts and people like Jimmy Murphy. You have got to have faith in your staff and he had been highly recommended so we bought him. He was needed... and quickly."

"The speed it all happened was crazy," says Jan Holton. "We'd only been married six months and had just moved into our new house. One day he is playing at Gay Meadow and the next he comes home and tells me 'by the way, I'm signing for Manchester United.' He then explained to me that meant that he had to go to Manchester and I was going to be left behind on my own in

Shrewsbury."

Jim's old landlady and friend from Shrewsbury Ruth Williams drove the Scot up to Manchester to complete the deal on the evening of Tuesday, 9 January. He was met at Old Trafford and shown round the trophy room by Crerand. He was then ushered in to meet Docherty and conclude the formalities of signing for United for a fee of £80,000 – a significant outlay for a relatively unknown 21-year-old. "Within twenty minutes or so the deed was done, I'd put pen to paper," said Jim. "I could hardly take it in. I was with a First Division club, and the way my new boss was talking I wasn't going to have to wait to get my chance of proving myself. I was walking on air."

As an aside, newspaper reports of Holton signing for United the following morning sat alongside another curious story – Harry Gregg had made an audacious attempt to lure George Best to Third Division Swansea on loan. It would have quite a coup for Gregg, but while he was able to celebrate Jim's slice of good news, he was left disappointed as Best chose to remain in self-imposed exile.

Meanwhile Maurice Evans, who had taken over from Gregg as Shrewsbury manager, accepted that his departing defender was always destined for bigger things than the Third Division. He predicted: "Jim was over the moon about joining United and you cannot blame a player for having ambition. I'm convinced he will make his mark in First Division football. He's got all the attributes to be a success in the top sphere. Holton looks a future Scotland centre half to me."

Jim himself said he "never dreamed this would happen" and vowed to make the most of a golden opportunity. "When I think of the big name players who are at Old Trafford it does make me feel a bit nervous," admitted, "but I realise it's entirely up to me now to make a success of the move."

Later, he would reflect, "When I joined United I faced a new kind of challenge – proving that I could measure up to the demands of First Division football. I reckoned that the extra training sessions I'd had in the afternoons at Shrewsbury had paid off handsomely, but I knew I still needed to work on my game. Manchester United had taken a calculated gamble by spending £80,000 on my transfer. It was up to me to prove to them, and to football in general, they hadn't spent their money badly. I was determined to justify the faith Harry Gregg had shown in me too. He had played for Manchester United for close to ten years and I didn't want to let him down at the club where he had been a star."

Docherty's first four signings came swathed in tartan, although they were soon joined by Irishman Mick Martin – signed from Bohemians for £20,000 – and much was made of the influx of Scots. "I always went for good players, no matter what nationality they were," insists Docherty. "Having been manager of the Scotland national team I'd seen a lot of Scottish players who were up and coming. When I went to Man United and saw the weaknesses that they had, I knew where to go to strengthen the club."

Martin Buchan, who 11 months earlier had been United's record signing when he joined the club for £120,000 from Aberdeen, agrees: "United were in need of fresh faces. I've always said there was a curious mix of legends – Law, Best and Charlton – and players that wouldn't have got a game in Aberdeen reserves, and I make no apologies for saying that."

Willie Morgan, who had been with United since the summer of 1968, had also witnessed the team disintegrate from European aristocrats under the management of Busby, to mediocre also-rans during O'Farrell's forgettable reign. "Doc inherited a bad team, no doubt about it. I had to play through those years of decline," says Morgan. "Doc brought a lot of Scots in, and he never stopped wheeling and dealing, but he also brought a lot of crap in at times. Bringing Jim in was a masterstroke though. We had Third Division players in the squad but with Jim, he came from the Third Division and looked a First Division player."

Forsyth and Graham turned out for United in a 2-1 friendly win against Hull - scorers Law and Charlton - on 30 December before making their competitive debuts in a defeat against Arsenal days before Holton and Macari were signed. United were dumped out of the FA Cup at Wolves the following week. It was a blessing in disguise as Docherty was at least allowed to devote all his attention to avoiding relegation. His spending spree had cumulatively made United the first ever £1 million team, and much was made of this in the build-up their clash with West Ham, which was billed as a meeting of 'Princes v Paupers'.

Holton and Macari were registered in time to make their United debuts, two of an incredible *eight* Scots in Docherty's starting XI that day. For the record, the line-up was: Stepney, Young, Forsyth, Law, Holton, Buchan, Morgan, MacDougall, Charlton, Macari, Graham.

"I made my debut with Jim that day and there were eight Scots in the team, something that will never ever happen again in the history of Man United," says Macari. "I've got to be honest, until recently I didn't even realise there were eight Scottish players in the team that day. I was absolutely amazed that at a club like Manchester United you could get eight Scots in the one team on any given day. Unlike nowadays where foreign players are the flavour of every season, it was Scottish players who were the big players – most clubs were keen to get them in."

Tartan scarves were worn by some supporters at Old Trafford, a nod to the new breed of player rather than the Bay City Rollers, and even the physio Laurie Brown was a Scot. Brown, who hails from Musselburgh, laughs, "When we were getting Jim Holton from Shrewsbury, I can remember the chairman, saying to me 'Thank goodness we're getting a Welshman'. I had to say: 'I'm sorry to tell you, it's another Scot!' People used to say to me 'you haven't lost your accent', but you didn't lose your Scottish accent if you were at Manchester United!"

The eight Scots became seven by the end of the game, when the injury-prone Denis Law was forced to make way for a Welshman, Wyn Davies. Another law – the one of averages - suggested it would be a Scot who grabbed the headlines, and Macari marked his debut by scoring a late equaliser in an entertaining 2-2 draw against the Hammers.

Within weeks Ted MacDougall would join West Ham. He had been signed by O'Farrell for £200,000 from Bournemouth just three months earlier, but was swiftly jettisoned by Docherty. Other

Scots would soon arrive though. By the end of 1974, Docherty had handed debuts to Stewart Houston, Jim McCalliog, Arthur Albiston and Martin Buchan's brother George.

Like Macari, Jim also impressed the 50,878 crowd in his first ever top-flight match against West Ham, even if he had been caught napping for the visitors' first goal. He had looked raw and a tad ungainly, but his commitment was there for all to see. United had at least shown some fighting spirit, having clawed their way back from 2-0 down to earn a point, and this was reflected when the attendance leapt up by 8,000 for the midweek visit of Everton four days later.

It was Mick Martin's turn to make his debut that night, "It was an exciting time for the club and the new boys bonded well. A whole load of us signed at the same time. We stayed in the Piccadilly Hotel in Manchester first and then eventually moved out to the Heath Mount Hotel in Salford, not far from the training ground. Guys that had never really met each other before were all of a sudden living in a hotel together, and in those circumstances you get to know each other quickly, get pally with each other and form lasting companionship. It was the start of a great period in my life.

"Two weeks before I made my debut I'd been playing in Dublin for Bohemians against Shelbourne in front of 3,000 people, and here I was playing for United in front of 59,000 people at Old Trafford. I didn't even know I was playing until 6pm. Tommy Docherty just came up to me and said 'You're playing wide left because Ian Storey-Moore has an injury'. I didn't have a left foot, but I never said anything to him because I'd have been happy to play anywhere. I played quite well in a 0-0 draw, and from there on in I became involved with the first team. I thought it might take me a good six months to get anywhere near the team."

The goalless draw at Old Trafford against Everton was quickly followed by a tough assignment away to fellow strugglers Coventry, where Jim made his mark with a goal and the type of ultra-aggressive display that became his hallmark. Docherty and his team laid down a marker that day, which Jim had ably advertised. With their First Division future at stake, United were going to stand up and fight. The days of them being outmuscled or pushed around were over.

"United's fight for their First Division lives is going to be a rugged one, and in more ways than one," warned David Meek in the *Manchester Evening News*. "It's going to upset the purists and there was much head-shaking at Coventry about the way the Reds got stuck in. But desperate situations call for desperate remedies. Manchester United are going to show their claws and reveal a mean streak that in the past has not been part of their make-up.

"The strapping Jim Holton leads the new approach. The Reds' strong man centre half crunched three opponents in the first quarter of an hour and then turned on his power up front to smash home a header that earned United their point in a 1-1 draw. Holton landed himself a booking but by that time he had made his presence felt."

After the bruising scrap at Highfield Road, The Doc lavished praise on his new enforcer Holton. "I think we have got a winner, a real hard diamond," he said. "Although he got booked at Coventry it was an honest tackle going for the ball. The Coventry fans may not have liked him, but I remember when they had George Curtis at centre half and he ate centre forwards for lunch! Jim Holton will get better with playing in the First Division. At present he may make mistakes because you cannot expect a 21-year-old to come suddenly into the First Division and know it all. At his present rate of progress, however, he will become one of the best in the country. In our present position we have got to play with strength and Jim Holton will help provide it. No-one will do us any favours between now and the end of the season which must be met equally hard by us."

After just three games in a United shirt, Jim had already won the respect of his manager, supporters and some distinguished team-mates. "I had no prior knowledge of him when he came to United," admitted Bobby Charlton, who had already announced his intention to retire at the end of the 1972-73 season. "I did not know whether he could use his head, whether he was left or right footed, until we were thrown together on the field. Any doubts I might have had were soon dispelled in the first few games. Here was someone big and strong and a great competitor. His heading was faultless and as good as anyone's in that position. My first impressions were certainly not misplaced."

Willie Morgan remembers the arrival of the wide-eyed Holton well. "He was a bumpkin, in the nicest possible sense," he says. "He was as raw as they come when he arrived from Shrewsbury. He was really eager to learn, but because we needed points, usually the best advice was: 'Jim, just kick anything in front of you and you'll be fine'. To be fair to Jim, he did want to play and learn, and eventually he did fantastically well, to have come from Shrewsbury and to be playing for Scotland – and not looking at all out of place – within a few months. It was an incredible achievement. Everyone wanted to help him because he did have the rawness about him. He didn't just want to learn, he *did* learn, but he was the typical centre half. He was the perfect centre half."

Goalkeeper Alex Stepney, another senior member of the United team, echoes Morgan's assessment of Jim's rapid improvement. "When you come from a lower division team and play with better players you've got to pick it up fast. When Jim came to the club there was rawness about him, but I was helping him, and other experienced players helped. He responded to that. He was always willing to learn, and that's why he went on to become a Scotland player."

Stepney was, at that time, competing for the gloves at United with Jimmy Rimmer. It was a tussle Stepney would ultimately win, with Rimmer first going out on loan to Swansea, then moving on to Arsenal and later - with great success - to Aston Villa. Rimmer went to Swansea at the invite of his mentor and former Old Trafford club-mate Harry Gregg, but before he departed from United, he was asked by Gregg to help Holton - his former protégé at Shrewsbury - settle into his new surroundings.

"Harry was a father figure to Jim and to me as well. When Jim signed for United, Harry asked me to look out for him and was always on the phone asking me for updates and checking on his progress," says Rimmer. "But he needn't have worried, Jim fitted in so well. We became great pals and he was a wonderful, lovely character. When he came to the club he brightened it up, because we were not doing so well at that time. No-one knew of Jim before because he had come from Shrewsbury, but he just boosted the place, instantly. Sometimes his brain didn't work and he did some daft, funny things, because he was a natural-born comedian and Tommy Doc loved him because he was so funny, but he knew when he was on that pitch it was time to be serious.

"When he pulled on a football shirt he was a different man and a total professional. I would describe him as a defender-cum-defender! Everything that went into the box, Jim would get his head on it. When he came to United he was just coming into his prime, and I was proud of the impact he made for United and Scotland. I thought the world of him and I still talk about him a lot. It didn't take him long to adjust from the Third Division to the top division, and believe me that takes some doing. People don't realise how hard is to come in and settle at a top club, only people who have been at Manchester United know how difficult it is to adjust, but Jim took it in his stride – incredible."

Lou Macari had also found his feet quickly at United, but believes Jim had a tougher baptism – coming as he had done from the Third Division. "It couldn't have been easy for him, coming from Shrewsbury," says Macari. "I was fortunate in that I was coming to United from a big club like Celtic. I had grown up with the Lisbon Lions, then I had played in cup finals at Hampden with 120,000 people at the game - so handling the crowds and pressure at Manchester United was quite easy for me.

"During my 11 years at Old Trafford, there were players who arrived with good reputations, but it didn't happen for them because they couldn't handle being at Old Trafford. Some couldn't handle even walking down that tunnel and hearing the noise of the crowd. But it was no problem to big Jim – that was down to his strong character. His game and his style were simple: it was attack the ball and attack whoever he was playing against and try and contain them right throughout the 90 minutes, and considering he came from Shrewsbury he did a remarkable job."

Like Macari, Sammy McIlroy also spent more than a decade at United, and is a good judge of who was able to handle the pressure that comes with the territory at Old Trafford. The Northern Irishman was a youngster on the cusp of regular first-team action when Holton first arrived and was impressed with the way the big Scot adapted to such a high-profile club. "A lot of people that came to Old Trafford would sink or swim with the pressure that was involved in playing for United," says McIlroy, "bigger name players have crumbled, I've seen it happen. It still happens. They were proven at other clubs but then sink under the pressure at Old Trafford. Not big Jim though. He had a heart the size of the pitch and everyone knew that. Players, team-mates, fans, everyone knew that when he was on the pitch he gave 100 per cent.

"At the beginning, coming from Shrewsbury a lot of people probably needed convincing, but he became a fans' favourite very quickly and was loved at Old Trafford. Centre halves in those days had a clear job to do - they had to head it and they had to tackle. But Big Jim was no mug with the ball at his feet, he could pass it and he was intelligent enough to know to pass it to people in front of him he knew that could help him out. He knew his position and he knew his job."

Physio Laurie Brown immediately took to Holton, and says everyone did. "Jim took it all in his stride," he says. "He was a character off and on the field. He was a likeable man and a good fellow to have in the dressing room. He fitted in no bother, and it probably helped that the club was full of Scotsmen at the time. Martin Buchan, in particular, was good for Jim, and that helped him settle in quickly. Martin was very fast and his pace allowed Jim to attack the ball, with Martin at the back of him tidying anything that got past him. It was a strong, effective partnership."

Buchan and Holton seemed to be made for each other as a defensive duo, and they hit it off immediately. "Jim settled in very quickly and was accepted by all the lads and all the staff. He was just a lovely bloke," says Buchan. "I'll be honest, I hadn't heard of him before he signed. In fact, Tommy Doc had barely heard of him before he signed – it was Paddy Crerand who went along to watch him. At the end of the day, he could play. You don't worry about which club a player came from. I mean, I went to Manchester United from Scottish football. We all started somewhere, not necessarily at the top, but he settled in very quickly and became a popular member of the squad."

Jim did not look out of place. He looked every inch a Manchester United player, and what's more he arrived with a professional attitude – determined to keep his feet on the ground and remain the same person.

His best friend John Hillan remembers his early days in Manchester, "when he moved to United it changed things in terms of his life and status, but it didn't change Jim as a person. I would see guys in the Players' Lounge and some of them could be a bit full of themselves, which they have a right to be, but Jim never went that way. The adulation never went to his head at all. I'm sure he loved hearing the Stretford End singing his name - you'd be abnormal if you didn't - but he was still the same guy. Jim never had the bravado thing or thought he was a big deal."

To friends and team-mates, it appeared that Holton had settled in seamlessly at his new club, but back in Shropshire Mrs Holton was getting more than a little impatient. With his focus firmly on United, Jim had overlooked the practicalities of finding them a new home so they could start living their life as a married couple again.

"Six months later I'm still in the Midlands and he's still in Manchester," Jan recalls. "If you can picture the situation... Jim had been married six months and then all of a sudden he's whisked off to Manchester, placed in the Piccadilly Hotel in the middle of Manchester. He can have anything he wants, he doesn't pay for a thing – everything's bought, paid for, sorted. He's picked up and dropped off for training. Basically, he slips very easily back into the bachelor life. He was 21 and all of a sudden he's a Man U player and personally I think it did go to his head at first, he was overawed by it all. I was very much forgotten, not intentionally but more through circumstance."

Jan took control of matters and put the couple's house in Shrewsbury on the market so they could look for a new home in Manchester. The property sold within a week but with Jim still living in a hotel room, Jan was forced to go back and live temporarily with her parents. "I had a dog by then, a Labrador, Tanya, so we moved back to mum and dad's and waited... and waited!

"I then got a job temping because I was getting bored doing my mum's housework. I think I left it about six months before I cracked. To be fair, he used to phone me regularly, as good as gold, but I remember I just lost it with him.

"What finished me off was that he was chatting away one night and telling me where he'd been, and then casually he mentioned he'd been to the Playboy Club in Manchester that afternoon. I just exploded! I'm a Gemini and I have a long fuse, but when I blow, I blow! He got it both barrels and he basically got told, 'Either you find us a house and I move up there within a month or I don't move at all.' So it was a threat really. It got the desired reaction because he found a semi-detached house in Urmston and I finally moved in within about six weeks.

"We loved Manchester. We loved the people. Although we were involved in football, it was the ordinary people – our neighbours and friends – that made it so wonderful. I'd come from Birmingham, then I'd got married then I'd gone to Shrewsbury where basically they rolled the pavements up at 10 o'clock at night. I was from Birmingham and was used to nightclubs, but I think they only had one in Shrewsbury. Nobody spoke to you, and if you smiled at anyone they looked at you as though you were mental. Nothing against Shrewsbury, but I was a city girl and used to city life. When I moved to Manchester it was like going home because they were so friendly."

The couple settled into a new home in Whalley Avenue in Urmston and Jan immediately fell in love with the city. Being a footballer's wife in those days was a world away from the WAG culture we are used to today, and Jan rarely went to watch Jim play, but she does recall the occasion when Bobby Charlton's wife almost choked on her sandwich when she learned that there were women in the 1970s out earning a living. "Jimmy Rimmer's wife and I both had jobs and when we told her she couldn't believe it. She looked down her nose and said 'You're not actually working are you? You don't actually have a job?' I was just a common Brummie bird and she was used to moving in different circles than us!"

On the pitch, for all the promise his new signings had been showing, Docherty had yet to register a win in his first five matches as United manager. The manager took advantage of United's inactivity during FA Cup weekend to squeeze a couple of friendlies into the schedule. First, United took on Martin's former club Bohemians in a friendly at a packed Dalymount Park in Dublin. With 40,000 inside the ground, and thousands locked out, United enjoyed a morale-boosting 3-1 win.

Next stop was Portugal, where United faced Docherty's former club Oporto. Jim's first taste of continental football, with all its customary off-the-ball nonsense, ended in a red card – the only statistic of note in a 0-0 draw.

United returned to the First Division and grabbed a vital 2-1 win against Wolves to open Docherty's account, but it proved a false dawn when they were soundly beaten 4-1 by Ipswich at Portman Road the following weekend. With 12 league games left, United were still in grave danger, and tension hung thick in the air over Old Trafford. Under such intense pressure, finding the balance between fire in the belly and cool heads was not going to be easy.

6: DIRTY TRICKS

*"When I snapped back to consciousness, the referee was sending Jim
Holton off and a great lump was developing on my head"*

Malcolm Macdonald

OF ALL the recruits Tommy Docherty made in his first three months as Manchester United manager, one more than any other was making the headlines, and usually for the wrong reasons.

Big Jim Holton's style, or lack of it, as some acerbically carped, was causing consternation in the Press Box. Most of the flak could be considered unfair. Holton's detractors failed to take into account that here was a largely inexperienced 21-year-old player, with many rough edges and a lot to learn, who had been thrust from the tough school of the Third Division into a high-pressure First Division relegation scrap.

Jim had the support of everyone within Old Trafford, but he was becoming viewed as the embodiment of a new, crude Manchester United, and when Newcastle United came calling in March 1973, an explosive clash with their iconic striker Malcolm Macdonald simply added more poison to the pens of his critics.

A self-enforced period of inactivity had left Jim chomping at the bit for the match against Newcastle. A booking in his third match for United at Coventry City tipped him over the 12-point disciplinary limit, thanks to three cautions for Shrewsbury, and he had served a two-match ban at the beginning of March. It would have irked him that the first of these games was against his old club West Bromwich Albion. Steve James deputised in a 2-1 win, with instant hit Lou Macari again on the scoresheet before a 3-1 loss to Birmingham City at St Andrews. Free from suspension, he was restored to the team against Newcastle. It was a game that would live long in the memory, with Holton and Macdonald in lead roles.

Holton went into the game on a personal high, having won international recognition for the first time, three days before the Newcastle match, when Scotland Under-23s beat Wales 2-1 in Swansea. One Glasgow-based reporter noted, "Scotland's strength was in defence where there was not a failure, although centre half Jim Holton certainly takes some getting used to. Especially, I'd imagine, if you're unlucky enough to be playing against him. He's as hard as nails and about as constructive as a B-52 Bomber – but by heavens, he's effective."

Macdonald was about to find out just how 'hard as nails' Holton was, and nearly 45 years on, the legendary striker still has vivid memories of a clash which brought simmering tension between the two clubs to the boil.

"There was always a bit of niggle between us and United during my time at Newcastle," says Macdonald, "and our trip to Old Trafford the previous season had only made matters worse. We'd just lost to non-league Hereford in the 1972 FA Cup third round replay, the game in which Ronnie Radford scored his famous goal. That defeat created massive headlines and was all very embarrassing for us. When we played at Old Trafford the following week we were sat in the dressing room getting changed and all we could hear was 50-odd thousand Manchester United fans chanting, 'Hereford, Hereford, Hereford'.

"We went out like men possessed and we absolutely murdered Man United, winning 2-0. From then on, I felt there was real bad blood between the two sides, and it was no surprise it all kicked off when we went back to Old Trafford in 1973."

Tommy Docherty left Jim in little doubt before the game that he expected his centre half to dominate the Newcastle star, the self-styled Super Mac. Arnie Sidebottom, Holton's affable understudy at Old Trafford, remembers the exchange. "I thought he was going to say to Jim, 'look be careful, Malky Macdonald is probably one of the best centre forwards in the world – don't let him get you out on the touchline because he's got rapid pace'. But he turned to Jim and said 'If Malcolm Macdonald kicks a ball today I'm not paying you for six months!' He got up and walked out, that was the team talk!"

Willie Morgan stirred the pot further by getting inside Macdonald's head when the two had a quick chat on the pitch before kick-off, which went like this:

"How are you Willie?"

"Jesus, what did you say about big Jim?"

"Why, what's wrong?"

"You must have said something nasty because he wants to kill you. He wants to kick your head in!"

"But I never said a thing'

"Well, if I was you, I would watch your back today."

Morgan laughs: "After that, Malcolm did his best to avoid him that day. He may have been a centre forward, but he played the whole game out on the left wing. It looked like Malcolm was frightened to death of him."

Jim, who spent most of the game clinging to Macdonald like a limpet, broke off from his defensive duties to give United the lead a minute before half-time. But the goal failed to dampen his appetite for a personal battle, and he emerged after the break with Macdonald still firmly in his sights. Armed with Docherty's instructions to stick on Macdonald, Jim instead stuck one on the livewire centre forward.

Recalling the flashpoint, Macdonald recalls, "It happened right in front of the two dug-outs. Frank Clark, the Newcastle left back, had knocked the ball up the line to me, and I was coming from the inside forward position, heading out wide towards the dug-out, with Jim Holton right up my backside. The ball bounced a few feet in front of me and was going to come up off the deck, so I slowed right down and spread my shoulders so that I could take it on my chest. Just as the ball was about to make contact with my chest, Jim Holton nutted me right on the back of my head.

"I literally saw stars and went down. Just for a few seconds, I lost contact with everything and didn't know where I was. When I snapped back to consciousness, the referee was sending Jim Holton off and a great lump was developing on my head. And there was

Tommy Docherty standing over me screaming, 'Get up! Get up you cheating bastard!' I'd just been nutted in the back of my head, and I was apparently the one who was cheating!

"It was quite comical actually because there was just no chance of him ever being able to make contact with the ball. One thing about me was that I was broad shouldered, and so once the ball was coming up on my chest, there was no way that he was going to get round me – so he took the option of deciding to go through me instead and it got him sent off. Jim Holton didn't argue with the referee or anything like that and he just stomped straight off."

The referee Tom Reynolds said he had been left with no choice, "All sorts of things were going on, but I was intent on taking the necessary action over the incident I had seen clearly."

With Jim in the dressing room, United held on. They had doubled their lead through Mick Martin before Irving Nattrass pulled one back, but the ten men held out for two prized points in their relegation scrap. "I remember it [the Macdonald incident] well, right in front of the dug-out," United's second goalscorer recalls, "That day I scored my first goal, Jim scored and we won 2-1. You could always be sure that Jim would get you three or four goals a year from corner kicks because he was such a good header of the ball, but the game against Newcastle was one of the odd occasions when he scored with his feet. He was loud, he was a massive influence on the pitch, he made sure the back four were right, he told them what to do. That's what his job was as centre half and he did it brilliantly.

"Whenever Jim got sent off he'd always say 'I didn't deserve that!' but I remember the Malcolm MacDonald one very, very clearly. He came barging into the back of him. Malcolm was protecting the ball with his chest and Jim was coming so quick I don't think he could stop and he just battered him, ploughed through him. By chance, his head hit the back of Malcolm's head. The referee had a good view of it and I don't think there was anything the big man could do. He just had to go in and have an early bath and that was it. But he was still protesting his innocence that night!"

Inevitably, the post-match chat centred around the moment Jim had mashed Macdonald. "From what the other players were telling me it was bad to watch," says Macdonald, "they were telling me 'He arched his back and then suddenly went whoooof and smashed his forehead into the back of your head'."

The incident still rankles with Macdonald and he didn't hold back at the time either as a war of words raged between the two clubs. The England forward said after the game, "In my opinion United were crude, not only in their tactics but in the way they played. It is a terrible shame that a great club should resort to such methods."

His Newcastle team-mate Terry Hibbitt also put the boot in verbally, saying he hoped United were relegated. "Manchester United used to be a credit to the game, now they deserve to go down. Kicking will not save them. They are degrading a great club. They just kept thumping Mac. Managers often shout from the bench, but not the sort of stuff that we heard from United's bench."

Macdonald also pointed the figure at Docherty and his coaching staff, adding, "I feel sorry for Holton. He got sent off for obeying instructions."

It is unsurprising that Macdonald's incendiary comments went down like a lead balloon with Docherty, who threatened to sue. United also promptly lodged an appeal against the red card, probably in the hope of delaying any suspension. "It's the old story of envy," Docherty raged, "people seem to have made their minds up that Manchester United are going down and perhaps they don't like it when we show them that it is not going to happen. Part of the trouble against Newcastle was that Malcolm Macdonald hardly got a kick at the ball, thanks to Jim Holton.

"Old Trafford is becoming a hard place once more for visiting teams to get away with the points. That is the way I want it to be, but I resent the accusations we are a dirty team. The players are challenging for every ball, but that doesn't mean they are going out of their way to hurt opponents."

Sir Matt Busby also had his say, effectively telling Newcastle to man up and shut up. "The first half at Birmingham the previous week produced far more heavy tackling against us than we experienced in the whole game with Newcastle. Yet we did not come away screaming. If I felt something was happening in our style of play that could destroy our image I would say something. It is just not there."

Busby was right about the treatment United had received at Birmingham. Holton had been forced to watch helplessly from the sidelines as he served the final game of his suspension, but when he saw Blues' defender John Roberts giving Lou Macari a hard time, he warned the Wales international, "I'll break you in two at Old Trafford for what you did to the wee dwarf today!"

With United stung by Newcastle's taunts and castigated by the press, the last fixture Tommy Docherty would have wanted was an away game against Lazio in the Anglo-Italian Cup. "I will be making the point to my players not to get involved in any trouble," Docherty - with his fingers firmly crossed - assured reporters on the eve of the match in Rome.

United's participation in the 1973 Anglo-Italian Cup, a convoluted consolation tournament for teams not involved in European competition, had started with a 1-1 draw at home to Fiorentina, in which Holton scored.

Lazio was the first of two away trips and Docherty, with his vast experience of football around the globe, must have known it would be a stern test of their discipline. The manager may have inwardly feared a free-for-all against the Italians, but before the game, as the players browsed around some of Rome's shops, he managed to mask his anxiety with a razor-sharp one-liner heard by journalists. When The Doc saw the bull-like Holton hovering close to a display of pottery and porcelain, he hollered: "Get Big Jim out of here – there's china in the shop!"

Against Lazio the United players heeded their manager's pleas and answered questions about their temperament impeccably. Under constant provocation, United delighted Docherty with an admirable show of restraint and discipline. Not that they behaved like choir boys mind you. A volatile 0-0 draw in the Stadio Olimpico produced a number of skirmishes and needless to say Jim was in

Jim mobbed by young fans at Old Trafford, where he was an instant hit.

the thick of them. One melee was so chaotic that referee Gordon Hill broke his finger separating rival players, but he had nothing but praise for United's reaction. "It was a credit to United that all their players showed such ice-cool restraint, and they certainly helped me in every possible way to keep the game going all the way to the finish," said the referee.

Hill may have shown a degree of restraint himself and it is conjecture whether he simply did not see Bobby Charlton being thumped in the face off the ball, or goalkeeper Jimmy Rimmer spat on, or chose not to pour oil on the fire by brandishing red cards in such a hostile environment.

Jim's first two months at United gave him an attention-grabbing record of: played 9, sent off twice, booked once, suspended for two matches, goals scored three. After the red cards against Oporto and Newcastle, Jim was forced to defend his character against a barrage of criticism being chucked in his direction. "I was concerned about my reputation after the sendings-off. If I was the sort of player who went over the top, then I'd deserve to be out of the game, but I'm not," he said, "I'm not a ball player or anything like that. I'm a winner of the ball and good in the air. You've got to be physical

– it's a physical position; you against him, a centre forward against a centre half. But I'm not a dirty player. I may have a few rough edges but it would be ridiculous to say I'm crude, and even more so to talk that way about United, with the talent we have here."

Criticism of United's robust style was reaching epidemic proportions in the press box, with many self-appointed guardians of the Beautiful Game wading into United, Docherty and scapegoat-in-chief Big Jim.

Jan Holton insists most of it was water off a duck's back as far as Jim was concerned. "It never used to bother him to be honest. Ninety per cent of the time he was fine with it. His attitude was if that's what they think, then that's their prerogative. There were journalists who thought he was a dirty player and they said as much. But there were plenty more who said he certainly wasn't a dirty player, he was a hard player – there is a big difference."

Not all of the barbs were vindictive. Derek Hodgson of the *Daily Express* injected some humour when he colourfully described an incident from Holton's first Manchester derby, a 0-0 draw with City at Old Trafford. He reported: "Tony Book, never a man to shirk a challenge, went galloping down the right in pursuit of a long ball. Then he heard from his left what must have sounded like the first Cavalry Charge in Manchester since Peterloo. Mr Book prudently braked, Holton thundered by to clear and Chorlton-cum-Hardy Baths were spared having to admit the first Manchester footballer ever to arrive in the middle of a derby match."

David Meek, of the *Manchester Evening News*, was better qualified than most to evaluate the defender's technique, and he opined, "The signing of Jim Holton has been a tremendous success. A big strong centre-half has been needed since the retirement of dependable iron man Bill Foulkes in 1969 and United have got one in Holton. I rate the signing of Holton as the single most important factor in the rebuilding of Manchester United. His impact during those first few critical weeks was tremendous and he influenced considerably the character and pattern of play of the whole team. He immediately revitalised the back line with his rugged strength.

"Jim Holton is a strong man who plays to his strength. No-one wants to encourage dirty play or reckless intimidation but it was high time United had a centre half capable of providing the aggression that is part of every successful team's make-up. The Reds were in danger of pussy-footing their way down into the Second Division. Holton, 6 feet 2 inches tall, lean and a little mean, will put that right."

Long-serving goalkeeper Alex Stepney meanwhile described Holton as the best number 5 that had played in front of him since Bill Foulkes. Foulkes, like Harry Gregg, had survived the Munich Air Disaster and courageously returned to the field of play within 13 days. A one club-man, who crowned his career by playing in the 1968 European-Cup winning team, he was unquestionably one of United's greatest ever players never mind defenders, and when he offered young Holton a ringing endorsement it must have done wonders for the Scots confidence. "He's the sort of player you can build around," said Foulkes, who was able to survey Holton at close quarters from his position on United's coaching staff. "He is extremely mobile, and for a big man he is exceptionally good with his feet. Jim Holton is the best centre-half playing in this country. He has been in top-class football for only five minutes but I would put him ahead of any of his challengers. The lad has a reputation for being a rough player, but I handed out more stick than he ever will without getting noticed. He certainly has no malice about him but a big man determined to win the ball always has problems. I only picked up one booking in my career because I was more cold-eyed going for the ball. Jim needs referees who know what is going on, especially when opponents start taking advantage of the situation."

And offering Jim some sound advice, which he would heed as his career developed, Foulkes added: "If Jim has one thing to learn it is patience. He is so anxious to get at the ball that he sometimes has a bite when he could shadow the man."

Jim put his red card against Newcastle behind him to play a pivotal role in helping United beat the drop. The victory against the Magpies sparked an eight-game unbeaten run which steered them towards safety. Pleasingly for Docherty, five of these eight games were built on clean sheets, prompting him to say, "We have a back four as strong as anywhere in the country."

Jim got on the scoresheet again in a 2-0 win at Southampton. The other scorer was Bobby Charlton – the last of 198 league goals the legendary midfielder would score for Manchester United.

United's final two matches of the season were at home to Sheffield United and away to Chelsea. They lost both, but the games will be remembered as the competitive swansong for the peerless Charlton. In his farewell home league match, he walked on to the pitch through a guard of honour to receive the warm congratulations of Chairman Louis Edwards and an emotional Busby. Sir Matt had known Charlton as man and boy and he said prophetically: "The name Bobby Charlton will stand forever. Time will undoubtedly add to Charlton's stature rather than diminish it."

After his 604th and final league match, a 1-0 defeat at Stamford Bridge, Charlton, soon to be appointed manager at Preston North End, said: "I leave Manchester United under the best possible circumstances. I have had more than 20 years with the club and I have enjoyed every minute of it. If the club had gone down I would most certainly have carried on."

Crystal Palace and West Brom were the two teams relegated, while United finished 18th – only ten points behind fifth-paced Wolves in a tightly packed First Division.

Despite the flirtation with relegation, Sir Matt underlined his faith in Docherty. "There is a spirit about the club again and I feel the future looks reasonably good. Tommy Doc has got the ability to communicate with the players. He makes them feel part of it. He gives them something and in return they give back. Before Tommy arrived it was like a nightmare. We were all under a cloud with embarrassments and headaches. I was beginning to lose hope."

By the end of the season, Jim had won over the majority of the sceptics, with *Goal Magazine* lauding the big Scot for the improvement he had shown and naming him bargain buy of the season. "Holton is dominating in the air, tackles with blockbusting power, and leaves a lasting impression on every striker who comes up against him."

Holton would build on a good season's work by winning his first full international caps in the 1973 Home Internationals, but when he got back down to club duty the following season, there were no shortage of enemies ready to accuse him of dirty tricks – most of them armed with a Biro. Brian Glanville, the eminent *Sunday Times* football writer, and Frank McGhee of the *Mirror*, filed fierce diatribes condemning Jim and United's forceful style under Docherty.

One typical example came after a ding-dong battle with West Ham at Upton Park in January 1974, when McGhee led the chorus of disapproval. Comparing his behaviour to Al Capone, McGhee wrote "The city of Chicago in prohibition days must have been more than a little like Upton Park was on Saturday." Pointing the finger at Jim for "a classically simple, brutal assault" on Billy Bonds in the first few seconds of the game, McGhee claimed to be so disheartened by the strong-arm tactics employed by United during a 2-1 defeat, that he didn't particularly care if his "first love" United were relegated, and warned, "if they want to go on playing as they did for too much of this game I want a divorce." To complete the hatchet-job, the *Mirror*'s sub-editors also had their pound of flesh. Under an unflattering picture of a snarling, gap-toothed Holton was the caption, "Hard man Jim Holton... eating strikers for breakfast can be mighty tough on the teeth."

However Jim was still very much adored at Old Trafford. 'Mr Manchester' Tony Wilson, the man who would later found Factory Records and discover Joy Division, New Order and the Happy Mondays, and was steeped in watching United, leapt to the defence of Jim in a passionate column he wrote for *Foul*, 'Football's Alternative Paper', in February 1974.

"Despite Brian Glanville's accusations of bestial origin and psychopathic leanings, I still believe that James Holton esquire is the best thing Tommy Docherty has done for Manchester and the best thing to happen to Old Trafford since they used to play a radio recording of the Benfica game at half-time. When he takes those enforced legal absences he's missed, like a junkie misses his needle. The most mindless aspect about the criticism heaped on

Holton has been the 'a disgrace to the tradition of Manchester United' approach. Remember the long-regretted Maurice Setters, the human scythe, so much part of the early Sixties team. And, of course, young Jim's precursor Norbert Stiles. Now that boy was rough but vital to any success that was achieved."

There were worse players to be compared to than Stiles. Indeed, when Sir Matt Busby first clapped eyes on Holton – minus his teeth – in the Old Trafford dressing room, he was heard to exclaim: "Good God, it's a giant Nobby Stiles!"

Holton himself admitted that he may have been a bit over-exuberant when he first played for United, but insisted that he had worked hard to adapt. "I'm ready to concede that in my early days at Old Trafford perhaps I was a bit rough at times. Maybe clumsy is a better word. The thing was that I was very conscious of being on trial, and I was utterly determined not to lose this golden chance of proving myself. In my enthusiasm maybe I rushed into the tackle a bit. I had to try to adapt very quickly to the change of pace. First Division football is a different kettle of fish to that played in the Third Division."

Sadly for Jim and United, First Division football was on borrowed time.

7: HAMPDEN ROARS

"It was great for us both to score that night at Hampden, the goals that took us to the World Cup"

Joe Jordan

S HOWING the strength and determination that would become his trademark, James Allan Holton made it out of the womb to take his place in the world in time for an England v Scotland match at Wembley. The infant Holton was just three days old when the Scots claimed a famous 3-2 win at the home of the Auld Enemy in 1951. Twenty-two years later he would be playing in the historic fixture himself.

That hadn't looked likely when he was playing with Shrewsbury Town in the winter of 1972 but in five remarkable months Holton defied convention to go from the Third Division to fully-fledged Scotland international by the age of 22. Jim's move to Manchester United was the launch-pad to the national team, but he was also fortunate to be in the right place at the right time.

When Tommy Docherty quit the Scotland post to join Manchester United, the Scottish Football Association chose Willie Ormond as his successor, appointing him in January 1973. Former international Ormond – who played in the 1954 World Cup - had been best known for his exploits as an outside left in Hibernian's all-conquering Famous Five forward line of the late 1940s–early 1950s, and had gone on to establish himself as a respected, intelligent, successful manager with St Johnstone before he was offered the Scotland job.

In contrast to the brash, authoritarian Docherty, Ormond took a more relaxed approach to curfews and discipline and though the likeable Musselburgh man was nobody's fool, players would occasionally take advantage of his good nature. More of which later!

The Doc had left Scotland boasting a solid record, only losing three of his 12 games in charge, although a 1-0 defeat in an ill-tempered kicking match against England at Hampden in May 1972 had cost the Scots the Home International Championship and was considered a blot on his record.

However, if a Scotland manager was to be judged solely on results against the Auld Enemy, Ormond would have been dead in the water after his first match at the helm, an utterly demoralising 5-0 thrashing at the hands of Sir Alf Ramsey's side. The friendly, played at a snow-cleared Hampden on 14 February 1972, had been organised to 'celebrate' the SFA's centenary, but there were crimson red-faces all round in the home camp – Ormond's perhaps the reddest.

The 'St Valentine's Day Massacre' may have been a chastening introduction to international football for Ormond, but inside a year he would use that bitter experience to transform Scotland from a collection of talented yet disjointed individuals into genuine contenders for the World Cup in West Germany. "We must mix skill and strength. That's the only way we will get to Munich," said the manager.

Before he was tempted to Old Trafford, Docherty had laid firm foundations for Scotland to qualify for the finals. Back-to-back victories over Denmark, home and away, effectively turned the three-team Group 8 into a shoot-out between Scotland and Czechoslovakia. Scotland's chances were boosted considerably when the Czechs unexpectedly stumbled to a 1-1 draw in Copenhagen. The equation couldn't be simpler: beat Czechoslovakia at Hampden in September and Scotland would be on the plane to Munich.

The Czechs' slip up in Denmark happened days before a youthful Scotland squad gathered in May for the 1973 Home Internationals – a demanding sequence of three matches in eight days. There were several new faces in Ormond's pool, but one was causing a bigger stir than any other – big Jim.

The tabloids had seized on the iron-man reputation he had quickly established in his first few months at Manchester United, and he was labelled a real-life 'Garth' – the muscle-bound superhuman comic strip hero from the *Daily Mirror*.

Interest in Jim went into over-drive when he was named in the starting XI to face Wales in the Home Internationals opener in Wrexham, one of six players under 23. As the squad gathered in Chester to prepare for the match, Hugh Taylor of the *Daily Record* wrote, "Look out for the fascinating partnership in defence of the mighty muscle-man Jim Holton of Manchester United and the brilliant Derek Johnstone of Rangers. This is probably the best example of the Ormond success recipe you could imagine - the power of Holton and the almost arrogant artistry of Johnstone. Many Scots are asking: Is Holton all that good? Just ask United's assistant manager Pat Crerand, who has this to say about the young giant: 'Would he be any use against Martin Chivers at Wembley? Why, if Chivers knew Jim was playing he wouldn't turn up!'"

Docherty reacted with glee to the news that Jim had been picked. Returning from United's end-of-season trip to Majorca, he predicted, "Jim Holton is going to be the best centre-half Scotland has had since Willie Woodburn. I played with Willie and now I am watching Jim every week as his manager. The fans at home will realise what I mean when they see Jim play. He is going to be one of the best centre-halves in football."

If Jim had read any of the hype surrounding his debut, it didn't show. He turned in a commanding performance at the heart of the Scotland defence to keep the Welsh attack subdued and help Ormond's team claim a morale-boosting 2-0 win. Jim's United team-mate George Graham scored both the goals, but would only play one more time for his country.

The win was obtained without the influence of talismanic captain Billy Bremner, who was rested after a gruelling series of matches with Leeds. Hibs' Pat Stanton captained the team, who unusually wore white shirts and navy shorts. They could have been mistaken for England until they opened their mouths! The inactive Bremner, never shy of opening his mouth, had taken a place on the bench to cheer on his countrymen at the Racecourse Ground and he couldn't resist chirping away at Wales substitute Wyn Davies when he saw the big centre forward being readied for action.

"You've got a big heart going on there against Jim," he laughed. Davies would suffer the same fate as his partner John Toshack – Holton never gave either of them a moment's peace.

Ormond was encouraged by the result and had praise for his debutant defender. "Jim Holton is effective. He gets everything in the air. He does the hard job I want him to do – that is to stop, and win the battles in the air. There are others around him to do the clever stuff."

Club-mate Willie Morgan played on the wing against Wales and was delighted to see Jim make the breakthrough alongside him and prove his international worth. "Jim adapted very well to international football, but you have to appreciate what a good player he was," says Morgan, who played 21 times for Scotland. "Unlike today where you pay £50 million for a dummy that can't play, in those days you played in a position and you were responsible for playing in that position. Jim's job was to stop the centre forward and he was brilliant at it. For two reasons: 1) they were frightened of him, because he looked like bloody Shrek and 2) he was a good player, a great defender. He kept it simple and did what was asked of him. I know I'm of the old school, but back then it really was about keeping things simple, not the way some coaches have over-complicated the game now."

Buoyed by their fluent victory against Wales, Scotland looked forward to a midweek match against Northern Ireland before the biggest test of all – England at Wembley.

The Irish had narrowly lost 2-1 to England at neutral Goodison Park, an alternative venue selected during the Troubles, and Ormond cautioned, "We have home advantage but we're not kidding ourselves it will be anything but a hard one."

Holton again dominated the pre-match build-up, and Northern Ireland striker Sammy Morgan – brought in for the injured Derek Dougan – was asked if he had found Jim an unfair opponent when the pair had crossed swords in the Third Division when Morgan was with Port Vale. "I don't accept the view that Jim is a dirty player and a hatchet man," Morgan insisted. "Our meetings have not been the most delicate affairs but I have never thought of him as a vicious player or a bad-hearted player. I think he has been maligned and called some unfair names because he has brought a touch of Third Division honesty into the First Division."

Jim's Old Trafford team-mate Trevor Anderson was also asked about the 'Holton effect', "I'd rather play with him than against him, but I don't think he deserves the criticism. In fact, I would say he's among the top three centre-halves in the First Division."

Despite the win in Wales, the visit of Northern Ireland did not capture the imagination of the Scottish public. Even admission prices ranging from 33p on the uncovered terracing to £1.10 in the centre stand could only attract a crowd of 39,000 to Hampden.

Those who stayed away were glad they had done so as Scotland perplexed Ormond with a lethargic, error-strewn display. Goals from Anderson and Martin O'Neill gave the Irish a thoroughly deserved win, and an 89th-minute Kenny Dalglish consolation goal could not prevent Scotland from being booed off. England had comfortably beaten Wales 24 hours earlier, so Scotland headed to Wembley with their expectations kept in check.

As is the custom ahead of this fixture, journalists on both side of the border merrily stirred the pot and played to the galleries, and Alex Cameron of the *Daily Record* questioned the bravery of England and Tottenham centre forward Martin Chivers ahead of his impending physical battle with Holton. "Chivers is big, fast and deadly but there are suspicions in tough penalty box battles he is not sure to stay around to win a Victoria Cross. Faced by Jim Holton, whose public relations men appear to be confusing him with Mick McManus (the wrestler) or George Foreman, it will be interesting to see what happens."

Legend has it that while the teams waited in the Wembley tunnel, preparing to enter the arena, an England player eyeballed Holton and rasped: "You're nothing but a big dirty Scottish bastard." Quick as a flash, Jim responded: "Aye! And don't you ever forget it!"

It was a bruising match, littered with fouls. The fiery Bremner and Holton were blamed for the bulk of them, with Norman Giller of the *Daily Express* accusing the pair of "kicking anything that moved". Looking beyond the understandable over-exuberance, however, Scotland had every reason to be proud of their performance.

The spoils and the Home Championship went to England, who secured a 1-0 victory when Alan Ball flighted a free-kick on to the head of Martin Peters in the 54th minute, Chivers distracting Holton with an intelligent run to the near post. However, only the brilliance of Peter Shilton denied Scotland a positive result, and German referee Kurt Tschenscher appeared to turn a blind eye when Lou Macari was bundled over in the penalty box by Peter Storey, much to the chagrin of Paddy Crerand who had a few choice words for ITV viewers from the commentary box!

Many Scotland fans viewed Alan Ball as the anti-Christ, a reputation cemented when he had scored the winner at Hampden 12 months earlier, and the sight of the passionate Englishman about to bag another win proved too much. Fuelled by a weekend of over-indulgence, one well-dressed assailant in a suit and tie rushed on to the Wembley turf with the England midfielder in his sights. After aiming a haymaker at Ball, he needed to be restrained by players and police in an unseemly melee, with Holton wading in like a nightclub bouncer. Ball's post-match response to the incident borders on the incredible, and shows how much times have changed. "I didn't see him coming and he caught me with a glancing blow," the England veteran told inquisitive reporters. "That didn't hurt me – but it still hurts me to see the way the police dragged him away. The man would be welcome in my house for a drink at any time. I think it's fabulous to feel that strongly about your country. Those Scottish fans were magic. I still can't get over it." Ball could have been having fun at the pressmen's expense, but it appears his comments came from the heart.

Holton's eagerly-anticipated contest with Chivers produced fewer fireworks that had been anticipated and it was clear the combative pair had the utmost respect for one another. Leeds United striker Allan Clarke, rather than Chivers, was the man who swapped shirts with Jim at the end of the match.

Watching from the Wembley stand was Jim's best pal John

Hillan: "I remember he had a good battle with Martin Chivers, who was a beast of a fellow. Len Cantello and a couple of other guys were with me, and there was a guy just along from us shouting at Jim for not doing this and not doing that. My mate Bluey turned round to him and said: 'You better watch what you're saying pal, this is his best mate and he'll knock your fuckin heid in!'"

Sir Alf Ramsey admitted it was the "best Scotland display I have seen in my 10 years as England's manager" and from both sides of the Press Box divide further praise was reserved for a mature performance from Holton.

Arthur Hopcraft, the *Observer*'s man at Wembley, said: "Surprising was the confidence with which Holton subdued Chivers. Holton has looked clumsy to a barely credible degree in his early matches for his club, but his improvement has been startling."

David Meek, football writer for the *Manchester Evening News*, says he admired Jim's metamorphosis from raw recruit to international footballer. "He built on his success and the confidence that came for playing for Manchester United and he became a more sophisticated defender which took him into international level. He was a bright, intelligent guy who profited from his experience."

Holton's Manchester United team-mate and compatriot Alex Forsyth says Holton was immediately accepted as one of the new faces of Scotland. "Every Scottish supporter liked him – as soon as he pulled on that Scotland shirt you got what you saw; a big, hard guy who would put his body on the line and give it everything he had. And that was a great Scotland team don't forget. Even though it was a fantastic squad, Jim would probably be the first one down on your team-sheet, 'okay, Jim Holton No 5, now who will the other ten be?' You could build your team around a guy like that. Up there, down there, he would win it, and alongside Martin Buchan – a guy blessed with pace who could read the game so well – he was brilliant for Scotland."

Scotland had finished only third in the Home Championship, but they had won plenty of admirers and optimism was tangible ahead of the crucial clash with the Czechs in September, which would decide their World Cup destiny.

Czechoslovakia had avenged their draw in Copenhagen by thrashing the Danes 6-0 in Prague, watched by a large contingent of Scottish football writers. Yes, the Czechs had looked good, but as Alex Cameron of the *Daily Record* noted derisively "Denmark were so poor that Drumchapel Amateurs could have scored against them."

Ormond had the luxury of two summer friendlies to tinker with his formula. The first, a match against Switzerland in June, taught him little. After gathering at Largs, the Scotland party endured a nightmare 12-hour journey when their plane was delayed with engine trouble in London. The travel ordeal seemed to affect Ormond's team and they succumbed to a sluggish 1-0 defeat. The second friendly, eight days later, saw World Cup holders Brazil welcomed to Hampden for a glamour fixture to mark the SFA's centenary. But those expecting to see a showcase of football at its glorious best were left sorely disappointed in a desperately ugly encounter, which only served as evidence that Brazil had unforgivably shifted the emphasis in their play from beauty to brawn. "They seem to think the physical important and skill, adventure and inventiveness, and dignity secondary," lamented *The Scotsman's* football writer John Rafferty.

Roberto Rivelino became engaged in a running battle with Billy Bremner, and the over-sensitive Brazilian also took umbrage at a few meaty challenges from Holton, unusually wearing the No 6 shirt that day. Unimpressive Brazil needed an own goal via the head of the unfortunate Derek Johnstone to secure a hollow 1-0 victory. In one swoop Johnstone had unwittingly filled the vacancy of scapegoat and the Rangers man, who had until then been Jim's international central defensive partner, would have to wait three long years before he was reinstated to the Scotland team. Mario Zagalo, Brazil manager, was not impressed with Scotland, sniffily saying: "The Scots played very like England – high balls into the middle all the time. They did not keep possession enough. They did not have ideas enough. They did not interchange positions enough." Almost three months would pass before the Czechs came to town.

★

If the Melbourne Cup is the race that stops a nation, this was the game that stopped a nation. On police advice, the crowd was restricted to 100,000, and it would be no exaggeration to say that the SFA could have sold double that number of tickets.

There was great news for those unable to attend: the match would be shown live on Scottish Television, following frantic negotiations which only resulted in a deal being struck on the eve of the match. Live televised games were a rarity in 1973, so this was an enormous coup for the broadcaster, and households rejoiced in the news, which made back page headlines on match-day.

This was billed as the most important fixture in Scotland's history, and Ormond and his team were determined to ensure the nation had an occasion to celebrate. They say fortune favours the brave, and the Scotland manager showed enormous courage by naming two debutants in his midfield – Coventry's City's tireless Tommy Hutchison and the delicate, but gifted, George Connelly of Celtic. He also brought back The King - Denis Law, who had by then left Manchester United for City - for his 50th cap at the age of 33.

"It was hard to believe that Scotland would want me again because I had felt really low when United allowed me to go," said Law. "It isn't age that counts it's how you feel and I felt like playing football. I reckon too that the idea of helping Scotland qualify lifted me again."

Jim almost never made it on to the pitch to face Czechoslavakia. He tweaked his groin during training at Largs on the eve of the match and was rated 50-50 but when the Scots ran out to deafening noise, there was the unmistakable figure of Holton.

A packed, boisterous Hampden Park was momentarily silenced when Zdenek Nehoda gave the Czechs the lead after 33 minutes. Somehow, his hit-and-hope angled drive from near the right-hand corner of the box eluded the grasp of Ally Hunter and sailed into the net. It would be the Celtic goalkeeper's final game for Scotland.

Eight minutes later Scotland won a corner on the left, which debutant Hutchison elected to take. Holton, the last man to arrive in the penalty box, had timed his run to perfection and with an almighty leap he out-jumped the Czech keeper Ivo Viktor and four bewildered defenders to head powerfully into the top corner from eight yards out, flattening Denis Law in the process.

"I got the most awful knock when that first goal of ours was scored," said Law afterwards. "I jumped, but I thought a tank had hit me and I was sent flying. As I got up, feeling sore and a bit aggressive I saw that it was big Jim Holton had hit me and the ball was in the back of the net. Jim never thinks to say 'excuse me' and I'm not sure I'm going to like playing against him in the Manchester City-United game in December!"

As the ball nestled in the net, Holton jumped for joy and raised his right arm in triumph before he was engulfed by captain Billy Bremner, who sprung a few feet in the air himself to wrap himself around the goalscorer in jubilation.

John Blackley hadn't yet made his Scotland debut, but as part of the squad he recalls that Holton's goal had been designed on the training ground. "We worked on set pieces on the morning of the game and exactly the type of corner that we scored from. Big Jim had obviously taken it all in, made the run as he had in training, and nicked a goal for us. Jim knew his strengths and he played to them. He always made the most of that stature he had in both boxes."

Scotland emerged for the second half full of belief and with the collective will of 100,000 and the millions watching on TV, squarely behind them.

In the 72nd minute, Bremner went agonisingly close when his effort struck the post and flashed across the face of the goal but the ball was only cleared as far as Willie Morgan, who cleverly beat his man and dinked the ball into the box with the outside of his right boot. There was Joe Jordan, on as a substitute for Kenny Dalglish, to stoop and plant the ball into the net with a firm header.

"Magnificent Scotland! Magnificent!" said a proud Arthur Montford, the STV commentator, enjoying his greatest night behind the mic. For those who watched the game on television, Montford's account of the game has lived long in the memory. It would be fair to say the broadcaster, a true gentleman of sport, kicked every ball with the Scotland team that night. He treated viewers to classics such as "C'mon lads hang on" and "Watch your back", before the 90th minute finally passed and he was able to declare "That's it. THAT IS IT! Congratulations Scotland, well done boys."

Match-winner Jordan's voice is thick with emotion when he recounts that night. "I speak to people all over the world who will tell you they were at the game or watched it on TV. It was a unique night because of the period of time the Scottish nation had been waiting to qualify for the World Cup, and we were playing against a team that were arguably the best in Europe at the time [the Czechs would go on to win the European Championships in 1976].

"Everybody was desperate to get a ticket, and all of our Scots team-mates at Leeds wanted to get there and support us that night. Billy and I were in the team, but David Harvey, Gordon McQueen, Eddie Gray and Peter Lorimer – who was suspended after being sent off against Denmark - came up in the car from Leeds to see the game with some friends. To players who weren't in that particular squad, they still wanted to be there to support their team. That's how huge it was.

"In those days, playing at Hampden in front of a 100,000 crowd, Scotland were capable of beating anybody and that's what happened. I remember what it meant to the older players in particular, Billy and Denis. They had achieved so much on so many fronts in their careers, but they hadn't been to the World Cup, and they'd finally done it."

Jordan is proud and delighted that it is he and Holton that are both remembered for the goals that night too. "It was great for us both to score that night, the goals that took us to the World Cup. Jim was a bit of a folk hero with the fans. That was not an easy thing to do in those days because of the amount of quality players that were around, but Jim was idolised by the Scottish supporters.

"I think they loved the way he played football. Not only could he do his job as a defender but he could, as he did that night, score crucial goals. I think he played in a way that the supporter could empathise with, could connect with, could understand. Jim epitomised what they would have done themselves by showing a total commitment to play for the jersey. The support that night – 100,000 people – and other nights before and after, saw Jim at his very best and that's why people could associate with him. The way he performed throughout the 1974 campaign, and during his time at international level, is why people still talk about him now."

Hutchison, who delivered the corner for Holton's goal, has still got to pinch himself that he was part of it all. "When you look at it now, it would never happen for somebody to make their debut in a qualifier. It just went so well for us on the night."

The Scotland players hugged each other at full-time, then with most of the team wearing the white shirts of their Czech opponents, they chaired manager Ormond around the pitch on a glorious lap of honour lasting 15 minutes, with fans chanting "Munich, Munich here we come!"

Later, captain Billy Bremner revealed how quiet man Ormond had to be coaxed out of the dressing room to join the celebrations. The emotion-choked Scotland manager said, "I just can't believe it's happened. That last period seemed to be the longest quarter of an hour of my life. Every 30 seconds, I checked my watch and the wait seemed never-ending I also lost my voice shouting at the lads but it was a tremendous victory. My team just refused to give up and admit that they would get any other result than a victory."

Most Scotland fans pinpoint the game as Hampden's greatest ever night. There was an unprecedented spirit of togetherness bonding players, supporters and press. "It was a wonderful time," reflected Montford in an interview years later. "Scotland kept qualifying for World Cups with great players, and it all started against Czechoslovakia. You just get that sixth sense during commentaries that something is going to happen and it did. The ground was jumping when Joe Jordan scored the winner and that was when the Hampden Roar died its last because the North Stand was going and the stadium was about to be refurbished. Willie Ormond, the

Goals from Big Jim and one of his best mates Joe Jordan took Scotland through to their first World Cup since 1958 sparking wild celebrations throughout the land.

manager, threw the dressing room door open and the media just piled in. It's unimaginable to think of any manager doing that now. Television, newspaper reporters, the lot were all in there."

Willie Morgan gets misty-eyed at the very mention of the triumph against Czechoslovakia. "It's probably the greatest night of my career as a footballer – the feeling was unparalleled," he says. "It was unbelievable. That night we stayed in a hotel out near the airport. We were in Jim's room celebrating with all the other lads who were going back to England the next day, it was some night!"

Full-back Danny McGrain agrees, "that night at Hampden was just magnificent. It had been building for months towards some sort of crescendo, and it turned into one of the best-ever nights for the players and the supporters. After falling behind, big Jim's goal gave us the encouragement we needed to go and win the game. We can laugh about it now, because we won, but Denis Law had a nightmare!"

In truth Law probably wasn't at his brilliant best, but it didn't matter one bit. "I don't think I have ever been happier in my life," said Law who was joined by Bremner, Jordan and others in Glasgow city centre that night as they soaked up the enormity of what had just happened. "I remember being out with Billy and Denis in Glasgow that night," says Jordan. "We went out, sat back and took it all in by thinking not only of what we'd already achieved, but what we could possibly experience the next summer. We didn't have a crazy night, we went and sat down, had a few drinks and just imagined what we were going to face.

"Through your career you don't really get many nights like that. There are many ups and downs in football, but if you're lucky you might qualify for a World Cup and experience playing in one, but it doesn't happen every day. You can't take anything like that for granted, and I never did. That night was unique because 16 years is a long time to wait. There was so much satisfaction and relief, particularly for guys like Billy and Denis."

The morning after, Law joined *The Scotsman's* football writer John Rafferty for a victory stroll round the streets of Glasgow and summed up how he and the nation were feeling. As sleep-deprived children headed into school bleary-eyed and euphoric punters went in search of a hair of the dog, Rafferty noted, "from taxi drivers and old women to staid businessmen, they all acclaimed the long flowing hair and slim figure of Law."

Walking considerably taller than his usual 5ft 9in, Law told Rafferty, "they're great people. There's nobody like them in the world. Even when they are giving you stick you can't help but like them. This is a bit different from the time we lost to Poland [in a World Cup qualifier in 1965]. Then they were shouting at Pat Crerand and me, 'Get out of town you English bums!' Imagine. . . Pat and me English bums!"

Turning to the influence of Ormond, Law said, "He left us alone to relax when the serious work sessions were over. We appreciated that. I have known a lot of managers and most of them seem to think that they have to keep on talking about the game. They get you jittery. Ormond talked little, but when he did it was about the simple things and in this game, the important things are simple. He began to grow on me and the others and there are not

Jim nods home the opening goal against West Germany in November 1973 at Hampden Park. The visitors grabbed a late equaliser but it was a promising performance from the Scots.

many managers that can be said about. A group of players at this level are hard to talk to. They have been around and know a bit about the game."

As an encore, STV repeated the entire 90 minutes again the following evening as Scotland milked the feel-good factor. The heroes who had booked a place in the World Cup finals were loudly saluted when they next played at Hampden against tournament hosts West Germany in a friendly in November 1973.

Big Jim picked up where he had left off with another international goal to give Scotland the lead after five minutes. Willie Morgan swung in a corner from the right which Law headed against the thigh of team-mate Dalglish in a crowded six-yard box, and as the ball ricocheted into the air, it fell perfectly into the path of Holton to nod past keeper Wolfgang Kleff, who was replaced at half-time by regular number 1 Sepp Maier.

Holton's goal separated the sides until the 82nd minute, and he would be the first to admit that he was culpable in handing the

Germans the opportunity to snatch a scarcely-deserved equaliser. Sandy Jardine took a throw on the right, but a heavy touch from Holton allowed West Germany to seize possession and after smartly moving the ball around, a cross found Uli Hoeness in the box, where he had the simple job of heading past David Harvey.

Scotland could and should have won, but a 1-1 draw against such stellar opponents made waves around the globe and it was widely accepted that Willie Ormond's side would be travelling to West Germany in the summer of 1974 as genuine contenders.

There was more to Jim's performance than his goal. He subdued the West German front two of Jupp Heynckes and Siggi Held, and left their main man Franz Beckenbauer pole-axed on the Hampden turf. One reporter remarked that the German great had been "bowled over like a lollipop man trying to halt a runaway bus." Jim himself laughed off the clash. "He attempted to obstruct me," he said, adding with a wink, "at least, that's my excuse."

Before the game, Holton had revealed that as a young professional Der Kaiser had been his role model. "I never started as a physical centre-half," claimed Jim, then still only 21. "I dreamed of being the Beckenbauer of West Bromwich – with the result that Alan Ashman gave me a free transfer!"

8: HARD BUT FAIR

"Jim Holton was perceived to be a dirty player, but I never saw it that way. He was graceful and talented as well as hard"

George Best

I N AN ERA WHEN Muhammad Ali, Joe Frazier and George Foreman were making history with Rumbles and Thrillas, big Jim Holton was involved in a few heavyweight epics of his own: Holton v Macdonald; Holton v Chivers; Holton v Anyone Brave or Silly Enough To Take Him On!

Holton may have been unheralded when he arrived at Manchester United, but within weeks he was a man of reputation among football writers and opponents, and carried a target across his broad shoulders. Uncompromising, committed and unflinching, this man mountain would attack the ball on the ground and in the air with little thought for safety – his own, or any unfortunate forwards who happened to get in his way.

He was also a manager's dream: a player who could be given a job and be trusted to do it well. Tommy Docherty had bought Jim Holton to apply some much-needed steel and aggression to United, something lacking somewhat since Nobby Stiles stopped patrolling the Old Trafford pitch in 1971. Docherty gave Holton a clear brief – get the better of your opponent and make them fear you. The eager young defender was only too happy to obey.

Holton's methods in early matches veered towards the clumsy and crude, something he himself would later acknowledge with the benefit of hindsight and experience, but at least he could say in all honesty he never once deliberately set out to injure an opponent. Hard? God, yes. But dirty? No way.

Even Malcolm Macdonald, victim of the infamous challenge which saw Holton red-carded when United hosted Newcastle in

March 1973, accepts that it was all part of the game.

It might sound over-nostalgic to say men were men back then, but that's the truth – plain and simple. Defenders could dish it out, forwards could take it, and both sets of adversaries could look after themselves, without the need to dive, roll around, or feign injury.

Holton's unforgiving style as a central defender was the norm rather than the exception. There was a production line of hard men operating in the 1970s. Chelsea had Ron 'Chopper' Harris, Liverpool had Tommy Smith, while Leeds United had almost an entire team of hard men, arguably headed by Norman 'Bite Yer Legs' Hunter, Johnny Giles and Billy Bremner.

But for Macdonald, who faced Jim for club and country, Holton was perhaps the toughest of them all. "I think he's the hardest wild man I've played against," says Macdonald, who amassed more than 400 games and 200 goals in his career. "You could have somebody like Tommy Smith, who would set a situation up so that he could demonstrate that he was a hard man. Jim didn't set situations up in any way; he just took whatever came along and reacted in the hardest of fashions to it.

"Jim Holton was right up Docherty's street. The Doc loved truly aggressive defenders and by heavens, there was nobody more aggressive on the football field than Jim Holton. It was all totally open, there was nothing sneaky. I've met other aggressive players and they used to do it sneakily, they would try and disguise it, but with Jim, there was no disguise whatsoever. He'd have been as well wearing a sign across his chest saying, 'This is how I am and I can't change'.

"There was just no gentle side to him at all; there was no easing off even in any way. It was totally 100% aggressive at all times, in everything that he did. If it meant putting somebody six foot in the air, so be it, he just did it. I don't think he ever really thought about it, but he certainly made referees think about it. You could see them puzzling as to which decision would be appropriate. In those days, by heavens, you had to do something bloody serious to get sent off, not like today.

"I've been looking for a word to describe the way that Jim

Holton went about his defensive duties, and 'agricultural' is what comes to mind. He was very basic, very physical. You know if it didn't move, he shifted it; if it did move, he stopped it. If he was told to mark somebody, you could feel him breathing on your neck for the whole 90 minutes.

"In the top division, defenders have often got a real confidence about themselves and they're happy to step off, knowing that they can just get tight as something develops. But Jim didn't wait for things to develop, he just stayed tight – that was his instinctive game, to stop the centre forward from playing, from scoring. He just went shit-to-a-blanket job. You just couldn't get away from him at all. I used to take him on walkabouts, and he would go everywhere with me. I'd go to the right back position, I'd have a wander across to the left back position and there was Jim, breathing down my neck all the while."

The art of defending wasn't just something Jim had to perfect on the pitch in the early days. He spent many an interview on the defensive, and he believed a lot of the mud being thrown in his direction was beginning to stick – particularly in the eyes of officials.

"The referees are on to me as soon as a game starts," said Holton back then. "It seems I have now got a bad name and they won't let me forget it. Before I have even committed a foul the referees are telling me to watch my step. 'Take it easy son' they say. I feel a marked man.

"I have never been in a punch-up on the pitch and nobody has ever been carried off because of something I have done. If I did, I would be sent off every week. Forwards have their tricks. They back into you, give you a sly elbow in the ribs, trample all over your feet, but I'm not complaining."

Jim had the mind-set, football intelligence and ability to change his game as his career developed, but the notoriety as a 'hatchet-man' which dogged him at United, is considered grossly unfair by those who knew him better.

"He was a bit clumsy, but I don't think he was a vicious man," says David Meek, the *Manchester Evening News* football writer who sadly passed away in October 2018. "He was big and he flung himself into situations that were a bit tough and he wasn't going to come out a loser. So he got this reputation, but I never got the impression that he was a tough guy that wanted to hurt people."

George Best, in his autobiography, also challenged the type-casting of Holton. "He was generally perceived to be a dirty player, but I never saw it that way," said the Irishman. "I thought he was graceful and talented as well as hard. My favourite tale about Jim is the one where his mother is chatting over the garden fence to a neighbour. Jim has just broken through at United and there is a lot of publicity about his highly committed style of play. 'I'm worried he is going to come home one day with a broken leg,' says Mrs Holton. 'Don't worry' replies the lady from next door, 'it won't be his.'"

A humorous anecdote from Best, but there is no escaping the irony that Mrs Holton's fears about her son breaking his leg would be realised not once, but twice.

Team-mates admired Holton's approach to football, and drew inspiration from the way he played. Sammy McIlroy says of him, "Jim was a proper centre half. He was told, 'you're up against a centre forward, make sure you head it, make sure you tackle and keep them as quiet as possible'. Big Jim did that job, he was not dirty he was a proper centre half that wanted to win every challenge and because of that he got stick for it. The players knew exactly what was going on and they loved to have him in the team."

Alex Forsyth agrees: "On the park, he was there to do a job – you were not going to get the better of him, and that was that. He'd even half you in two at training! If you were going to go through and score, or tried to take the mickey out of him, then you were getting it. At least at training he would do it with a smile. He'd say 'sorry wee man, ah didnae mean it' and just lift you up off the ground."

Fellow Scot Jim McCalliog, who joined United in 1974, says: "Jim was more clumsy than brutal. I wouldn't say that Jim Holton would go over the top – no way – but he was a big hard guy and he would go in to win a tackle. If he tackled you, you would feel it, but that's what a defender's job is. He would go for everything in the air and Martin [Buchan] would cover round the back of him, guiding and helping big Jim. But he was physical, there's no doubt about that."

Lou Macari experienced playing with and against Holton, "For me, 4ft nothing and him, 6ft 2 and huge, he was a tough opponent. I was just delighted I wasn't playing against him on the Saturday because it was just during the week at training you realised how powerful a man he was and of course that was his big asset – his strength and his power.

"You've got to play to your strengths and Jim's strengths had got him from Shrewsbury to Man United, so why would he change? He had power and strength and an ability to make it uncomfortable for whoever he was playing against. If he'd gone out there and all of a sudden tried to be Franz Beckenbauer, it would have been a joke because he was no Beckenbauer. The accusations and criticism against him were just ridiculous. There were a lot of real tough, aggressive central defenders who let you know that you were in a game back then."

George Telfer, the former Everton forward, said in a recent interview, "There were a number of tough opponents in those days. I can remember being marked by the likes of Jim Holton and he was terrifying as he used to kick lumps out of you."

Holton always enjoyed testing himself against the best centre forwards in the country and he had some memorable jousts with Martin Chivers. The Tottenham legend insists that there was always a great deal of respect between the pair, particularly during the England v Scotland encounters.

"Certainly against the Scots it was always a physical battle," says Chivers. "It was the end of the season, it was the home internationals, and they were fantastic games to play in. The build up to it was fantastic and there were more Scottish fans at Wembley than English fans. The build up to the game could be nerve wracking. Little Billy Bremner would be having a go at Alan Ball – the verbals always tended to come from the small players, it was the big players like Jim and myself who decided what the result

United v Birmingham City - Jim clears from the feet of Alan Campbell as a young Trevor Francis watches on. It was this type of no-nonsense defending which made the Scot a Manchester United icon.

was going to be. All the talking was over before the game and once we went out on that pitch, the two little ones might have a go at each other, but that was nothing compared to what the big fellas were up to!

"Jim was a great big fella, I had to be on my toes, but thank goodness I was a little bit quicker than him. He was a tough opponent and you had to be wary of that left foot of his. He was physical, but the whole game was physical in those days. We always used to have a chat on the field. Not many centre-halves did. For me, it was one way of distracting them, you could ask him a question and then nip away while he was trying to come up with an answer!"

Jim also traded verbal exchanges with Macdonald, even if the former Newcastle and Arsenal man couldn't understand a word that was being said! "He would talk to me on a regular basis, but his accent was so broad I didn't understand any of it," says Macdonald. "All I knew was that half of it was swear words, and the other half of it was equally derogatory. There was no gentlemanliness about him at all, there was no real sportsmanship – he was there to play against you and to beat you and to stop you and he wasn't going to be polite about it. You could turn round, look over your shoulder and you could sense him snarling, and it wasn't a put-on thing - that was him, that was how he played. Everything was physical and he sought to be frightening."

For Chivers, that was the nature of the beast. "We expected it to be hard," he says. "It could be a real physical battle at times, but there were always ways to look after yourself. If you've got some ability which is better than the opponent, you make the best of it. Jim did an effective job then; there were a lot like him, centre halves were in demand in those days - Ron Yeats was another one – great big fellas. We accepted that and it was up to us to try and get past them and get the ball in the back of the net - that was the only way to hurt them."

Yeats – such a linchpin in Shankly's great Liverpool side - was one of Holton's heroes, but the contemporary he most aspired to be like was Roy McFarland of Derby County.

As for his hardest opponent, Holton could have picked from many. He certainly found Liverpool's Kevin Keegan a real handful, but the man he usually named as his toughest adversary was a much more obscure name from his days playing in the Third Division.

Jim 'Pancho' Fryatt may have been your archetypal lower division journeyman, but he was spring-heeled and fantastic in the air, deadly in front of goal, and was a fans' favourite at Oldham, Stockport and Southport before he moved to Las Vegas in the 1970s. During his spell at Shrewsbury, Holton must have been given a torrid time by Fryatt on more than one occasion to rate him so highly.

Supporters of Manchester United and Leeds United must

have expected sparks to fly whenever Holton came up against his international team-mate Joe 'Jaws' Jordan. But they would be disappointed. Although both were fearsome, fearless competitors, an unwritten pact seemed to exist whenever they lined up in opposing teams.

Jim's friend John Hillan laughs: "People would see Joe Jordan playing with nae teeth and be scared, but I've been in his company umpteen times and off the pitch a more placid fella you couldn't meet. When Jim used to play against big Joe, they seemed to take it turn about who was going to win the high balls. Jim and Joe were never going to fall out or make each other look stupid. Kevin Keegan was a different matter. Jim always saw him as a pest to play against - he could make a right dick out of you with his low centre of gravity."

Gary Gillespie, who would go on to partner Jim in Coventry's defence, agrees with Hillan. "Joe Jordan was his big mate and Joe always had that reputation for putting his arms and elbows everywhere, smashing centre backs – but he would never do that with big Jim. I think Jim and him had a pact and a wee word with each other before the game – 'let's just have a calm game, no fighting, no head butts, no flailing arms' - and the pair of them would both sail through the game. He looked after me in that respect because big Joe stayed away from me as well!"

Jordan, ever the professional, isn't having it though. "Jim never held back, I didn't expect him to, and nor did I," he says. "We got on really well and he was always good company, but it didn't make any difference that we were friends and team-mates in the national team. When we played against each other, Jim wouldn't take any prisoners.

"Throughout my career, whether it was in the tunnel or out on the pitch, I would purposefully not want to speak to opponents prior to a game. I know that they shake hands before games now, but that never went on when I played. I had no interest in speaking to people before the game and Jim was the exact same. He was playing for his club and I was playing for mine and that was it. Jim would deal out what he dealt out and that was fine by me. He

Jim tangling with England's Roy McFarland, a player he admired, at Wembley in 1973. As ever, Jim was hard but fair.

wanted to win the game and the same applied to me. Once the whistle was over and the 90 minutes was up we would go in and have a beer and that would be it."

9: UNITED WE FALL

"Certain members of the squad thought we were too good to go down because we were Manchester United. I was never of that mentality'

Martin Buchan

CALLING THE DOC may have saved Manchester United from the malevolent threat of the drop in season 1972-73, but the new manager could only administer a brief tonic rather than a cure for their ills. Soon United would lurch their way back on to the critical list. Season 1973-74 would prove even more testing, and this time the prognosis was relegation.

In the fullness of time, Manchester United's humbling fall from grace would be seen as a blessing in disguise. When they lost their place in the First Division in April 1974, Tommy Docherty had at least started the revolution needed to rebuild the club. A year in the Second Division would allow them to return with renewed confidence and swagger.

Docherty's revolution wasn't without controversy. Before a ball was kicked he had banished The King. Legendary Old Trafford figure Denis Law was handed a free transfer at the age of 33. Law had scored 237 goals in 404 games in an unforgettable decade at Manchester United, but Docherty felt that injuries and age were diminishing his powers – a view not shared by his former club, Manchester City, who gratefully snapped him up. To say United had not seen the last of the Law Man is an understatement!

It was a bold but contentious move by Docherty, who had also lost the services of Bobby Charlton at the conclusion of the 1972-73 campaign. The third member of United's Holy Trinity, George Best, had 'retired' but would try one last hurrah with the club under Docherty before walking away for good. "Denis needed a fresh spark, a kick up the backside if you want to be basic," said

Docherty. "He got that in his move to Manchester City."

After reporting back for pre-season training, United began with a series of four away friendlies – against Hamburg and Ross County, followed by a pre-season tournament in Spain against local sides Penarol and Real Murcia. The only victory United mustered was against the Scottish part-timers, so perhaps it was no surprise that Arsenal made short work of them at Highbury on the opening day of the new season.

United, wearing yellow shirts and blue shorts, were given a torrid time in the North London sunshine by the rampant Gunners, who won 3-0 thanks to goals from Ray Kennedy, John Radford and Alan Ball. It is worth noting that 200 miles away on that same afternoon, Denis Law was busy scoring twice for Manchester City against Birmingham.

Holton was on the scoresheet himself in the second of two successive wins at Old Trafford, against QPR and Leicester, but this brief interlude of optimism gave way to deep concern when they lost three league games on the spin – home and away defeats to Leicester sandwiched by a loss at Ipswich.

The Old Trafford defeat against Leicester had a bizarre sub-plot, when 2-0 down, United's goalkeeper Alex Stepney – who had scored in a shoot-out during the friendly in Murcia against Penarol - was suddenly handed the responsibility of taking a penalty midway through the second half. Facing his opposite number Peter Shilton, Stepney coolly slotted home from the spot, and in doing so became United's designated penalty taker.

When he again took a penalty a month later to score the only goal of the game against Birmingham, he found himself in the position of being the club's joint top-scorer in the league with Sammy McIlroy. A novelty it may have been, but Stepney did not seek such attention, and Docherty was pilloried by many for what was seen as unnecessary show-boating. "That was Tommy's mistake, I've got to say," says Stepney. "I missed one against Wolves and that was the last one I took, but I should never have been taking them anyway."

That win against Birmingham would be the last league victory

United would taste for more than two months. Ironically, it was the same match in which George Best returned to United's first team. Having been asked back to the club by Sir Matt Busby, Best was given a chance to prove himself by Docherty. He returned in September and 7,000 fans turned out to watch him play in the reserves against Aston Villa. Best impressed the manager enough with his attitude and application to earn a first-team recall, and he was back... but for how long?

Best was way short of his top form but, on the plus side, United turned in some outstanding displays defensively, with Holton, Buchan and Stepney particularly impressive. They drew 0-0 away to Leeds – who would win the league comfortably that season – then held reigning champions Liverpool 0-0 at Old Trafford, Jim doing an excellent job in keeping Kevin Keegan quiet.

After the draw against Liverpool, Denis Law was given a rousing reception at his testimonial match against Ajax at Old Trafford. It didn't matter that he had crossed the divide to sign for City, United fans rose as one to acclaim a living legend.

Jim missed three games through injury in December, and United lost them all - Steve James and then Arnie Sidebottom deputising in the number 5 shirt. A nine-game winless run was finally snapped in their final fixture of 1973 – a 2-0 victory over Ipswich.

The pattern of United's season was very much one step forward, two steps back, and sure enough league defeats followed at QPR and West Ham. The 3-0 humbling at Loftus Road on New Year's Day 1974 is more famously remembered as being Best's final appearance for Manchester United. It was Stan Bowles rather than the forlorn Best who stole the show, although one positive for United was an impressive debut from Stewart Houston, signed from Brentford.

As 1974 arrived, recession-hit Britain, much like Manchester United, was enveloped by deepening gloom. New Year's Day had been decreed a public holiday for the first ever time, but celebrations were thin on the ground as the "three-day week" came into force that same day. An energy crisis and escalating dispute with the National Union of Mineworkers threatened to paralyse the country and the crisis forced Prime Minister Edward Heath to declare a State of Emergency. Among the drastic measures he introduced to reduce electricity consumption and conserve coal stocks was the three day week.

The lights literally went out on Britain. Commercial users of electricity were limited to three days' consumption each week and only essential services were exempt. Football received no special treatment, and until March midweek floodlit matches were forbidden and kick-off times had to be re-arranged.

In some cases, special permission was granted to play the first ever Sunday matches in the FA Cup, a competition United would be out of before the end of January. Having scraped past Plymouth Argyle in the Third Round, they fell at the next hurdle at home to Ipswich.

After his New Year's Day performance at QPR, Best was abruptly dropped by Docherty less than two hours before the Plymouth tie. Docherty claimed it was because the Northern Irishman had missed a training session, while Best insisted he had been given permission, allowing him to host a New Year's party in his new nightclub Slack Alice. It was the final straw for the mercurial Best, who sat alone in the Old Trafford stand after the match, tears in his eyes, as he contemplated a future without United. Days later Best was officially out the door, gone but never forgotten. This time there would be no last chance for Best at Old Trafford, nor did he want one.

"The tragic thing is that Best had done the hard part," The Doc told the press, "he'd broken the back of the training that was designed to help him to peak fitness again. Now all the repair work is being undone and he's wasting the greatest flow of natural talent there's been in modern day football. I'm genuinely sorry that he couldn't make the final effort just when it looked as though we were succeeding. We're better off now without him and I don't mean that disrespectfully."

With or without Best, United were struggling. Dire away form and lack of goals were the main problem. It would be March before

United won a game on the road that season, a scrappy 1-0 win at Sheffield United - two days after a snap General Election had resulted in the first hung parliament in the UK since 1929.

Ted Heath was clinging to power and United were clinging to their place in the First Division. Both would eventually lose their grip. Heath was gone within a week, as Labour formed a minority government led by Harold Wilson. United's fate would be sealed by the end of April.

The three-day week came to an end on 7 March, and within a week United would be back under the floodlights in a crucial midweek match with their rivals Manchester City at Maine Road. It didn't help matters that United were idle on the Saturday before the Manchester derby, as the FA Cup quarter-finals took centre stage that day. So to keep his side sharp Docherty hastily arranged a friendly at Old Trafford against Glasgow Rangers, who were also at a loose end having been eliminated from the Scottish Cup. It was anything but friendly!

Holton must have been chomping at the bit from the moment he heard Rangers were coming to town. When he trained with Celtic as a youth, he must have dreamed about throwing himself into Old Firm battles on a regular basis. Fate took him on a different course, but this unexpected chance to play against Rangers had presented itself, and Holton must have been relishing the chance to get stuck in to Celtic's arch-rivals.

Unfortunately for Jim and United, he got stuck in a bit too much and was sent off. He wasn't the only one to get carried away with the occasion. More than 8,000 Rangers fans had piled down the M6 for the match, and violent clashes between supporters raged in and around the ground, the tension spilling on to the pitch.

"I don't know if it was just because we were playing Rangers, but big Jim got himself sent off," recalls Alex Forsyth, who lashed home a free-kick for United in a 3-2 defeat. "To be honest, it didn't matter who we were playing, Jim would be going 100 per cent into his tackles. Nowadays, he would be off every week!"

Forsyth recalls that the Scottish players at Manchester United took particular interest in this fixture, particularly as they were all inundated with requests from would-be lodgers from their pals north of the Border.

"The game against Rangers was a hot ticket," he says. "I had 20 coming down and Jim had a load down too. Most weeks, we would have a mixture of Celtic and Rangers fans that came down to watch us. We would pool our complimentary tickets, and then a whole load of them would travel down to spend the weekend with us. It didn't matter who you were, as long as you got on. If you didn't get on and behave you wouldn't be asked."

As a Rangers supporter, Forsyth was also looking forward to the game, although he knew that their fans had a tendency for 'over-excitement', particularly in the 1970s. "I remember playing for Partick Thistle against Rangers at Ibrox. I was only 18 or 19, and I was playing against wee Willie Johnston. He had loads of pace, but I got in there with a good tackle and got the ball off him, only to be shown a red card. I remember leaving the park, everyone spitting on me, calling me a dirty Fenian so and so, but I was just laughing. Little did they know that I supported them and that years later I would be back to play for them. But that's the Scottish mentality - people can go absolutely crazy when it comes to football."

'Crazy' doesn't really do justice to what went on that March weekend. Little was recorded in the press about the match or the widespread disturbances that surrounded it, prompting writer Gordon Williams to enlighten the public the following weekend in his *Observer* column.

"Something like 8,000 battle-hardened Rangers veterans came down on special trains, coaches and cars for Saturday's little-publicised friendly," wrote Williams. "According to the survivors it went something like this: The Stretford End decided to try what Franco's police, Cumberland's butchers and the Roman cavalry all failed at – the pacification of the heathen Scot. Four hundred or so sports lovers had a battle on the park before the game. Policemen were savaged. Flying bottles injured 40. The police arrested 77 people and ejected a mere 400. Fighting went on all night in the city centre. In the Manchester courts last week one man was fined

£100 for assaulting a policeman. Another Ibrox acolyte was fined £175 for hitting a cop who was insisting that swinging a fireman's axe at people is a bit strong even in Jim Holton territory!"

Forsyth conceded that it was a "wild weekend" but he said the folk invited down by him, Holton and the other Scots in the United squad, were a good-natured bunch, who only came to the attention of the police when they were given a lift home at the end of the night. "I used to get the polis calling round at mine in the middle of the night, delivering them back to my house because they were lost, stoatin' about Manchester at three in the morning. When the police would ask them what they were doing and where they were staying, they would say 'We're doon here for the weekend and we're staying with Jim Holton or Alex Forsyth'. So the police would drop them off at our houses. I could have 16 people staying and we would have to have four sittings for breakfast! It was great fun."

The derby match against City was also a feisty clash, although most of the trouble was confined to the pitch. Lou Macari and Manchester City's Mike Doyle were unnecessarily red carded by referee Clive Thomas following a spot of 'handbags' then refused to walk. Thomas reacted by ordering both sides off the field. When they returned, the two 10-man sides played out the remainder of a tense 0-0 draw.

Denis Law missed this game through injury, but City fielded their new record £275,000 signing Dennis Tueart, who recalled in his autobiography: "Every time I ventured near the United dugout I could hear Tommy Docherty and Tommy Cavanagh urging Jim Holton and Alex Forsyth, in fact any United players who got near me, to 'break his legs'. The match was more of a war of attrition than a game of football. Jim Holton, United's massive defender, a Scot with a Desperate Dan jaw line, spent the entire first half trading kicks and shoves with our centre forward, Mike Summerbee."

The draw did nothing to ease United's relegation worries. To fortify their ranks Docherty made a shrewd signing by bringing in another Scot, Jim McCalliog from Wolves. "I arrived just before the transfer deadline, when United were second bottom," says

McCalliog. "I was about to sign for Aston Villa, but decided against it because I didn't want to be in the Second Division. I went to United because I thought we had a good chance of staying up, because there were some great players there.

"I had nearly signed for United seven years earlier, but I was priced out of a move by Sheffield Wednesday. I'd been really excited at the prospect of playing for Sir Matt Busby and I was cut up when that fell through. So I'd always wanted to go to United and this was my chance. Man U has always been a glamorous team, they always had that edge on the rest. As much as Leeds and Liverpool were successful at that time, it was Man U who always had the glamour.

"But when I walked in I thought to myself 'it's no wonder that they are down near the bottom'. The atmosphere wasn't great. The Doc had an awfully difficult job because of what had gone before him."

The arrival of McCalliog coincided with a brief upturn in results. United, without Jim in the side, won 3-1 at Chelsea, and when he returned to the centre of defence, they followed a 3-3 draw with Burnley with three wins and three clean sheets in a row against Norwich, Newcastle and Everton.

When Stepney gladly handed over penalty duties, it was McCalliog who picked up the baton. "It was embarrassing having the keeper taking them, so I volunteered, although it kind of happened by accident," says McCalliog. "We were playing away to Southampton. I was sitting on the coach next to Willie Morgan, just chatting away about the game, and he mentioned that we hadn't had a penalty in ages. I said: 'Who is it that takes the penalties Willie, is it Alex Stepney?' He said: 'No, if we get one today, I'll take it.'

"Sure enough, about 20 minutes into the game we got a penalty. There was a lot of pressure on us that day, and I could feel someone at my back saying 'Go on Jim, take it'. It was bloody Willie – he'd ducked out! Thankfully I scored."

McCalliog's penalty at The Dell gave United a point, but a midweek defeat at Everton left them staring at the abyss with two matches to play. Failure to win their penultimate fixture at home to

Manchester City on 27 April could be enough to send them down.

In contrast to the spring sunshine, an ugly, funereal atmosphere swirled around Old Trafford, and an unbearably tense game was frequently interrupted by pitch invasions and crowd trouble. With eight minutes left, City counter-attacked and when Francis Lee played the ball across, deep inside United's penalty area, who else would the ball fall to but the deadly Denis Law. From the edge of the six-yard box he instinctively back-flicked the ball into the net. Holton was a yard away from his old team-mate when the fatal blow was struck, and United players hung their heads in resignation.

Law hung his head too. You could see him thinking to himself, 'Why Me?' Even his City team-mates realised that this was not a moment to be celebrated. A pitch invasion brought the game to a halt, as fans did their utmost to have the game abandoned. Many of them made a beeline for Law, consoling rather than confronting him. The referee decided to take the teams off the field, but they never returned. There was no need for any official abandonment, the damage was done.

Law, whose love for United was beyond doubt, trudged disconsolately from the pitch in the belief that he had relegated his old club. He hadn't. They would have been relegated that day regardless, as Birmingham City had beaten bottom club Norwich to beat the drop and confirm United in the second relegation spot. "Denis didn't put us down – that's a myth, results elsewhere put us down anyway," says Willie Morgan, an ever-present for United that season. "It was heart-breaking for us and for Denis too, because he thought at the time he had put us down."

"Denis will always be remembered for that back-heeler," says Alex Forsyth, "I was right next to him when he did it. Jim wasn't far away either. I remember the ball came in to a crowded penalty area and he back-heeled the ball almost without thinking. He just walked away, not a flicker of joy or celebration on his face. There was only a few minutes to go and the next minute there was bedlam, the fans were invading the pitch and the referee said 'right, everybody off'. We were down anyway, so the ref just called it a day. It was bad day for us and a bad day for Denis."

Jim McCalliog remembers how cut-up Law was, pretty much from the moment he scored. "It was a funny game to play in, and I thought there would be quite a few goals to be honest. It wasn't like we played defensive, because Docherty didn't know how to play defensive. I wasn't so far away from Denis when he scored. He just nicked it. It never even registered with him. He just walked off the pitch. He was just a goal machine and his natural instinct was to score the goal. It was so weird that day, it really was. When we came in after the game, I was one of the first to come in, and there sitting in the corner of our dressing room was Denis – still wearing his Manchester City shirt. When the Doc came in I thought there might be a ruck, but there was no problem – The Doc just gave him his space."

When Law finally made his way to the City dressing room, nothing could snap him out of his personal hell. Rodney Marsh reveals: "In the dressing room afterwards, Denis was as miserable as I've seen him. His goal hadn't relegated United but he later told me that only one other game had made him feel as bad and that was England winning the World Cup!"

Law himself would reflect: "I just felt depressed, and that wasn't like me. After 19 years of trying my hardest to score goals, here was one that I almost wished hadn't actually gone in. I was inconsolable. I didn't want it to happen. The subject always crops up. It's one of those things. It's always there and I am always remembered for it. That's a shame. I played with all those guys. They were pals. I didn't want them down. It was the last thing in the world that I wanted."

Martin Buchan has great sympathy for the tormented Law. "I will never forget the look on Denis's face. That's etched on my mind and always will be. From our point of view, it was a scruffy goal. The pitch was dry and dusty - as they were in those days - and it just bobbled into the net. It was great execution from Denis, though, there is no getting away from that.

"Afterwards we were very flat and empty. Relegation is a dreadful thing and the fact is we hadn't been good enough over the season. The fact that it was confirmed against our 'noisy neighbours' didn't make it any better but we didn't go down because of that game."

Alex Stepney, who watched helplessly as Law's back-heeler trundled past him, remembers, "We actually played well on the day. But when Denis Law is dancing around the six yard, there is always danger. We weren't good enough and actually it was the best thing that happened because it made us go into the Second Division and come back stronger."

Two days later United – under a massive cloud - completed the formality of their final league fixture – a dispiriting 1-0 defeat at Stoke. The reasons for their relegation were simple. In 19 of their 42 fixtures they had failed to find the net. The defence at least could point to 13 clean sheets, and only four times did they concede more than twice. Despite United being immersed in turmoil, Jim Holton had continued to shine and his displays were recognised by supporters who named him their runaway choice for Player of the Year. It was a notable personal accolade, but against the backdrop of United's relegation, it was a hollow award.

Holton's partner in defence, Buchan says: "Jim, personally, played exceptionally well that season. Our goals against record was very respectable, we just didn't score enough at the other end. Defensively our record was better than a lot of teams that stayed up. It sounds a bit obvious, but we didn't win enough points because we couldn't put the ball in the back of the net.

"When we got relegated it gave Tommy Doc time to do a proper clear-out. There was a feeling with certain members of the squad that we were too good to go down because we were Manchester United. I was never of that mentality. The reality is, you just need to look at the points total, and we were not too good to go down. Tradition counted for nothing, you've still got to win the points. Even though we had won the European Cup six years previously, for various reasons we just weren't good enough."

Morgan agrees: "It was a tough season for all of us – it was as if it didn't matter how well we did, how well we played, we just never got a break. It happens to most teams that get relegated. We weren't playing badly, that was the odd thing. There were a lot of 1-0 defeats, and it was heart-breaking."

Morgan, Holton and Buchan at least had the World Cup finals with Scotland to look forward to before the reality of playing for Manchester United in the Second Division hit home.

Before Jim had even got on the plane to Germany, Harry Gregg was urging him to look for a new club after the World Cup. "He is too talented to be anywhere but the top division with a top club," insisted his mentor. "The big fellow and I have never lost contact and between us there's a great deal of mutual respect. Jim knows he can trust me all the way. He contacted me and asked my advice about the move to Manchester United. At the time, I was sure he was doing the right thing, but I reckon that position has altered with United's drop to the Second Division."

United, recognising the importance of Holton to their side and wary that the forthcoming World Cup would only make him a hotter property, quickly made their centre half an offer he couldn't refuse, handing him what was effectively an unprecedented 10-year contract. The deal was an initial five-year deal with a further option of five years. Only George Best had been handed a similar length of contract, by Busby in 1970.

The contract put to bed unfounded rumours that Docherty might seek to replace Holton. "I already have the best centre half in the game. That's why we gave him a ten-year contract to keep him with us for the rest of his career," said Docherty. "As soon as he got into the World Cup squad with Scotland I gave him the new long-term contract."

As Jim prepared to go the World Cup, he reflected on his career so far, and thanked Gregg, Docherty and Willie Ormond, for making him the player he now was. "I owe a hell of a lot to Manchester United for the chance they took on me. I've got much to pay back Tommy Docherty. I owe it all to the three men who have changed the course of my career, and I've got much to prove to myself and most other people.

"There's nothing like falling flat on your face, as I did when West Bromwich gave me a free transfer, for making a player eager to do well. Harry Gregg, Tommy Docherty and Willie Ormond gave me chances to make good after everything had fallen apart.

Now I realise West Brom did me a favour when they told me they had no further use for me.

"I didn't lose faith in myself because other clubs quickly began to enquire about me. Then along came the first man who set me right back on course – Harry Gregg. He told me if I joined Shrewsbury he would help improve my game and get me back into the First Division in two years. Harry is a straight-shooter. There are a lot of con-men in football, but he always gave it to me straight and thrashed me if I needed it.

"He worked so hard with me that he was out by six months in his two-year plan when I joined Manchester United. My first thought about the transfer was that £80,000 was a hell a lot of money for me. But I quickly realised I was in the hands of another straight-shooter in Tommy Docherty. He boosted my confidence when he said he thought I could win a Scottish cap in 12 months. His forecast was out too – thanks to the faith of Willie Ormond I got my first cap in five months!

"It has filled me with gratitude, though at the same time it has made me much more conscious of the fact that I've still for much to learn."

10: YABA DABA ... DON'T!

"The Scotland team were like one big travelling circus. When you had guys like Jinky Johnstone and Billy Bremner things could occasionally go awry"

Willie Morgan

NINETEEN SEVENTY-FOUR. Not just any year, a World Cup year and the football-crazy nation of Scotland had qualified for the biggest tournament in the world for the first time since 1958. Although 1973 had yielded just two wins from nine internationals, blinkered euphoria was the order of the day.

Willie Ormond had started his reign as manager in 1973 with a nightmare 5-0 thrashing against England on Valentine's Day, but there was love for him in every Scottish household by the end of the calendar year after he had led his side to a World Cup qualification-clinching win against Czechoslovakia. The fact that Scotland wrapped up their 1973 fixtures by giving tournament hosts and hot favourites West Germany an almighty fright in a pulsating 1-1 draw in Glasgow only fuelled optimism further.

Expectations weren't exactly dampened by the release of Scotland's World Cup record, which included the lyrics '*Yaba daba doo, we support the boys in blue and it's easy, easy!*' The squad recorded this and other tracks featured on a 12-track 'Scotland Scotland' LP released by Polydor, which included contributions from Lulu, Rod Stewart and the Bay City Rollers. 'Easy Easy' made it to number 20 in the UK singles chart – once heard never unheard!

The draw for the 16-team World Cup finals was made on 5 January 1974, in the main hall of Radio Hessen in Frankfurt. Pride of place in the hall was given to the new FIFA World Cup trophy, Brazil having been awarded permanent custody of the Jules Rimet version after winning it for the third time in 1970. A rather bewildered looking member of the Schöneberger Sängerknaben boys' choir was entrusted with the task of making the draw and the youngster pulled Scotland's name from what looked like a sweetie jar to face Brazil, Yugoslavia and Zaire in Group 2.

Scotland would play their group matches in Dortmund and Frankfurt, and wisely a March acclimatisation friendly was arranged with West Germany in the Waldstadion, the venue for their fixtures with Brazil and Yugoslavia. Jim Holton missed the trip to Frankfurt due to injury as an experimental Scotland side again emerged with credit despite a tight 2-1 defeat.

Jim was fit again and back in the squad by the time the home internationals rolled round in May, with three games in eight days designed to whip the Scots into peak physical and mental condition for the World Cup. An added bonus was that all of three matches would take place at Hampden Park, Northern Ireland having again been forced to relinquish home advantage due to the Troubles.

In theory it looked nicely teed up for Scotland, but with firebrands like Billy Bremner and Jimmy 'Jinky' Johnstone in the team, it was never going to be plain sailing.

A tumultuous week began with a dire 1-0 defeat against Northern Ireland at a rain-soaked Hampden, leaving an apologetic Ormond to splutter, "Our attitude was all wrong."

While the forwards were pilloried for a toothless effort, Holton was one of the main reasons the defeat wasn't even more damning. "It was fortunate for Scotland that Holton was at his most effective, sweeping up trouble with the functional thoroughness of a street-cleaning truck," said Hugh McIlvanney in the *Observer*.

Holton – who was trying to put the disappointment of Manchester United's relegation to one side – was again in commanding form three days later as Scotland bounced back with a 2-0 victory over Wales, secured through goals from Kenny Dalglish and Sandy Jardine from the penalty spot. The squad returned on that Tuesday night to their training base at the Ayrshire seaside town of Largs, greatly relieved to have returned to winning ways.

The 'big one' was the visit of England four days later. It offered Scotland the perfect platform to send confidence soaring skywards again for the World Cup. There was also the considerable incentive of trying to secure a first win over the Auld Enemy since the Scots had out-dazzled world champions England at Wembley in 1967.

With spirits revived after the win over Wales, the Scotland players were rewarded by Ormond with some free time to enjoy a couple of drinks and unwind − a gesture which catastrophically backfired. What was meant to be a team-bonding exercise over a couple of quiet pints unravelled into a full-blown scandal when Jimmy Johnstone decided on the way back from the pub to the hotel that it would be a hoot to test his maritime skills in a rowing boat with no oars.

In the wee small hours, a gaggle of tipsy team-mates − including Holton − loudly encouraged Johnstone's caper from the shoreline. But as the wayward winger, lustily belting out Scotland anthems, started to drift hopelessly out into the Firth of Clyde, they eventually realised the gravity of the situation and started to panic. Only the intervention of the emergency services ensured the errant 'Jinky' was rescued and returned to dry land.

Willie Morgan, having initially joined the group for a few beers, was fast asleep in his hotel bed by the time the drama unfolded but he remembers the rumpus well. "The Scotland team were like one big travelling circus," he laughs, "when you had guys like little Jinky and Billy (Bremner), who were massive drinkers, things could occasionally go awry. As an older team-mate, I remember warning big Jim, 'Don't you be hanging around with those two too much' and he would say 'No, I won't Wullie'. Willie Ormond was a lovely man, but he took his eye off the ball that night.

"I was sharing a room with Jim at the Queen's Hotel and we had a room upstairs facing the sea. We had all been out for a couple of drinks. I was getting tired and I said to Jim, 'I've had enough, I'm going back to bed, are you coming?' Big Jim said: 'naw, I'm just going to have another'. I said: 'Well, whatever you do, don't fuckin wake me up when you come in'. So off I went and got myself to bed.

"I think I was asleep as soon as my head hit the pillow, but the next thing I knew I was being woken up unceremoniously by Big

Jim. It was daylight, and there he was at the side of the bed saying 'Wullie, Wullie, you've got to see this'. I wasn't impressed and said 'Ya bastard, I told you not to wake me up!' He said: 'I'm sorry Wullie, but I had to – look out the windae!'

"So I got out my bed, went to the window and of course the wee man is in the boat with no oars, still singing away to himself. The other lads that were still with him were running up and down looking for bits of driftwood to go and get him before the Coastguard arrived. When he first got into the boat he'd been singing away quite happily. The lads who had shoved him out to sea didn't know any better. But then he started to disappear and the next thing there are sirens. It was hilarious, but he was lucky because the wee man couldn't even swim!"

After a rude awakening, Ormond could have been forgiven for escaping to a darkened room for a long lie down. Instead he manfully faced up to a long list of embarrassing questions from reporters. This was one of these stories managers dread – one with enough clout to generate 72-point headlines on the front and back pages, and he knew he was on a hiding to nothing. He had placed trust in his players and it had been sadly misplaced. Johnstone's escapade, and the outcry surrounding it, had heaped the pressure back on the squad ahead of the England showdown.

England, still smarting after missing out on the World Cup finals, arrived in Glasgow in a period of transition. Joe Mercer was in charge in a caretaker capacity following the acrimonious exit of Sir Alf Ramsey, and he was forced to reshuffle his side for Hampden with Leicester City's Frank Worthington and Martin Peters of Tottenham coming in for Stan Bowles and Kevin Keegan, while Holton's main rival from 12 months earlier, Martin Chivers, was another absentee.

Emlyn Hughes captained England and Peters was one of few experienced men in their ranks, and there was much more familiarity to the Scotland line-up. It quickly became clear that the storm surrounding Jimmy Johnstone's ill-judged boat trip had only brought them closer together and turned them into a determined unit.

In driving rain Scotland started with real purpose, roared on by a 94,000 crowd — incredibly the lowest Hampden attendance for this famous fixture in 50 years. Joe Jordan sent them wild when he gave Scotland the lead in the fourth minute, his effort diverted into the net by the despairing Mike Pejic. England were rattled and could not establish any foothold in the game, and fell further behind on the half-hour mark when Colin Todd diverted Peter Lorimer's cross past Peter Shilton to make it 2-0 to Scotland.

With the atmosphere crackling, Scotland steamrollered their way to an emphatic victory. Holton must have been licking his lips when he saw Malcolm MacDonald sent on as a substitute for Frank Worthington with 20 minutes to play. The Newcastle striker again made no impact against the man who had laid him out at Old Trafford the previous year.

With his Manchester United colleague Buchan sidelined, Holton was partnered at the centre of a well-disciplined Scotland defence by John Blackley, who effectively booked his seat on the plane to the World Cup with an assured display. The young Hibs defender proved to be one of the stand-out performers for Ormond's side, which was built around the Leeds United spine of Harvey, Bremner, Lorimer and Jordan. Celtic's David Hay was also outstanding, but then so were the entire Scots team.

"I was brought up with the Scotland-England game," says Blackley. "My brothers would go down on the bus to Wembley and be away for what seemed like days. The fixture was special to me, so to get the opportunity to play alongside Big Jim at Hampden that day, when Martin Buchan was injured, was unbelievable. It was a great experience and a great day for me."

A party atmosphere engulfed Hampden at full-time and Jimmy Johnstone — first topless then wearing the yellow goalkeeper's shirt of Shilton like an outsized hand-me-down — danced on the sodden turf during a lap of honour, intermittently snarling and flicking well-aimed V-signs at the Press Box where some of his detractors sat. This time, Johnstone's ship had come in!

Officially, Scotland and England shared the 1974 Home International Championship, as goal difference wasn't then a deciding factor, but in the partisan eyes of the Hampden faithful there was only one winner. As the triumphant songs sweeping the old ground indicated, the World Cup was once again a source of excitement rather than trepidation.

Monday's newspapers carried adverts for an 11-day trip to the finals in West Germany costing £115. One fan who would struggle to scrape the cash together was the 18-year-old fined £100 in court that morning for breach of the peace – he had been arrested after being seen by millions of TV viewers risking life and limb as he celebrated the win over England on the South Terracing roof!

That same day Ormond revealed the final 22-man squad he would take with him to West Germany. The list, with squad numbers, read: 1 David Harvey (Leeds), 2 Sandy Jardine (Rangers); 3 Danny McGrain (Celtic), 4 Billy Bremner (Leeds), 5 Jim Holton (Man Utd), 6 John Blackley (Hibs), 7 Jimmy Johnstone (Celtic), 8 Kenny Dalglish (Celtic), 9 Joe Jordan (Leeds), 10 David Hay (Celtic), 11 Peter Lorimer (Leeds), 12 Thompson Allan (Dundee), 13 Jim Stewart (Kilmarnock), 14 Martin Buchan (Man Utd), 15 Peter Cormack (Liverpool), 16 Willie Donachie (Man City), 17 Donald Ford (Hearts), 18 Tommy Hutchison (Coventry), 19 Denis Law (Man City), 20 Willie Morgan (Man Utd), 21 Gordon McQueen (Leeds), 22 Erich Schaedler (Hibs).

With Scotland still at fever pitch after the 2-0 victory over the Auld Enemy and the World Cup squad announcement, Jim was whisked back to Hampden by a Sunday newspaper where he posed on the empty terracing with a kilt and bagpipes. Holton, looking handsome in Stewart tartan, admitted it was the first time in his life he had worn a kilt.

Jim's star was rising and his flawless display against England had not got unnoticed. Argentina coach Vladislao Cap was an interested spectator at Hampden, as his team were due to play England at Wembley in midweek (a 2-2 draw). He praised Jimmy Johnstone, but added: "Your Jim Holton too is another great player. He will become a big name in the World Cup."

The Home Internationals, despite Jimmy Johnstone's mishap, had been a success. The squad would regroup at Largs before two further fixtures would see them on their way to West Germany – away matches against Belgium on 1 June and Norway five days later.

Jim missed the match against Belgium in Bruges when a knee cartilage problem flared up during training. Gordon McQueen took Jim's place and made his Scotland debut alongside Blackley in a 2-1 defeat. The consensus among the newspaper men was that Scotland had missed the influence of Holton and that they desperately needed to get him fit in time for the World Cup.

Martin Buchan had also missed the match in Belgium after reporting back late to the Scotland training camp. A cable from Manchester United to the SFA to say their player would be a day late had not gone down well with Willie Ormond, who said: "It's just not good enough. It's ridiculous. You would have thought Buchan – of all people – would have been here on time. He has a groin injury and we wanted to see how he was."

Buchan's delay had actually been due to him concluding formalities on a new two-year deal with United. Ormond was too diplomatic to say publicly that Tommy Docherty was getting under his skin, but he must have bristled when his predecessor had his say on Holton's injury. The Doc aimed a thinly-veiled swipe at Scotland for not keeping him fully updated, and even offered to fly out to Norway with United physio Laurie Brown to help get Jim fit in time for the World Cup.

"I am not trying to denigrate the Scottish trainers or anything like that, but we know the case history of this injury," said Docherty. "It has troubled Jim off and on throughout the season. Sometimes it has looked really bad, then it has improved again. I'd be ready to fly out with our own man if Willie Ormond thought it might help. I would hate to see the lad lose this chance of playing in the finals. It is the greatest honour and opportunity he has had in his career so far and it would be a tragedy if he missed it now.

"The trouble can come and go. He didn't miss too many games for us because of it and he played all three Home Internationals at Hampden. Anyway, I'm ready to travel to Oslo. I think Scotland need Jim in the World Cup and anything we can do as a club to help will be done. Mind you, I'm a little disappointed that no-one has officially told us about the injury. I only know about it through the television and newspaper reports. Still, all that matters is having Jim fit. I honestly feel he can recover - as he has done throughout the season."

The recurring injury was to Holton's right knee. He had twice gone under the knife to have cartilage removed, but a piece of gristle was beginning to affect a nerve in the knee. It was a serious situation, with Ormond admitting the Norway friendly might be make or break in terms of Holton being fit enough to play in the World Cup. "Jim will be given a severe test in this game and if he isn't 100 per cent then he is out and I'll have to get a replacement," warned the Scotland manager.

It was indeed a severe test. James Sanderson, covering the Norway match for the *Mirror*, watched the Scots train and reported: "Holton, watched by Willie Ormond and two medical officials, had to survive a series of blood-curdling tackles and then play in a practice match." The scribe added: "I still think Ormond is taking a risk with Holton. I've always thought of Holton as essential to our team, but there must be nagging worries about him."

Big Jim had been given every chance to prove his fitness, and had done so, but the biggest problem facing Ormond was a fresh outbreak of indiscipline. If the manager had read the players the riot act after the Largs rowing boat rumpus, then it had fallen on deaf ears.

Hugh Taylor of the *Daily Record* chronicled the latest episode of hell-raising in diary form. He reported: "Scotland's tour de Farce reached such a peak of hilarity in solemn Oslo today that Morecambe and Wise seem like amateurs. At home, loyal fans must wonder what is going on...

"Sunday: Early rise and complaints from players about boring bus run and early charter flight out of Brussels. Champagne flight brightened the mood. Everyone left the plane at Oslo carrying two or three bottles of the best wine. The Panorama Hotel in Oslo horrified the players. Like a students' hostel. Players, however, glad to go to bed. Except two − Bremner and Johnstone, who couldn't sleep and visited the bar. Billy argued with reporters, Jimmy sang a few bars of "Scotland, Scotland." Willie Ormond rushed in and said: "God! Not you two again." Players left.

"Monday: SFA secretary Willie Allan called a conference. Two players reprimanded for breach of discipline. No names. Press decided to name names in fairness to the innocents.

"Tuesday: Evening training session. Norwegian manager George Curtis told us that Scottish press was barred then goes back into the ground. Ormond confirms he didn't want journalists in because of what they had written.

"Wednesday: Ormond back to smiling, admits 'Some of the stuff written did annoy me' but says he wanted to practice new moves privately. Why then did he allow Curtis to watch. 'Oh dear, I didn't know he was there or he'd have been outside with you!' Laughter. Then Allan walked over and told one journalist [John Mackenzie of the Scottish *Daily Express*] he was banned from the charter flight which will take us on to Frankfurt."

Somewhere amid the maelstrom, Scotland had played a game of football – and won. The part-timers of Norway had given Ormond's side a stern test, taking the lead in the fourth minute. The introduction of Dalglish for Johnstone 20 minutes from time galvanised sluggish Scotland, and Jordan soon equalised. Dalglish then grabbed a late, morale-boosting winner.

Holton and Buchan didn't look at their best in Oslo, but at least both had used the 90 minutes to prove themselves fit and ready to participate in the World Cup. "I had a twinge or two in my knee against Norway but I feel good again," said Jim. "I wasn't at my best but I'll be ready by next week." Next stop Frankfurt.

11: SCOTLAND THE BRAVEST

"The way Jim played against Brazil,
he could play against anyone in the world"

Martin Buchan

FOR THE WORLD CUP Scotland had booked themselves into accommodation far from the madding crowd, in the Weilna Hotel in the wooded hillside sanctuary of Erbersmuhle. But as they arrived at the hotel, they found themselves ambushed by the German press. Tales of the Scots' drinking escapades of the past month had circulated ahead of their arrival, and when champagne cocktails were mischievously offered to the players as they walked through the doors of their hotel, the German TV cameras were ready to pounce. None of the players fell for the trap however, and after drinking nothing stronger than tea, they got down to some hard training.

As Britain's sole representatives at the World Cup, security surrounding the Scotland party was intense, particularly as there had been explicit threats made against the team and this was only two years after terrorism had blighted the Munich Olympics. When the Scots' chartered Trident jet touched down in Frankfurt they were met by armed police and dogs at the airport.

Journalist Hugh Taylor, sharing the experience for a special World Cup edition of his annual The Scottish Football Book, said: "A yellow and blue bus roared out to the plane doors and the Scottish players were given the top VIP security treatment. With a motor cycle escort, the bus, on which was emblazoned the flag of St Andrew, immediately took off for the Rodweil, the Taunus resort at which the Scots were quartered."

A cordon was thrown around the hotel and every room was searched for bombs before the players settled in to their HQ. Despite the close attention of the security forces, the Scotland players and officials seemed relaxed. By way of apology for the friction in Oslo, SFA president Rankin Grimshaw went on a charm offensive and wined and dined the Scottish press corps – without a single journalist being banned.

The newspapers and TV stations back home could not get enough news about the Scotland team. The World Cup had gripped the nation and one tabloid carried a two-page feature on the players' mothers in which Mrs Mary Holton said of her son: "Jim was always in trouble for playing football in the street. I hope his injured leg is improving."

As if to prove that his knee could withstand anything, Jim was one of a number of players involved in a blood-and-thunder training session in the town of Wehrheim. Playing three 20-minute sessions, the Scots turned the exercise into a match of cup tie intensity. Hundreds of German onlookers were captivated as they saw Holton clash with Peter Cormack, John Blackley tangle with Jimmy Johnstone and Martin Buchan battle with Joe Jordan. Of all people, it was skipper Billy Bremner who ended up the peace-keeper. "Sure there was a bit of needle. But that made it a really good training session," said Willie Ormond. "All the lads are beginning to fight for their places."

William Hill were quoting Scotland at 25-1 to win the World Cup, while betting to win Group 2 was 4-6 Brazil, 11-4 Yugoslavia, 7-2 Scotland and 40-1 Zaire. Billy Bremner underlined Scotland's belief that they were genuine contenders by telling reporters: "Hell, if I didn't think we were here with a good chance I would be sunbathing on a beach in Majorca."

As tradition dictated, the reigning champions would open the tournament, so Scotland were given an early chance to see their group rivals Brazil and Yugoslavia in action in Frankfurt, 24 hours before they would start their own campaign in Dortmund against African underdogs Zaire.

The match in the Waldstadion on 13 June was cagey and uninformative. With both teams desperate not to lose, it finished a flat 0-0 stalemate. Scotland couldn't afford to be distracted, all their attention had to be on Zaire, of which little was known.

Zaire had made history by becoming the first ever black African nation to qualify for the finals, but they arrived under the stifling, oppressive glare of President Mobutu Sese Seko – the notorious dictator who months later would famously bring the Ali-Foreman 'Rumble in the Jungle' world heavyweight title fight to Kinshasa.

Mobutu expected the team to showcase his country on the world stage, and they were under unbearable political pressure to succeed. It was accepted that the team, who wore their 'Leopards' nickname on their shirts, had a technically gifted squad, but pundits had widely dismissed them as mere makeweights. In the run-up to the match, Bremner said: "We'll beat them okay but we must not under-rate them. After all, it's a sad part of our football history that we lose to those we think on as mugs and do better against the giants."

Scotland looked tense as they lined up for the anthems. Jim standing second from right as the two teams fanned out across the Westfalenstadion pitch. To Jim's left stood John Blackley – preferred by Ormond for the opening match to Martin Buchan. To his right stood Denis Law, named in the starting XI and fulfilling his lifetime ambition of playing in the World Cup finals.

A curious sight was that most of the Scotland team, including Jim, were wearing sheer black boots. A stooshie over endorsement payments for wearing Adidas products had led the players to rebel and physically cut the distinctive three-stripes off their footwear in protest.

Scotland started on the front foot and took the lead after 26 minutes when Celtic pair Davie Hay and Danny McGrain combined on the left to cross for Joe Jordan, who knocked down for Peter Lorimer to smash home a magnificent volley. Eight minutes later, Jordan made it 2-0, Zaire keeper Kazadi Mwamba making a hash of a tame effort and allowing it to squirm into the net. And then Scotland relaxed. Boy did they relax!

Instead of going for the jugular, Scotland protected what they had and they were jeered for a 10-minute spell where they kept possession without any real attacking intent. Law, aged 34, was given the full 90 minutes in what turned out to be the last international appearance of his illustrious career, while a subdued Dalglish made way for Tommy Hutchison.

There had been tittle-tattle about witchdoctors and juju in the Zaire camp, and there were some worried looks exchanged when the floodlights failed for four minutes in the second half. Soon after light was restored referee Gerhard Schulenberg harshly booked Holton for handball, an offence officials had been instructed to clamp down on at the World Cup.

The World Cup was the first time Jan Holton had seen her husband play live on television, but she admits the tension made it difficult to watch. "It was nerve-wracking watching Jim," she says. "My mum and dad were up in Manchester and I had to go out to the garden because I was too nervous to sit and watch him play. My Dad kept shouting through the window, 'There's our Jim!' but he kept getting Jim mixed up with Joe Jordan, because they were of a similar build and had the same mullet hair-styles. My mum was saying, 'that's not Jim, our Jim's not number 9, he's number 5!' but Dad was convinced that Joe Jordan was Jim and the pair of them spent the match arguing in the lounge while I was busy mowing the lawn!"

Scotland coasted their way through the remainder of the match, and walked off 2-0 winners but straight into a wave of criticism for not being more ruthless. Ormond admitted, "My team slackened off" and the great Jock Stein, an observer, said: "I thought there was some irresponsibility in the team in the second half, they messed about a bit when they should have gone for more goals."

John Blackley says: "Looking back, the big problem was that we didn't know what we were facing. We didn't know if they were good players, we didn't know what was going to come at us. It was a difficult game, more difficult than it ought to have been, but it was still a win."

Buchan, who has no gripes that he sat this one out, says: "We settled for a narrow victory when I think we might have pushed on towards the end of the game to get more goals. There were one or two players showboating actually, thinking that the job was done."

Zaire's Yugoslav coach Blagojev Vidinic, meanwhile, tipped Scotland to qualify along with his home nation at the expense of Brazil. "Scotland had a very good first half and a very bad second half – but I am sure it will be Scotland who go through with Yugoslavia."

Holton picked up a mild back strain during the match, but Ormond was confident he would be able to put out his first choice XI against Brazil. To raise spirits ahead of the crucial clash against Brazil, one of the nation's favourite comedians, Billy Connolly, was summoned to the camp to entertain the players.

The win against Zaire, irrespective of the margin, had fuelled confidence at home that Scotland could topple Brazil. Charter flights were scrambled from Glasgow and fans started arriving in West Germany in droves, with at least 15,000 Scots expected for the Brazil match in Frankfurt.

British Consulate staff were promptly placed on 24-hour alert with leave cancelled. Alex Cameron of the *Daily Record* reported: "Already two penniless Dundee fans have asked for tickets to get them home plus their £3 eating allowance for the journey. Once they had been given this by a polite member of the consul staff, the pair jokingly asked if it would be all right to stay over and watch the Brazil game." Only 26 would ask the consul for help in the end.

Another fan from Edinburgh said he had given up his job as a TV mechanic just to be there. "We are living rough and existing mostly on coffee and crisps," he said.

Holton's back injury had thankfully eased off and he was declared fit to play alongside club-mate Buchan, restored to the team in favour of a crestfallen Blackley. "Martin Buchan was a very, very good player, and I had no complaint at him being picked," says Blackley. "My disappointment was the fact that I was missing out on playing against Brazil. Martin was gifted with pace; and while I could read the game all right, I wasn't as pacey as Martin, so I could see the thinking, but at the end of the day the hurt in myself was evident." Law also dropped to the bench, with Willie Morgan fit again and introduced to provide Scotland with some width and menace.

Sadly, Brazil were a crude shadow of the great team who had lit up the world so gloriously in Mexico four years earlier. They started the game strongly in the first 20 minutes and came closing to scoring through Rivelino, but soon a pattern of petty, cynical fouling emerged, discrediting their name. Brazil were taking full advantage of the leniency of Dutch referee Van Gamert, who only booked Mario Marinho and Rivelino, who should have been sent off.

Scotland were the superior team for 70 minutes, and they came agonisingly close to a deserved triumph when Bremner sent the ball millimetres past the post from less than a yard out after Brazil keeper Emerson had palmed a header from Joe Jordan against his feet. It was a miss that has long haunted Scots, but in truth Bremner had no time to react and he was blameless. He was also, arguably, the best player on the pitch that day with the Brazilian press hailing him as Scotland's 'small giant'.

There was action of a different kind unfolding at the other end of the pitch too.

Buchan explains: "In the Brazil game, my main job was to mark Jairzinho. I still jokingly say to my pals that I'm the man who tamed Jairzinho, although in fairness he must have been about 53 at the time! But they had another guy in their team called Mirandinha, who was 6ft 2 with a big afro. The first thing he did was put his studs right down my shin, and I wasn't very happy about that, particularly as I wasn't wearing shinguards.

"In football, I had always been taught that if someone had a go at you, don't go chasing after them in the heat of the moment. Instead, wait until the next time you are playing them, then sort them out! But I thought to myself, 'it might be a long time before I play against Brazil again'. We were into the last couple of minutes of the game and while everyone was watching the action in the Brazil goalmouth, I walked past Mirandinha and I'm ashamed to say I gave him an elbow in the face and I walked smartly on.

"I then heard a commotion behind me and I look round and Mirandinha is grappling with big Jim. So after the game I said to Jim 'I'm very sorry, I smacked him in the face because he'd put his six studs down my shin. He must have been dazed and thought it was you.' But Big Jim said: 'No, no, I saw you do it, but straight after you did that I booted him up the arse!' So there was an example of Man United teamwork at its very best!"

Prime Minister Harold Wilson, who had arrived by helicopter shortly before kick-off, had watched Scotland come within a whisker of a famous victory. "Scotland played well and deserved to win. They should have had a great victory," the PM said afterwards, before the Huddersfield Town supporter mischievously added: "I thought Lorimer should have been moved to the inside left position in the last 15 minutes." On hearing Wilson's analysis, an unimpressed Ormond retorted, "You stick to your job and I'll stick to mine!"

Ormond also found himself handing out a rebuke to his opposite number Mario Zagalo, who tried to deflect criticism of Brazil by accusing the Scots of being over-physical. "If he thinks that he should come down to our dressing room and look at the shins of our players. There is hardly a man unmarked."

He was backed up by his captain, "They did not want to let you play. I feel sorry we couldn't give our fans a victory. They deserved it – but I don't think we let them down."

They certainly hadn't. Under the headline, "The night magic was just not enough", the *Daily Record*'s Hugh Taylor enthused: "The bagpipes shrilled and the bongo drums were silent as the bravest and brightest Scotland team for years hammered world champions Brazil on to the ropes. Alas Scotland did not have the knockout punch to gain the victory they deserved."

Danny McGrain believes Scotland missed out on a golden chance, but he insists, "That's all in the history books now. We had the chance to beat them and we didn't. That wasn't the best Brazil team ever, but they were still Brazil, they were still the reigning world champions. Every time they got the ball you were thinking, 'oh no what are they going to do now?' Yeah, we did great getting the 0-0 draw but we'd have done better beating them 1-0 and qualifying for the next round. Big Jim played very well, I think we all did. It was great for us to experience an occasion like that –

for us as defenders to be playing against that calibre of player was magnificent to experience."

Bremner, Hay and Holton commanded the lion's share of praise, with Jim's performance lauded as "dazzling". He had proved beyond doubt he could play in the very best company. After the game, Buchan agreed: "The way Jim played against Brazil, he could play against anyone in the world. Those who regard him as just crude will now have to change their minds." And Ormond insisted: "Too many people have run away with the idea that the big fellow is a player without craft. He is not." Adding to the shower of praise was Bremner, who said of Jim: "He is a super fellow, friendly and dependable. Everyone likes him."

Unlikely as it would have seemed, Holton had emerged as the face of this vintage Scotland team, and comparisons were made between him and the great George Young – the granite-featured former Scotland and Rangers captain from the 1940s and 50s. "I have never modelled myself on any player," said Holton. "I heard a lot about George Young, but never saw him play. I met him in Manchester last season and was quite honoured to spend time with him."

Holton's popularity was not contained to a partisan Scottish press either. *Bild*, Germany's mass-selling sports daily newspaper, carried a banner headline – in English – across its front page declaring 'Big Jim Is After You' while reporters from around the globe, including Japan, had been jostling for interviews with him.

Reacting to the *Bild* headline, Jim – talking at Scotland's hotel – said: "What a laugh. In 16 months I seem to have gone from nothing to the moon. I think the singing began at Manchester United but the Scots have certainly taken it up in a big way." Modestly, he added: "Look, if I'm doing well in this side it's because there are so many players with me. How can you do badly with Billy Bremner around?"

Alex 'Candid' Cameron of the *Daily Record* picked up on international interest in Jim, writing: "A phenomenon of the World Cup, with greats such as Cruyff, Oblak and Deyna thrilling TV audiences, is that Scotland's big Jim Holton is the most talked about player."

Full-back McGrain, who showed his immense versatility by playing on the left for Scotland rather than his favoured Celtic slot on the right, said Scotland's defence was a proud unit and Holton was an inspirational figure to his peers. "We had a tremendous defence, Jim gave you real confidence because his commitment was always 100 per cent. He would go for every ball he could, sometimes he did miss, because we all miss, but it wasn't often. To have that bulk of a frame coming towards you frightened a lot of players, including myself! I think if I was playing against him I would be a bit worried. Jim didn't have the experience of some of the other lads at the World Cup but what he lacked he made up for in physical stature. He was a centre half who just won the ball, defended the 18 yard box and did it brilliantly. The physical attributes of Jim were fantastic. He was a big beast of a man, but he was our big beast."

Two games, two clean sheets and three points represented a solid start to the tournament. Yet Scotland headed into their final game with Yugoslavia knowing only a victory would assure them of a place in the second phase.

The Leopards of Zaire, who had shown stubborn resistance against the Scots, were thrashed 9-0 by Yugoslavia in their second match. Years later, this landslide win was given some context, when it emerged that the African players had staged a near-mutiny before the game after promised payments failed to materialise. It didn't help that Zaire's Yugoslav coach decided to substitute his regular keeper Mwamba early in the game and replace him with Tubilandu Ndimbi – height 5ft 4in!

"The result that really did us was Zaire losing 9-0 to Yugoslavia," says John Blackley. "I thought back then there was a conspiracy and I still do to this day. Zaire had a Yugoslav coach and we had Yugoslavia in the group. I'm not saying there was any hookery crookery, but their result against Yugoslavia just didn't ring true because although they didn't have the same quality as Brazil or Yugoslavia, they were half-decent defensively. There was no way Zaire were a team who should be losing 9-0."

Yugoslavia's goal difference gave them the luxury of knowing that a draw against Scotland would see them through, regardless of how Brazil fared in their final match against Zaire. As both teams traditionally wore blue, the toss of a coin decided strip colours, with Scotland losing and settling for an all-white kit. Thousands more Scottish supporters had flown out for the Yugoslavia game, including the Scottish Secretary William Ross.

On match day, Saturday 22 June, the *Daily Record* decided anything *Bild* could do they could do better and the Scottish tabloid featured a picture of a grinning Jim Holton, stretching the full length of the front page, with the headline, "Six foot two, eyes of blue, big Jim Holton's after you."

The accompanying text said, "He's big. He's hard. Thankfully, Big Jim Holton belongs to Scotland. And according to that little ditty, he will be after the Slavs today. He doesn't bite, as some schoolboys will have you believe. But he certainly does get his teeth into a game." The article also featured a quote from his mother Mary, who admitted that she had never watched him play. "I couldn't bear it. I'm terrified in case Jim gets hurt."

The back page further stoked national fervour, referencing the 1314 Battle of Bannockburn – the 660th anniversary of which would fall on that very weekend and adding that Billy Bremner, a "man born on the touchlines of that Bannockburn victory", was the perfect captain to lead the Scots to another great victory.

The mercury was nudging 30c in the Walstadion that Saturday afternoon, as an energy-sapping battle began. Joe Jordan missed a good chance on his less favoured right foot early in the match as Scotland tried without success to unpick Yugoslavia's turgid defence. News filtered through from Gelsenkirchen that Brazil, needing a 3-0 victory against Zaire, had taken an early lead, although encouragingly the scoreline remained 1-0 at half-time.

With Scotland and Yugoslavia still deadlocked in an absorbing contest, Brazil edged 2-0 ahead after 66 minutes then – unbeknown to Ormond and the supporters inside the ground in Frankfurt – added the killer third goal in the 79th minute. Events 150 miles away had already sealed Scotland's fate unless, of course, they could find a late winner. But it was Yugoslavia who struck first, with nine minutes left, when substitute Stanislav Karasi powered a header past David Harvey. The Scots showed immense spirit and with only two minutes on the clock, a sweeping move up the pitch ended with Jordan volleying from close-range to make it 1-1.

Ormond desperately tried to get Jimmy Johnstone on for Martin Buchan but the referee didn't notice the Scots were signalling to make a substitution, and the incomparable wing wizard was sadly denied his bow on the World Cup stage.

With Scotland mounting one-last gasp attack and the ball at Morgan's feet in a dangerous position on the right, referee Alfonso González Archundia blew the final whistle to confirm that Ormond's brave side were out of the World Cup. It would be Morgan's last touch as a Scotland player, while another long-standing servant David Hay would also never play for his country again.

"That was the best Scotland squad ever," says Morgan. "Willie Ormond was a lovely man, but as much as I hate Tommy Docherty, I still maintain that if he had stayed on as Scotland manager we could have won the World Cup that year."

Tommy Hutchison, who came on for Dalglish against Yugoslavia, said the feeling was indescribably awful. "I think the saddest thing for all of us was the disappointment of the supporters, even if they still treated us like heroes. I can remember big Jim saying to me at the end of the Yugoslavia match 'Have a look at their faces'. We walked round the pitch, just looking at the fans in the terraces, a lump in our throat. For us, it wasn't a lap of honour, just a lap of the pitch. We clapped them and showed our appreciation as much as we could, but they were distraught and I think it got to all of us. Jim was a big softie at heart really, and that was one time it showed. It wasn't a time for bravado."

"We were silent in the dressing room," Willie Morgan remembers, "but when we got back to the hotel after that last match we drank the place dry. We had quite a party and they reckon the bill for Scotland for booze was more than every other country put together! I was sharing a room with Erich Schaedler of Hibs, and we ended up with Billy Connolly and Rod Stewart as our guests that night. They couldn't get a room, so I told them they could kip on our floor and the two of them just crashed out on the floor between Erich and I. Things were different in those days!"

The hotel must have been quite a sight the next morning/afternoon as bleary-eyed Scots bodies surfaced one by one and started to pack their bags ahead of their flight home on Monday. But the hangovers would have been banished by the sight that greeted them at Glasgow airport. A crowd of 10,000 gave them a heroes' reception. Amid the throng fluttered the giant banner: 'Welcome Home Scotland's unbeaten heroes'.

Missing from the returning Scotland party were Jim and his fellow Anglos Morgan, Law, Harvey, McQueen and Cormack who headed to Manchester instead. Bremner, however, was asked especially by Ormond to join the Glasgow-bound players, as a gesture to his captain's leadership. "To go home to Glasgow, where it all started, without Billy leading the boys would be rather like having a Rolls Royce and no petrol," explained Ormond. "He is the spirit of Scotland and so much credit is due to him for our showing at the World Cup. And he must be first off the plane to take the bow he and the team so thoroughly deserve."

Bremner did just that, and after stepping off the plane, the bus that took them onwards was loudly cheered on every yard of its journey out of the airport. A German TV reporter, sent to Glasgow to cover the incredible scenes, was seen shaking his head as he said: "My God, what would it have been like if you'd won!"

"We were a good bunch. Willie Ormond, bless him, gave his all and we could have gone further, who knows how far," reflects Danny McGrain. "We had the gel of Billy Bremner, Denis Law, Peter Lorimer, older guys of that time, and the younger guys like Kenny [Dalglish], Tommy Hutchison, Jim Holton and Willie Donachie. We blended really well, but when it came down to it at the World Cup in '74 we just didn't score enough goals."

CHAPTER 12: THE BFG

"He looked like a big thug, yet his personality was so soft and so gentle"

Willie Morgan

CENTRE FORWARDS who felt the full force of his Size 11 boots up their backside might find it hard to believe, but away from the football pitch Jim Holton was a big friendly giant.

Team-mates, to a man, will tell you what a great character big Jim was to have around the dressing room, training ground and to meet socially, while the old saying 'you should never meet your heroes' never applied to his relationship with supporters. He would stop and sign every autograph book proffered outside the stadium and pose happily for photographs with grateful fans. If Holton had played in this age of endless selfies, he would have been a social media sensation!

Shrewsbury fans took to Holton because of his unflinching will to win every ball he contested, and those traits immediately endeared him to Manchester United fans. The more he was pilloried in the press, the more they rallied behind their man.

His lifelong friend from Lesmahagow, John Hillan, remembers many an evening where a post-match pint had to wait because Jim was busy ensuring that autograph-hunters were not left disappointed. "The dressing room at Old Trafford used to be up at the halfway line near the railway station and every game there could be 100 or 200 people outside waiting on autographs. Jim never walked past anybody. It was never any trouble to him. I actually had to help Jim write his autograph fluently because at first it was like an Egyptian hieroglyphic! Jim never let anything go to his head and he always recognised how important fans are to a football club. He never forgot his roots or got above himself – if you came from our scheme in Lesmahagow you didn't!"

Iain McCartney – a lifelong United fan and fellow Scot - was one of the supporters who occasionally rubbed shoulders with Holton at the stadium and United's training ground. "Jim Holton was my last Old Trafford hero. No-one has replaced old 'six-foot-two' and no-one will," says McCartney. "Big Jim didn't even have 'eyes of blue' as the legendary terrace anthem proclaimed, but he did have eyes that would instil fear into the heart of many opposition forwards at home and abroad, letting them know that their Saturday afternoon was not going to be an easy one. His presence always lifted the Old Trafford faithful, as they knew with big Jim in the line-up, he would give his all in the attempt to secure victory for United.

"Being Scottish didn't influence my admiration for the gentle giant. Despite his on-field presence, he was a nice unassuming lad. He certainly was when I met him at United's Cliff training ground back in the 1970s – and my memories have not been clouded over the years. In his early days he was raw, but he had just stepped up from the lower leagues with Shrewsbury Town to the First Division with United. He was a young lad, doing a job that we couldn't and we admired him for it. We forgave his errors and blamed his opponents and the referees for the free-kicks given against him. He wasn't dirty. Clumsy at times? No, it was nothing more than boyish enthusiasm!"

I contacted a few United supporters via Twitter to ask for their memories of Holton and was overwhelmed by the response. TV presenter Eamonn Holmes revealed: "The days of man-mountain centre halves! On my first visit to Old Trafford I bought his picture in the souvenir shop!" Another well-known celebrity United fan, Terry Christian, said: "My memory of Jim is a great 50-50 with Peter Osgood of Chelsea - both big lads - Osgood left in heap. I saw Osgood pulling out of the next few challenges."

Sue Jones, a United fanatic, was so taken with Jim that she sometimes went to watch him play for Sunderland and Coventry on weeks when United weren't playing. "He was a colossus in our defence. He took some shifting! It's just a shame that he suffered so many injuries. I loved him and he was a nice jovial chap off the park."

United midfielder Sammy McIlroy could see why the fans adored Jim so much. "He was a wholehearted player, great in the air and just a big, loveable character. The fans loved his do or die attitude, and recognised that he was winner, determined to give his all for them and for United. All the players liked him and he gave 100% in everything he did."

The adulation that came with being a Manchester United player was new to Jim, and his wife Jan too, but she says he always coped well with attention when they were out and about.

"People always knew who he was, particularly after the World Cup, but it never affected him," she says. "After he'd become a Stretford End favourite, you'd get random people walking past chanting 'Six foot two, eyes of blue', but he never got harassed. You could be out for a meal and overhear someone saying 'That's big Jim over there', but the nice thing was that even though people knew who he was, they didn't tend to intrude and when they did come up to speak to him, they were always polite. On the rare occasions that I was allowed to go to Old Trafford with him, he'd have all these little girls, 14, 15 and 16 year olds saying 'Is that your wife Jim?' When he said yes, they were always as good as gold."

The 'Six Foot Two' song was the ultimate recognition of Jim's popularity, and although team-mates used to tease him when it was belted around Old Trafford, Holton wasn't bashful — it was music to his ears!

"I laughed when I first heard it," says Holton's wife Jan. "I think on the quiet he was quite chuffed because they had made the effort to come up with a song for him. To him it was acceptance by the United fans and that was important. If you got the Stretford End on your side, you'd cracked it. The blue eyes reference is hilarious though. I remember he joked to me 'Do you think I should go and get contact lenses, Jan?' Six foot two, eyes of brown would never have had the same ring to it!"

Mick Martin said the song was a source of amusement, and pride, to Jim. "He loved the 6 foot 2, eyes of blue chant. I kept saying to him 'God, they absolutely love you Jim, it must be great hearing your name', so he decided to make up a song for me. I came in one day to training and he burst into a chorus of '5 foot 10, eyes of green, Micky Martin's on the scene!' I was breaking my heart laughing, but I had to admit to him 'I don't think that will ever take to the terraces big man!'"

Not many of United's players had the honour of a song in their name in those days, but one who did was popular winger Willie Morgan. "Jim was the first defender that they ever had a song about as far as I remember, he became a big favourite," says Morgan. "They loved Jim because he was one of them, and he loved that adulation. He looked like a big thug, yet his personality was so soft and so gentle and he had this very infectious smile. It's only great memories I have of Jim, no bad ones whatsoever, and I think everyone would say the same. For the size of him, he had a fearsome reputation, but he wasn't like that at all. He was just a big happy-go-lucky guy."

Within months of his arrival at Old Trafford, the honour of a 'Jim Holton Fan Club' was bestowed upon him. The club, run by Stockport-based Manchester United fan Bryan Nield, quickly built up a solid membership base. For 50p a year (£1 overseas), fans received a typewritten newsletter, car sticker, poster and photo. A bumper sticker with a cartoon of smiling assassin Holton and the obligatory phrase 'Six foot two eyes of blue, big Jim Holton's after you' proved particularly popular – not that many people had a car in the early 70s.

The Fan Club newsletters were crammed with reverence for Holton from far and wide. Paul Flight of Ramsbottom wrote in to say: "I think Jim is one of the finest centre halves in the country and gives all is effort in every match. He is a real asset to the inexperienced players and the big occasion doesn't seem to bother him", while Hilary Payne of Rossendale, insisted: "He is the best centre half around. He is king in the air!"

The newsletters reproduced press articles, while also giving their own guest writers a platform to sing the praises of their favourite player.

Looking through the newsletters, there are many contenders for the title of 'Number 1 Fan', but articles by Mark Shutt particularly catch the eye. In an impassioned defence of Holton's playing style, the author captures what made the big number 5 such a hero in the eyes of supporters. "Jim wasn't bought just to stand around and look pretty, but nobody could possibly have envisaged just how big an asset this colossus would turn out to be. What he lacks in style and poise he more than compensates for in tenacity and physical power. Dedication is the word for this buffalo of a man, and honest graft is in short supply nowadays. As he thuds around the Old Trafford pitch his mere presence fills the arena. He is compelling to watch. At one end he will be hammering opponents to the ground, and at the other he will be soaring in for set-pieces and smashing in the headers. There is no striker in the country that can hold a candle to him in the air.

"Let the critics jeer and call him awkward in his movements. The truth is that Jim is a superbly built athlete, a man with the build of a heavyweight boxer. Centre half is a physical position, and there can't be many who fancy their chances against this tank-like stopper. I once asked a bloke at Old Trafford what he thought about Jim Holton. The reply was 'He's a rough bugger, but by hell I know none better!'"

Shutt, writing in the next issue, went even further. He claimed: "His popularity is nothing short of phenomenal. I reckon he's as popular now as any player in United's distinguished history. Many football followers like to see the game played with a bit of blood and thunder and there's just isn't anything more thunderous than a Jim Holton tackle. What is more, he is proving nowadays that he can play a bit as well. Thrown into his growing repertoire of talents is the ability to beat an opponent with nifty footwork, although it has to be said that a Jim Holton body-swerve is like an elephant negotiating a bend in the road. Best of all, however, is Jim when is airborne. Low-flying aircraft come over Old Trafford at their peril. He can head a ball further than lesser mortals can kick it. Holton is so big, both upwards and across that when he wades in with a challenge, bodies are seen to move through the air. It's no wonder that naughty boys in the Manchester area are threatened by their mums with 'behave yourself or I'll send for Jim'."

The truth is that, off the pitch, Holton was a gentle, genial soul. "I don't think he would ever hurt anybody," says former United team-mate Jim McCalliog. "He had a glint in his eye and was always taking the Michael. He was sharp-witted, liked the banter, and he and Mick Martin brought out the best in each other – both had a bit of devilment. Jim was very outgoing, very accommodating and just very nice to have around."

In a dressing room crammed with characters, Jim more than held his own. Martin Buchan says Holton was always up for a laugh and loved a wind-up. "One story that still tickles me is that he was involved with Jimmy Rimmer and one of Jimmy's pals in a cavity wall insulation business," says Buchan. "After training Jim would sometimes go and sit in the office during the afternoons and have a cup of tea. Apparently if the phone went and there was no-one there to answer it, Jim would pick it up and say in his broadest Scottish voice: 'Good afternoon, Crazy Foam here, how can I help ye?' The partner was not very happy with that, and Jim was quickly banned from answering the phones."

Mick Martin, who was nicknamed 'Bunjy' by Tommy Docherty after the Irish character of that name in the sitcom 'Me Mammy', shared many a laugh with Jim and says he was one of the biggest personalities in the dressing room.

"Jeez, he was a funny character," says Martin. "He came up with some great stuff, always on the wind-up. You'd be standing in the shower after training and he'd be chatting away to you, with a big grin on his face. He'd be saying 'You all right Mick? Will we go out for a bit of lunch later?' He would just be keeping the conversation going, until one of the other lads would say 'Bunjy, he's pissing all over you!' He was such a wind up merchant.

"The team morale at that time was fantastic. We'd go out together to George Best's club Slack Alice, on a Saturday night for a couple of pints before getting back into the routine on a Monday. He was great company and he always fun to be around."

Even though Jim was a relatively young player himself, he

would always take time to encourage the youth and reserve players at Old Trafford. Dave Bradley, who was also a central defender, was at the club at the same time and cites Holton as a huge influence. "I found Big Jim very relatable and it was great to have that relationship as a youngster with a first team player and Scottish International. He had no ego," says Bradley, who went on to play for Doncaster Rovers under Billy Bremner. "I would often see him on the toilet, door open, reading the paper! I also remember going in the club mini van with Norman the kit man to pick Jim up from his house to take him in to The Cliff. Just to be around him and treated as an equal was priceless, especially as we were both specialised centre halves with a not dissimilar style of play, meaning take no prisoners. His on-field personality was ruthless but his off-field demeanour was gentle, something I related to also. All in all he was a great guy and very helpful and influential to me. I needed that role model at that early stage of my development."

Journalists and broadcasters also warmed to big Jim. They admired him for his honesty and accessibility, and he made a firm friend in Tom Tyrrell – the man known as the 'Voice of Manchester United' on Piccadilly Radio, and stadium announcer for some time at Old Trafford. "They saw each other socially and had a good friendship," recalls David Meek. "That perhaps illustrates that Jim was a more rounded personality than his tough guy image suggested. To be a footballer and have a friend who was a journalist in radio was slightly unusual in those days."

Jim and Jan were never fussed about courting celebrity, and besides Jim's team-mates and their families, most of their close circle of friends were in 'ordinary' jobs – miners, police force and fire service. They did, however, occasionally mix with the great and the good and Jan remembers the time that Billy Connolly played a trick on his fellow Big Yin by trying to set him up with a gay aristocrat! "At a gathering in London Billy tried to set Jim up with a high-profile Lord, who was gay, and because Jim could be so naïve, he had had absolutely no idea what was going on," laughs Jan. "It was so typical of Billy Connolly and his sense of humour; he'd just stood back and thought it was hysterical. Jim's face went beetroot red when he knew the truth."

One of Jim's greatest honours was when he met the Pope in 1973. Manchester United visited the Vatican during their trip to Rome in the Anglo-Italian Cup, but Holton had a little trouble with Papal etiquette. "He said he didn't know what to do when the Pope held his hand out," says Jan. "He was actually going to shake the Pope's hand until somebody told him to kiss the ring. Jim was a very lapsed Catholic – he was well out of practice!"

Willie Morgan also remembers the visit to the Vatican with amusement. "When we had our audience with the Pope we were all given a gold papal key ring as a souvenir. I said to Alex Forsyth [a Rangers fan]: 'C'mon you blue-nosed bastard, you can't be taking one of them! Give it here!'"

13: ADDING INJURY TO INSULT

*"Riding along in the ambulance I thought a
broken leg could not happen to me"*

Jim Holton

NOT SINCE 1937 had Manchester United started a season in the second-tier of English football. It was an insult to a proud name, but in 1974 the club that had gloriously lifted the European Cup under Sir Matt Busby just six years earlier, took its medicine and prepared for life in the Second Division.

"Don't weep for Manchester United," said a defiant Tommy Docherty as he absorbed United's relegation after 37 unbroken years in the top flight. "Out of the ashes of last season will rise a team good enough to take on the world."

In a rallying call to United fans, he said: "We are being made to suffer, but sometimes it has to be that way before you can succeed. I would rather shoot myself than quit this club now. It's not the end, more the beginning of something that should be eventually very, very good."

His optimism was shared by Sir Matt, who said: "In all my 40 years as player, manager and director, I've never been in the Second Division. It's a terrible disappointment. I can't tell you how much of a loss I feel. We are down but all the movement is towards an upwards direction. Tommy's made it a happy club again. He's made some good buys whatever people say. He was criticised for buying Jim Holton, but the lad will mature."

Busby's direct reference to Holton was made before the World Cup, and the dependable defender – United's player of the year in that relegation season – returned from football's biggest stage with his credentials at an all-time high after three tremendous displays against Zaire, Brazil and Yugoslavia.

Holton was quickly back on club duty, joining up with his team-mates for two friendlies in Denmark, then returning to the less cosmopolitan surroundings of Boothferry Park, Hull, for a final pre-season outing.

The gloomy memory of losing to Manchester City at Old Trafford and succumbing to relegation in April had been replaced by a mood of pragmatism, hope and steely determination. If United were to get out of the Second Division quickly, then togetherness had to be the key. "We are looking like a Manchester United team again and we have complete faith in the manager to take us back," insisted Busby. "In the Second Division we're not going to feel sorry for ourselves. We're going to get our backs up – and get out."

Certainly Docherty had started to build a team full of flair and panache, capable of delivering his flamboyant style of football. The addition of centre forward Stuart 'Pancho' Pearson from Hull City for £170,000 plus Peter Fletcher, was further cause for excitement among United supporters – who, even in their relegation season, could boast the highest average home attendance in the land at 42,712 a game.

"We went into the Second Division with the right attitude and a lot of optimism," says Jim McCalliog, signed towards the end of the relegation season. "Tommy had a really good mix by that time of great club men like Alex Stepney, and Willie Morgan, experienced guys like myself, and then the younger guys like Jim, Lou Macari, Stewart Houston, Alex Forsyth, Brian Greenhoff and Sammy McIlroy. We were all buzzing."

It wasn't just the players that were buzzing – United's Red Army had mobilised and was ready to converge on every away ground in massive numbers. Football was a magnet for hooliganism in Britain in the mid-70s, and the reputation of United's travelling fans went before them. The district of Leyton in east London was the first to batten down the hatches, with many local shops in and around Brisbane Road boarding up their premises in anticipation of trouble as an unruly invasion of United fans headed en masse for their team's opening fixture of the Second Division at Orient.

This represented a tough introduction to the second tier for

United, given that the doughty Londoners had only just missed out on promotion to the First Division by a single point the season before. Nearly 18,000 fans were packed sardine-style into the ramshackle ground, some scaling floodlight pylons in the hope of securing a vantage point and ignoring pleas from the stadium announcer to come down quietly. Orient mirrored the first-choice colours of United – red shirts, white shorts and black socks – so Docherty's side played in an all-white kit. The last time Jim Holton and Willie Morgan had worn these colours was two months earlier for Scotland in their World Cup clash with Yugoslavia.

Morgan gave United the lead in the 28th minute and a second half goal from Stewart Houston ensured the return journey to Manchester was a happy one. "That first game was a bit of a shock to the system," says McCalliog. "We won that game quite comfortably but I hurt my Achilles and had to go off. It was quite a scary injury for me, but the physio Laurie Brown worked wonders and got me back quickly."

Victories against Millwall (4-0) and Portsmouth (2-1) quickly followed at Old Trafford, three of those goals coming via Gerry Daly from the penalty spot, before United's next away trip – this time against Cardiff – was again played against a backdrop of bedlam and arrests. Daly scored the only goal of the game in the Welsh capital – again from the penalty spot. United were happy to accept any help that came their way, and they sat proudly at the top of the table.

A draw against Nottingham Forest helped keep United's feet on the ground, and they were also held away at West Brom – on Holton's return to the Hawthorns, where he faced some of his old apprentice pals, including Ally Robertson and Len Cantello, although Asa Hartford had just left the club to join Manchester City.

Holton picked up a knock and was probably not too disappointed to miss out on a game in the white-heat cauldron of The Den against Millwall, although he watched the match – played on a Monday night - from the stand with his celebrity pal from the World Cup, Scotland fanatic Rod Stewart! "Going down to the Second Division was a culture shock for us and going to Millwall was certainly an experience. It's safe to say they weren't too pleased to see us at The Den," laughs Martin Buchan. "You had to be professional and blot out some of the abuse coming your way at these away games. Everyone wanted to beat us, and we had had no choice but to accept it and get used to it. It was character building." United had to dig deep to come away with another single-goal victory, yet again courtesy of a penalty from that man Daly. Ironically the Irishman would acquire a variant of the six foot two chant with the Stretford End soon singing 'Five foot eight, underweight, Gerry Daly's f**king great' in tribute.

Jim returned to the side for the 3-0 win at home to Bristol Rovers, but was back on the sidelines for the next two matches, including United's first league defeat of the season, at Norwich. A pattern of niggling injuries was emerging for Holton, but when he played, United were undoubtedly at their most effective. With so many gifted attacking players in their ranks, they didn't have to rely on the defence the way they had in previous seasons, but when called upon – Holton and co did their job.

"We adopted a really attractive style and we quickly got back to winning ways in the Second Division," says Buchan. "Willie Morgan and Gerry Daly were firing in the crosses for Stuart Pearson to finish. We almost played a 4-2-4, but we had the ability quickly adapt to a 4-4-2 when the opposition had the ball. The funny thing was that we didn't really have a midfield enforcer as such – all of our midfield were nippy and quick. We became the best team in the country at winning the ball back when the other team were in possession – they call it 'pressing high' nowadays, but we were doing that back in the 70s."

The club were on the crest of a wave, and a League Cup date at home to Manchester City offered Docherty's men the perfect platform to show they were still a side to be taken seriously, despite the drop in division. City had enjoyed bragging rights in Manchester for years, winning six out of seven league matches between 1968 and 1974, and United were desperate to challenge the equilibrium.

In one of the great Old Trafford nights of the Docherty era, a goal from unerring penalty king Gerry Daly 12 minutes from time, was enough to seal a dramatic victory. The United back four, which included 17-year-old debutant Arthur Albiston at left-back, were magnificent, keeping Rodney Marsh, Mike Summerbee and Colin Bell at bay, and the bulk of the 55,159 crowd loudly celebrated a famous triumph over their neighbours.

Jim had further cause for cheer around this time when he learned that his wife Jan was pregnant with their first child, with the due date in late June.

With Holton at the heart of the defence United also went on a winning run in the league, going five games in a row without conceding a goal, but when the big Scot went away on international duty – to face East Germany at Hampden– he would last only 12 minutes before having to be carried from the field with a chest injury following a collision with Konrad Weise. His replacement, Kenny Burns, got on the scoresheet in a 3-0 win, while a 21-year-old Graeme Souness made his debut. Alex Forsyth had been restored to the Scotland team and would go on to win four more caps, but unfathomably this would be the last time Holton played for his country.

Holton duly missed most of November as he recuperated from his injury, and both Scotland and United immediately wobbled. Scotland slumped in their European Championship qualifier against Spain at Hampden, while United lost at Bristol City and Hull. Before his return against Sunderland on 30 November, 1974, Jim was chomping at the bit after missing five games, although he admitted he was feeling the heat ahead of such a pivotal match, with Sunderland now only four points behind with a game in hand.

"I've never been so nervous before a game in my life – and that includes the World Cup," said Jim. "This is undoubtedly the match of the day and it's a tremendous prospect coming back to play in front of a near 60,000 crowd. Whatever the result it won't be the end for either team – which is the way a lot of people see it. There are plenty games to play yet and although this is a very important match, promotion will not necessarily depend on it. But the way United have been playing I fancy our chances."

United took an 11th minute lead through a Pearson pile-driver, but found themselves 2-1 behind within three minutes. The Doc's team talk at half-time did the trick, however, and Holton came close with a towering header before second half goals from Morgan and McIlroy earned them a priceless 3-2 win.

The top of the table clash had lived up to its billing, full of blood and thunder, in front of Match of the Day cameras and a bumper crowd of 60,585, the highest in English football that season, an astonishing turnout for a Second Division fixture. "Everywhere we went we had a huge support," says Willie Morgan. "When we were in the Second Division I think we broke every ground record away from home. After the heartbreak they experienced the previous season, the United fans still showed an amazing amount of loyalty."

"We had huge crowds home and away that season," agrees Jim McCalliog. "It made me laugh, but the Doc would never let us go out on to the pitch first. We would be dying to get out, and Tommy Cavanagh and the Doc would tell the officials 'no, we're not ready yet'. Only once the other team was out would they let us go. What the Doc wanted was for us to walk out into the middle of the pitch and wave to the crowd. He wanted the other team to hear that roar of the United fans. He used the crowd to our advantage, it was a fantastic ploy. He was also one of the first managers to send you over to applaud the fans at the end of the game, especially the away games.

"They had another trick they used to try and boost our confidence before matches. Cav would go down and get the team-sheet from the other team and he would bring it back to the Doc and the Doc would make sure all the boys were watching him. He would then crumple it up and bin it, as if we had no-one to fear. Of course, as soon as they went away, we were retrieving the team-sheet from the bin because you wanted to see who you were playing against! The spotlight was well and truly on us in the Second Division, but we handled it well and played some great games."

Next stop for United's juggernaut was Hillsborough, on what proved to be a shocking, fateful day for Jim Holton – his final competitive appearance for the club.

As outlined at the beginning of the book, United were leading 1-0 when Jim was involved in a bone-crunching tackle with Sheffield Wednesday midfielder Eric McMordie. Other players in the vicinity of the clash knew immediately that Holton was badly hurt as he crumpled to the turf, roaring in agony, his right leg shattered.

Photographers caught the extent of Holton's pain as Laurie Brown and team-mates tried to help the stricken Scot from the field. Instinctively, Holton himself knew he had suffered a bad injury, although he clung to the hope that it was not a leg break. When he recounted the incident later, he was insistent that no blame should be put on McMordie.

"I heard the crack as I collided with Eric McMordie, but it was certainly no fault of his," said Holton magnanimously. "I had to blame my own over-enthusiasm. I went in for an impossible ball that, with better judgment, I should have left well alone. It was nobody's fault. I had gone in to tackle Eric. As he jumped over me, going out of his way not to hurt me, his boot just caught my leg. I heard a crack. I knew I had done something out of the ordinary but I did not think it was broken. In the dressing room the Sheffield Wednesday doctor thought it might just be a trapped nerve. Riding along in the ambulance I thought a broken leg could not happen to me but the plaster they put on showed that it had. That night, lying in a hospital bed, I was quite content. Broken legs had happened before, I told myself, and I would get over it."

The game was unforgettable for plenty of other reasons. A 4-4 draw, pitch invasions, more than 100 arrests and widespread condemnation of the behaviour of United's supporters, meant that day at Hillsborough lived long in the memory.

Tommy Docherty was straight on the phone to Sheffield Infirmary after the final whistle. Before the manager had a chance to ask about Jim's well-being, the ever-loyal Holton asked him what the final score was. "I told him, of course, but said he shouldn't worry about the result because we were going back up and his job was to get ready for First Division football next season," said The Doc.

Although there is YouTube footage of the match it doesn't include the flashpoint between McMordie and Holton. McMordie was already well known to Manchester United having been the companion who travelled to the club for a two-week trial with George Best when the pair were teenagers, only to return homesick to Belfast. Best was, of course cajoled back to the club by Sir Matt Busby, while McMordie first played locally for Dundela before he was tempted back to England by Middlesbrough. He was displaced by Graeme Souness at Ayresome Park and was coming to the end of a short-term loan at Sheffield Wednesday before the fixture with United. As far as Holton and United were concerned, he was in the wrong place at the wrong time.

While Holton absolved the Irishman of any blame, Martin Buchan still sees it differently. "In my opinion it was a shocking tackle. You don't remember things like that 40 years on without reason," he insists. "I know Jim always said there was no malice but all I would say, that in my opinion, I felt at the time that it was a very poor tackle and my view to this day remains the same."

Veteran Welsh striker Ron Davies was the United substitute at Hillsborough and was thrown into the fray, but the loss of Holton left a gaping hole in Docherty's defence, and Sheffield Wednesday exploited it. All things considered, a point represented a good result for United.

As he faced up to the extent of his injury, Holton was overwhelmed with the flood of 'get well soon' cards and messages he received. "I had over 400 cards, chocolates and other presents," he said. "I never thought I would be as popular."

With Holton's broken leg and a long period of rehabilitation confirmed, Docherty first turned to Arnie Sidebottom to fill the number 5 shirt. Raw and slightly ungainly, Sidebottom acquitted himself well, playing in three successive clean sheets before Christmas, including a victory over Middlesbrough which took United into the semi-finals of the League Cup.

However, after that Sidebottom only played five more times for United, three of them defeats and one a disappointing exit to Walsall in the third round of the FA Cup. Steve James was the next player entrusted with filling Holton's boots at centre half. Sidebottom credits Holton for bringing on his game and taking him under his wing – 'I'll sort this one out young man, you just get behind me!' – but although he was a talented enough footballer, the Yorkshireman was always preoccupied by another sport. "Cricket was always my first love," says Sidebottom. "I had a clause in my contract that once I finished playing at the end of the season I went to play cricket for Yorkshire during the summer months."

When I interviewed Docherty, he still affectionately (I think!) referred to Sidebottom as 'The Cricketer'. The dual sport arrangement was never going to last when United made it back to the First Division.

Sidebottom eventually left United for Huddersfield Town who were happy to accommodate his cricketing commitments but he has a good story to tell of how he nearly went straight from United to Brian Clough's Nottingham Forest. "I made a big mistake – I went on my own. A secretary told me 'Mr Clough will see you now' and when I went into the office he was sitting behind a big desk, with Peter Taylor standing behind him, with his hand on the back of the chair. Cloughie said, 'We'd like to give you a contract.' He threw it across the desk and just said 'sign it'. He didn't say how much money it was, what length of contract it was, anything else. I couldn't get any words out, I was tongue-tied, so he said, 'Sign it or bugger off!' So… I buggered off!

"I went to Huddersfield instead. I was there a couple of years before they said, 'make your mind up, you either choose football or cricket'. Geoff Boycott offered me a five-year contract at Yorkshire so it was a no-brainer really. I enjoyed my football days though, particularly at United." It proved the right decision as Sidebottom went on to represent England in the Ashes a decade later.

And he wasn't the only player to fall out of favour as Docherty continued to reshape United. One surprising casualty was Jim McCalliog, who had been a solid addition to the squad. Although

Gorbals-born McCalliog had previously played under Docherty at his first club Chelsea, and the pair generally got on well, their relationship soured in early 1975. "I had a bust-up with the assistant manager Tommy Cavanagh, which didn't help," reveals McCalliog. "He and I never got on, although I suppose I brought it on myself because he was a fiery character and Sammy McIlroy and I used to try and nutmeg him in training. Cav loved five-a-sides, but I would wait and see what team he was in and then get on the other side against him. Sometimes we would play two or three-touch, and I would push the ball a bit – as if I'd lost control – then flick it through his legs when he got near. The boys would be laughing, but he would be raging. I would go out of my way to take him on. It wasn't a battle royale between the two of us, it was just one of these things, and I was out the door after only 13 months."

McCalliog's final game for United was in February 1975, and it was a sticky month – as the goals dried up and they slumped to three league defeats. A 2-0 reverse against title rivals Aston Villa would be their final loss as the introduction of future England winger Steve Coppell added verve and purpose to a faltering campaign as United marched to the title with eight victories and three draws from their final 11 fixtures.

First, promotion was clinched with three games to spare when Lou Macari scored a late winner at Southampton. The following week, with the pressure off, United ensured they would return as champions when they beat Fulham 1-0 at Old Trafford.

Macari says: "We waltzed away with Division 2. We found our rhythm quickly and the fact that we kept winning gave us the confidence we needed to kick on when we did go back to the top league. It was a new United, with different players, and it was always going to take time for those players to click. It's even more difficult to gel at a club like Manchester United where the pressure is on you every week, in front of massive sell-out crowds. You have got to perform, and we did."

A 2-2 draw at Notts County meant little before Docherty and the players basked in a party atmosphere as United celebrated the title in style, thrashing Blackpool 4-0 in front of a jam-packed Old

Trafford, then paraded the championship trophy round the pitch on a lap of honour. United finished three points clear of Villa, who also won the League Cup that season, while Norwich also sealed promotion back to the First Division, in third spot.

Jim had featured in 14 of the 42 games, as well as three League Cup games – and was never once in a losing team. Reflecting on the season, Holton said: "We got stuck in without anyone thinking we were a bit classier than the other teams. And clearly the turning point came when I broke my leg! Obviously that has been a big upset for me and I am just glad the lads went on to win promotion."

With a month-long World Tour planned, Holton was desperate to return to action after a series of minor setbacks had prevented him making any kind of end-of-season cameo. "With injuries like this you have highs and lows of morale," explained Jim. "The worst moment came when I first went to have the plaster off. I had been doing body exercises to keep myself in shape. The doctor had told me the plaster would be on for six to eight weeks, and when I went to see him I was in the eighth week. I was really happy. I thought he would just whip off the plaster and say 'Away ye go son!' Instead, he decided to give it another 14 days in plaster. That shattered me. That was a setback. I had been looking forward to playing in the Easter games.

"Still, I got over it. I have been running and working with weights and kicking a ball just recently and I am only waiting for the stiffness to go from my ankle. Right now my morale has never been higher."

Having not played since early December, Holton could not even be considered by Willie Ormond for the Home Internationals, but his disappointment was quickly assuaged when Tommy Docherty gave him the green light to join the party on the plane for United's World Tour.

Absent from the tour, however, was Willie Morgan, who was instead placed on the transfer list after a bitter bust-up with The Doc, who had a ready-made replacement at No. 7 in the shape of emerging star Steve Coppell.

Morgan says: "I shouldn't have been surprised, because I'd seen him do it to other players, and there had been tension between us throughout the season. On one occasion I had been away with Scotland, and returned to see a headline in the paper: 'Will Willie Morgan keep his place this weekend?' I went in to see Doc to confront him.

"The Doc, said 'Bastard! Do you want me to ring him?' So he called up the journalist, who was a pal of his, in front of me and gave him what for. When I left the office and shut the door, I listened in and, sure enough, he was back on the phone to the journalist, saying: 'Sorry about that, he was standing right next to me'. From that moment, I knew what was coming.

"At the end of the season, after we had just won promotion, he said: 'I want to be friends, let's stop all this unpleasantness. Do you and your family want to go on a nice holiday somewhere, get a nice rest? You don't have to come on the tour' I agreed, we shook hands, and the following day the headline in the *Manchester Evening News* was: 'MORGAN REFUSES TO GO ON TOUR!' I went looking for him, but I couldn't find him for love nor money. They had an emergency board meeting and put me on the transfer list. He was clever, I'll give him that. My time at United was over after seven years, and I went back to Burnley."

Meanwhile Buchan, Forsyth, Macari and Houston reported for Scotland duty, with a friendly against Portugal preceding the Home Internationals before they could hook up with their United team-mates in Hong Kong. Rising star Coppell also missed the early stages of the tour to sit his final exams at Liverpool University.

'World Tour' is no exaggeration of the adventure United embarked on. Eight fixtures were arranged between the end of May and the end of June, taking in Iran, Indonesia, Hong Kong, Australia and New Zealand. The only defeat of the tour came against Ajax in Jakarta in a match watched by 110,000!

A rejuvenated Holton played in each and every one of the eight tour games. He already had cause for celebration, but the icing on the cake came hours after United's penultimate fixture – a 3-0 win over Queensland in Brisbane - when he got word from home that he had become a Dad.

The Scottish press reaction to Jim's injury focussed on the prospect of him missing the 1976 European Championship qualification campaign but he had already played his last game for both his club and his country.

Baby boy Neal arrived on 22 June, 1975, with his proud dad on the other side of the world. "They drank the hotel dry of champagne apparently," laughs Jan. "I think they were on a bender for three days celebrating Jim's good news. I went in to labour and got taken in to a little cottage hospital which was run by the midwives. My mum was with me and I had Neal at ten to eight. He was born 9lb 1oz - a big boy. United arranged for Jim to phone and his first words were, 'Were you able to walk to the phone?' I said 'Of course I can walk, what do you think I am, an invalid? I've just had a baby, that's all!' Neal was about four or five days old by the time he saw him, but he was so proud."

Jim returned from Down Under feeling on top of the world. Everything was rosy. He was a new dad, he had proved his fitness, and he was looking forward to returning to the First Division with a brave new Manchester United. What could possibly go wrong?

14: UNLUCKY JIM

*"Jim changed his style of play. It probably dawned on him
that to have a longer career, he'd have to settle down a bit"*

Manchester United physio Laurie Brown

A BROKEN LEG in the 1970s didn't necessarily signal the
end of a footballer's career, but plenty of patience and
mental and physical resilience, not to mention luck, was
needed to make a return to full fitness. For Jim Holton, it's safe to
say there were complications.

Boredom was the first problem. Holton, with his entire right
leg encased in plaster, from the tip of his toe to the top of his thigh,
was doubtless one hundred per cent committed to his treatment
and rehabilitation at United's Cliff Training ground, but when he
returned home from those sessions with the medical staff, he was
susceptible to bouts of restlessness.

On one such occasion, he decided to break the monotony by
cleaning his car, which was parked in his drive at Whalley Avenue.
Not just any car, but the top of the range Vauxhall VX4/90 saloon
that each member of the Scotland squad had been given for a year
as a reward for qualifying for the World Cup.

The car-washing itself went without a hitch, but a frightening
experience began when Holton decided he wanted to return his
gleaming motor to his garage. Because his right leg was immobilised,
to perform such a feat he would need his wife Jan to help work
the pedals.

Jan hopped into the passenger seat, while Jim, with his right
dangling precariously out of the driver's door, attempted to steer
the car into the garage, using his left leg to work the brake and
accelerator. They almost pulled the stunt off, until the pair managed
to hurtle into the garage at full speed, crashing full tilt through the

back and straight into the adjoining neighbour's shed. If that wasn't bad enough, they managed to kill the neighbour's hamster in the wreckage!

"It was terrifying," said Jan. "At first, I think I was upset about the poor hamster. But then one of the firemen said, 'You do realise Mrs Holton, if Jim had been an inch or two further over to the right, he would have torn his leg off at his hip. He would have bled to death and you would have gone through the windscreen and ended up with a face like a roadmap.' That's when I started to shake like a leaf. I was in shock – it could have been so much worse."

Manchester United physio Laurie Brown was one of the first on the scene after the accident, and he remembers it well. "His right leg was completely in plaster, so I wasn't expecting to see him for a while. It was a Sunday morning and I was in at Old Trafford, the only physio, treating the lads that had been injured on the Saturday. I was working away when I got a phone call from Jim, sounding a bit agitated, and asking me if I'd be able to come round to his house straight away.

"I finished up and headed round, and I could see there had been a bit of an accident. Jim was still outside with the plaster on, looking sheepish. I could see the back of the garage had been bulldozed, and there was no fence anymore on the adjoining garden – it had all been completely demolished. The neighbours had a shed with a fridge in it and that had been flattened as well. The first thing he said was 'Laurie, don't say a word!' I don't think I was able to say a word, I was speechless! He had scratches on his toes beneath the plaster, and I realised with his leg hanging out the car, he must have just missed the stanchions on the garage by inches. If he'd hit that with his leg rigid in plaster, who knows what would have happened. He was a bit shaken up, but he was laughing about it – that was Jim to a tee."

The Holtons had somehow escaped relatively unscathed, although the plaster cast on Jim's leg was cracked in the incident, and had to be re-set at nearby Park Hospital.

News of the smash was swiftly relayed via reporters to Tommy Docherty, who did not see the funny side. "I feel both angry at what has happened and relieved that he does not seem to have been hurt," said a nonplussed Doc. "He should not be driving a car at all in his condition."

Holton was at least in good hands working with Laurie Brown, who in turn admired the big man's determination to return to action.

"In those days everybody wanted to play, and Jim was desperate to get back out there," says Brown. "My job was to try and hold players back until they were ready, to give them a proper chance of recovery. I was quite pleased when they were in plaster – not because they were injured – but because managers saw that and left them alone. Once the plaster came off and a player is walking about and then jogging, then your problems started, because immediately the player and the manager would be in your ear, asking when they could get back on the pitch.

"I don't know if it's just my imagination but players didn't seem to be out for as long in those days as they are now. I'm not saying that's a good thing, but I think players in my day came back quicker because club's didn't have such great depth in their squads as they do now. I used to worry about players being paid and missing a few games, but gee whiz, now some of them are getting paid £200,000 a week and not playing for weeks. If that had been the case when I was physio, my hair would have gone grey and fallen out a lot quicker than it did! Generally, in my day, players wanted to be out on the pitch. Men were men back then and players were tougher, and nobody came much tougher than Jim!"

With his broken leg healed, Holton had proved his fitness on the World Tour of 1975, and was poised to make a return to the United defence for the 1975/76 season. With a good pre-season under his belt, he was looking leaner, fit and hungry. However, less than two weeks before the First Division curtain-raiser away to Wolves, his luck began to take a serious turn for the worse.

The first problem arose when Holton was controversially red carded during a low-key August friendly in Denmark against a Halskov Select XI. 'Simulation' wasn't even recognised as a term in football in 1975, but Holton appeared to be the victim of some

Oh baby! Dad's put his foot in it again

CRUNCH! ... Big Jim Holton's jinx has struck again.

Jim's disastrous attempts at washing his car ended up as headline news. .

unnecessary gamesmanship when Danish player Reidar Hansen collapsed theatrically after minimal contact in the penalty box as United teenager Peter Loughanne swung in a corner. The local referee immediately brandished the red card, and a crestfallen Holton trudged off, well aware that strict UEFA suspension rules meant that the dismissal could potentially trigger an immediate three-match domestic ban.

"It was a faked job," protested Holton after the game. "We just bumped each when I challenged. Next thing I saw their player on the ground clutching his face. My comeback has been going so well and now I'm bitterly disappointed."

Tommy Docherty agreed: "It was just a brush between two players and the Danish lad went down like a log."

Thankfully for Holton, UEFA deemed that the sending off was sufficient punishment, and decided not to take any additional disciplinary action against Holton. His First Division comeback was back on... for just a few more days as it turned out.

A glamour match against Red Star Belgrade had been arranged at Old Trafford four days before the start of the season, to further whet supporters' appetites ahead of United's triumphant return to the top-tier. Holton, like the rest of the team, was looking forward to testing himself against a top European side. He was lost in his own thoughts during the pre-match warm-up, when suddenly a stray ball whacked at pace by team-mate Alex Forsyth thumped into his head, knocked him off balance, and sent him crumpling to the ground in agony as he twisted his knee.

Forsyth remembers the "million to one" freak accident well. "When we were warming up I used to love whacking the ball as hard as I could from 30 or 40 yards," he explains. "Before the Red Star game I was hitting a couple towards the goals. Jim just happened to be running across the 18-yard line at the same time, minding his own business. I hadn't seen him when I whacked it and the ball smashed him right on the side of the heid. He went down like a sack of tatties and I'll never forget his face as he was getting stretchered off. He didn't have his teeth in, and he was looking up at me saying 'ya effin so and so!' All I could keep saying was 'sorry big man, I didnae mean it!'. It was bad enough to put him out the game for a while and I felt terrible about it."

Holton, always one quick to forgive, put it down to the bizarre accident it was. "Alex must have miscued but I didn't know anything about it until I came round and tried to pick myself up," he told reporters. "I know that nobody could damage my head, so there was no problem in that respect! But my knee ligaments were damaged as I fell."

Coincidentally, the match against Red Star finished 4-4 – the same scoreline it had been at Hillsborough nine months earlier when Jim broke his leg. "We all felt terrible for Jim, as he was so close to coming back for us. It was shockingly bad luck," says Martin Buchan. "I remember it vividly. We were knocking balls back and forward to each other and Jim had a ball coming to him. As he put his right foot to stop it, out of his line of sight Alex Forsyth was trying to hit a 50-yard pass across the field and it hit

Jim on the back of the head. As it turned out, Brian Greenhoff, who was due to play in midfield, was pulled back to play alongside me. We went a few goals behind and were in disarray but we managed to scramble a draw." It was a move that would be fatal to Big Jim's long term Old Trafford future.

The outing against Red Star obviously sharpened up United, as Docherty's side opened the season – minus Holton – in whirlwind fashion, winning five and drawing one of their first six league games. By the end of August, United sat proudly at the top of the First Division, one point clear of West Ham.

The versatile Brian Greenhoff quickly established himself in the centre of defence alongside Martin Buchan, and the pair immediately clicked. Although Greenhoff stood only 5ft 9in, his ability to read the game together with his incredible work-rate and link-up play, made him a class act. Added to the considerable talents of skipper Buchan, the duo proved an instant hit. It was the key to United's dynamic new style.

The Holton-Buchan partnership had also been one of the best defensive combinations in United's recent history, but Docherty was never afraid of trying new ideas to feed his attacking ethos, and he deserves enormous credit for recognising what Greenhoff had to offer in the back four. The Yorkshireman's seamless transition into defence was bad news for Holton, as he first rested then got back into the gym at The Cliff to strengthen his damaged knee.

Worse was to come for Holton in September. With the knee ligaments mended, Jim set off on the comeback trail again, returning to action in a reserve match against Bury he ended up leaving the field, close to tears of utter frustration, with his right tibia broken for the second time in ten months. Same leg, same rotten luck.

The big Scot was simply in the wrong place at the wrong time when team-mate Lindsay McKeown tackled Bury winger Peter Farrell. "I was holding back waiting to see what happen when the Bury player fell over my leg," Jim told reporters from his hospital bed that evening. "As soon as it happened I knew it was broken. It was a pure accident. The break is about three inches above the ankle, in exactly the same spot as the first break. But it is a clean break and I don't think I will be out for long."

Mentally it must have been extremely testing for Holton. Although he had come back from a broken leg once, he must have been well aware that the journey back from the latest break would require patience, willpower and a lot of mental strength. His mood can't have been helped by a brutally insensitive comment from Docherty, who as he waxed lyrical about Buchan and Greenhoff's performances, told reporters: "With due respects to Jim Holton, I think we have shown that the days of the stopper centre-half are over."

Holton took the remark on the chin and got on with the pressing business of rehabilitation under the watchful eye of United physio Laurie Brown, who did all he could to keep the big man's spirits up. "When players are spending a lot of time in the physio room, they're not happy bunnies. If they are happy you start thinking something's not right," says Brown. "You don't really see the players when they're at their happiest if they're coming into the treatment room, but big Jim always tried to keep his head up. We got on well and we had some laughs. Jim was a great lad - one of the very good ones.

"The way he played, you could say I saw a lot of Jim! He was one of the most wholehearted players I knew, there was never any holding back with Jim. He never really thought of his own well-being half the time. He did pick up a lot of injuries - that was just the way he played. Jim and Kevin Moran, who came to United a few years later, were much the same. People would ask me if they had fragile bones, but it was simply the way they both played. They didn't think to themselves 'hold on a minute, this may not be a very good idea for my wellbeing'. They went into everything 100 per cent and never thought about their own safety. I also used to hear people say about Jim, and particularly Kevin Moran, that they got so many head wounds because they 'cut easily'. No! It was because players like that put their heads where they shouldn't have been putting their heads.

"Over the years, Jim seemed to calm down and change his style of play. It probably dawned on him that to have a longer career, he'd have to settle down a bit. He used his experience to adapt. I can remember Denis Law saying it's not how many games you play in a season it's how many seasons you play. The way that Jim was playing at United, unless he changed a bit, then he wasn't going to have many seasons."

While Jim knuckled down to his recovery, Greenhoff had made the number 5 shirt his own as United continued to impress, quickly establishing themselves as title contenders. While the defence were doing their job admirably, Steve Coppell was having a terrific season on the right wing, while the arrival of free-scoring winger Gordon Hill from Millwall in November 1975 gave Docherty another exciting option.

With United still riding high in the league, the FA Cup – which they hadn't won since 1963 - offered another realistic chance of silverware. Docherty's side came from behind to edge out Oxford in the third round, then beat Peterborough and Leicester to reach the quarter-finals. Wolves represented the toughest test yet for their aspirations, but after a 1-1 draw at Old Trafford, the young United team came back from 2-0 down to win 3-2 after extra time in the replay at Molineux, Greenhoff scoring the equaliser. Winning the semi-final at Hillsborough, against hot favourites and reigning League Champions Derby County, proved surprisingly straightforward; Hill scoring in each half to take United to the FA Cup final at Wembley.

Not only that but United were, incredibly, challenging for the double - just two years after being relegated. With five games remaining in the league, Queens Park Rangers narrowly led the way from United, Derby and Liverpool. Derby were the first to drop from contention, before United suffered a couple of hammer-blows to their title chances, going down 3-0 at Ipswich and then 1-0 against Stoke at Old Trafford – their first home defeat of the season.

With their fixtures complete, QPR led by a point and needed Liverpool to lose their final match to clinch the title. They didn't, the Reds winning at Wolves to snatch the championship in dramatic fashion, with United finishing a highly creditable third in their first season back.

Jim had been rendered a frustrated spectator during this exciting spell for United, and he took a seat in the stand for the 1976 FA Cup final against Second Division Southampton. Many pundits suggested United simply had to turn up to collect the trophy but in a competition famed for its shocks, a massive upset unfolded on May Day at Wembley.

Holton must have felt dizzied by a whirlpool of emotions as he sat with 100,000 other spectators, on the outside looking in. Win or lose, it was always going to be a day where Holton felt alone and uncertain. Docherty had given Holton no signs of encouragement that he was in with a chance of ever winning his place back, and the Scot was feeling unwanted by the club he loved. Even if they won the cup, on a personal level, Holton would have felt like a spare part, having played no part in the success.

As it turned out The Doc's hopes of delivering Manchester United their first major trophy of a success-starved decade were spectacularly shattered by unheralded Southampton. Docherty sat squirming on the bench when the only goal of the game from Bobby Stokes was fashioned from a defence-splitting pass from none other than recent United cast-off Jim McCalliog.

In the stand, Holton also sat uncomfortably, his energy spent after kicking every ball through his mind's eye. He would have backed himself 100 per cent to stop Stokes in his tracks too. Jan Holton, who accompanied her husband to the match, recalls: "Jim was just coming back from his broken leg the second time, and he was on edge. I almost had to sit in his lap to stop him standing up, because every time a high ball went over he was halfway out of his seat. I had to keep telling him 'You're not on the pitch!'"

Despite his bit-part role, Holton shared the deep disappointment felt at the end of the game by his friends and team-mates. Most of them would return 12 months later to banish that bitter experience and taste FA Cup glory. However, a year can seem like an eternity in football, as big Jim was about to find out.

15: WELCOME TO MIAMI

*"We were really lucky to have him, not only for his
playing ability but for his personality"*

Miami Toros coach Dr Greg Myers

HE WASN'T THE first player to experience going from hero to zero in the eyes of Tommy Docherty, but Jim Holton was floored in the summer of 1976 when he learned that he effectively had no future at Manchester United.

Docherty, who had previously coveted and championed Holton, left his fellow Scot in little doubt that he was now surplus to requirements. Buchan and Greenhoff had become his undisputed first choice-pairing in the centre of defence, and to rub salt into Jim's wounds, the United manager went out and bought Burnley stalwart Colin Waldron as cover.

As The Doc told Holton he would not be taking him on United's summer tour and let it be known on the grapevine that his former favourite defender was for sale, a timely opportunity arose for Jim to join the flow of players heading to the North American Soccer League (NASL) on temporary contracts. The Miami Toros invited Holton out to join them for the outdoor season, and he jumped at the chance of some game time and sunshine.

In an interview years later, Jim explained: "Tommy Docherty made it plain that there was no future for me at United, and I was so low I was thinking of packing it all in. I was playing in the reserves and there were a number of newspaper reports saying other clubs were interested. I went to the United States for three months to get myself fully fit."

Holton, wife Jan, and their son Neal flew out to Florida, but the experience got off to a horrendous start when the baby boy was scalded by hot water not long after their arrival, tipping a teapot over himself in a hotel room. "The football club couldn't have been better when Neal got scalded, they were absolutely amazing," says Jan. "As luck would have it that year they had changed their insurance to cover the families and not just the players, it was really fortunate in that sense."

Neal was given the best possible treatment, and although he was left with a scar on his leg, he fully recovered. Despite the accident, the Holton family quickly settled into their new sunshine surroundings. "We rented a bungalow on Key Biscayne that the club organised for us and we generally had a whale of a time," says Jan. "Jim thoroughly enjoyed playing, and we enjoyed the life. A lot of the players were British and the captain was a Scot, Ronnie Sharp, so were made to feel incredibly welcome."

Indeed, there were several Britons in the 1976 Toros squad or 'roster'. The big-name signing was Chris Lawler, a pivotal player in Bill Shankly's great Liverpool side, but there were several other English imports; Steve Mills (Southampton), Cliff Marshall (Everton), Gordon Fearnley (Bristol Rovers) and John Evanson (Blackpool).

Besides Holton, the only Scot was midfielder Sharp, who arguably boasts the most flamboyant story among the Toros' class of '76. Sharp started his working life as a humble coal-miner playing part-time for Cowdenbeath to supplement his wages. When he found himself beleaguered by a gambling addiction then divorce, he decided to try a new life in Florida in 1973. It would transform his fortunes, and by the time Holton arrived in 1976, Sharp was well on the way to re-inventing himself as a playboy and NASL legend.

Sharp taught himself Spanish, and used his new-found language skills to meet, woo and marry the daughter of a well-connected Mexican in the border town of San Louis Potosi. Toro's American goalkeeper Bill Nuttall remembers how Sharp's unlikely romance blossomed. "Myself, Ronnie Sharp and Steve Baumann were sent to San Luis Potosi, a little Mexican town about the size of your living room, to play on loan for five or six matches. We would train in the morning and then we would go to this coffee shop and this gal caught Ronnie's eye. Every time she came into the coffee shop Ronnie was doing a little spade work. Finally they agreed to go out which is very difficult in the Mexican culture - as a single girl you just don't do it. Her father, who was a Mexican aristocrat, went crazy, thinking 'What the heck, this crazy foreign guy is in our country, plus he's a footballer'. But they kept seeing each other and Ronnie married her."

So powerful were his new in-laws that they commandeered the entire front pages of both local newspapers for pictures of the society wedding between Sharp and his bride Guadalupe 'Lupita' Rodriguez, held in a grand cathedral and attended by 600 guests and 10 violinists – all a far cry from Cowdenbeath!

While Jim's stay in the Sunshine State was confined to one memorable summer, social climber Sharp would go on making a name for himself on the front and back pages. When the Toros later morphed into the Fort Lauderdale Strikers, Sharp used his new-found wealth and connections to become owner of the franchise in 1984, only to relinquish control when he became embroiled in a Texas marijuana-smuggling operation, eventually making a plea bargain and testifying as a witness for the US government. Back in 1976, to Jim, the man known to Mexicans as El Rubio Escocés (the blond Scotsman) was just "wee Ronnie fi Cowdenbeath" and the pair hit it off immediately.

Sharp went out of his way to welcome Holton and his family to Miami with open arms, and the pair would socialise at family barbecues and pool parties. "The weather was fantastic, a bit different to Manchester, and we spent a lot of the time in and around the swimming pool," says Jan. "We did have an episode when we came face to face with a snake. I was lying on my stomach reading and I looked up and saw something draped in a bush. I turned to Jim and said, 'I think there's a snake!' Most people would have stayed well clear, but Jim just went striding over in his shorts and started trying to poke it. I was screaming at him, 'You do realise there's lots of venomous snakes that can kill you here?' But no, he ignored me and had to investigate!

"The whole lifestyle could be an eye-opener at times. When

Jim was out at training I decided I'd push the baby round to the local shop. Wrong move! You didn't go out with a pushchair in 80 degree heat with no sidewalks. I was wondering why people kept giving me strange looks as they went by in their cars until it dawned on me – nobody walks in America. Other than that, the day to day life was much the same there as it was at home – he'd get up, go out to training. But when he came back we used to go sightseeing and shopping. Key Biscayne was an amazing place to live. We were next door to millionaire's mansions and you would see their yachts moored at the end of their gardens. It was another world."

The Toros were founded in 1973 and were owned by Joe Robbie, founder of the Miami Dolphins and although the club shared the Orange Bowl for a time, they played at Tamiami Field during the 1976 summer season. As well as the British imports, the Toros assembled a cosmopolitan squad containing Peruvians, Argentines, and a couple of pacey strikers from Trinidad and Tobago - Steve David and Warren Archibald. League rules dictated that there had to be a quota of home-grown players, and Nuttall was delighted to be learning from the likes of Holton and Lawler.

Goalkeeper Nuttall was one of the home-based players and admits he was awestruck when the Toros brought Holton to Miami, "I was just a young American goalkeeper and when they told me that this guy Jim Holton is coming over on a rehab assignment I was ecstatic. What a defence! I knew Jim had been centre back for Scotland and for Man United, and suddenly he was playing in front of me, with Chris Lawler on the right who had played more than 300 matches for Liverpool under Bill Shankly. I was a bit star-struck when Jim showed up and what made it even better was that he could not have been a nicer guy. I never saw the guy upset, he was the happiest guy you'd ever want to meet, just glad to be alive..

"I could not have been more thrilled knowing big Jim Holton, playing with big Jim Holton, learning from big Jim Holton. He was obviously a world-class player so it was a treat for me to have that kind of a player playing in front of me for those matches.

"There was nobody going to beat him in the air, and he was

very dangerous from corner kicks in the opposition's box. From a goalkeeping stand point he was great to have because he took a lot of balls out of the air. I think he was very good at organising the defence, keeping everybody in place, and he was unbelievably strong. A lot of times Jim would be up against big target men. They were huge guys, but Jim always enjoyed matching their size, strength and physicality. He was also pretty fast, although he was smart enough to never put himself in difficult positions where he had to really use speed.

"Like Jim, Stevie Mills was brought over to Miami for rehab because he had been in a car accident and was trying to re-establish his fitness. But Jim was fully fit and trained very hard because he knew he was going back to top-flight football, whether that was United or somewhere else. He also wanted to get back into the Scotland team, so it was clear that he wasn't coming to Miami Beach for a holiday. He was really motivated to get as fit as he could."

At the helm of The Toros was Dr Greg Myers, then an inexperienced coach who had a talented, but inconsistent multinational assortment of players at his disposal. He recognised that the recruitment of a big-name Manchester United and World Cup player was a coup and was delighted to see his new charge more than live up to expectations.

"We were struggling at the time and he was a really good addition," says Myers, "I knew I was getting a top class player, but I was surprised at Jim's all-round ability. I knew he was one of the world's great headers of a ball, but I had no idea how good he was on the deck. We had already had a number of international players – three Trinidadians and four or five South Americans who had played on their national team. We had a really nice club and Jim fitted right in.

"He helped the American kids a lot, because at the time we had to have three home-based players on the field. They were decent players, but they weren't on the level you see now, so there was a teaching process, and guys like Jim were central to that. I didn't have that much experience on that level either, so Jimmy and some of the players that had played in the World Cup were really, really good with me as well as the American kids.

"At training, he gave 100 per cent all the time. He was one of the first ones on the field and one of the last ones off, talking to the younger players all the time. He was almost like a coach on the field; he was a delight to be around. The American kids just loved him because they just got so much from him."

The Toros played in the Eastern Division of the 'Atlantic' Conference, grouped with teams like the Tampa Bay Rowdies, Washington Diplomats, and the star-studded New York Cosmos, who had Georgio Chinaglia and Pele in their star-spangled ranks that season.

Results were largely inconsistent, but what was never in doubt was the team's morale. Nuttall, who later became General Manager of the US National team and a successful businessman with sportswear firms such as Mitre and Diadora, looks back on the 1976 season with Toros as one of the best years of his life. "We trained about 10 o'clock in the morning or sometimes a little bit earlier because the Miami heat was brutal. We trained for a couple of hours and then everybody headed home and then later circle back many times for a swimming pool party at somebody's apartment complex. We'd throw some burgers on the grill, occasionally have a couple of beers, and have a very nice time. There was lots of camaraderie."

Myers says Holton was an integral part of the team and remembers him with great affection, referring to him as 'Jimmy the Jokester'. Elaborate pranks were rife and the fun-loving big Scot could usually be found in the thick of them.

"We had a trainer by the name of Tom O'Neill," says Myers. "Tom was only 5 foot 8, weighed 200lbs, and he and Jimmy for some reason were the best of friends. When we went on the road, they would usually room together. We had just played a game in San Diego and were staying overnight in a hotel. We had to get up that next morning to catch a flight to Vancouver for our next match, so I took Tom aside and told him to make sure that he got us up and on the road by 7. Jimmy was aware of this and decided to have some fun. When he got up in the middle of the night to go to the bathroom, he changed the time on his watch, the time on Tom's watch and the clock in the room. Then he made enough noise to wake up Tom.

"Tom says, 'What time is it Jimmy?' and Jimmy replies 'It's quarter after 7'. Tom jumps up, shouting 'Oh my god we're going to be late for our flight and I'm going to get fired!' He's screaming bloody murder, so Jimmy tells him to go and wake up the players. All our rooms were on the one floor, and we were damn lucky that no-one else was on that floor. Tom rushed outside to wake up the players. You've got to picture this... he had no shirt on, his belly was hanging out over his underwear briefs and he was in the hallway trying to wake up people. As he was doing that Jimmy went over and locked the door. He then got on the phone and called the lobby, telling the receptionist 'There's a wild man up here running around in the hallway!'

"Tom was busy trying to wake people up, and when one of the players came to the door, he said 'Tom, what's the matter? It's 3 o'clock in the morning, what are you doing? Look, it's dark outside!" The penny dropped and Tom went, 'Oh my goodness!' Eventually they sent the manager up and took Tom to Jim's room. When Jim came to the door, the manager said, 'This guy says he's your room-mate', but Jim - poker-faced - replied 'I've never seen him before in my life' and closed the door! Thankfully, we got it all sorted out but we were all rolling about the floor at the airport when Jim told us the story. That's the kind of personality Jim had and that's why everybody on the team just loved him. We were really lucky to have him, not only for his playing ability but for his personality."

Nuttall says players resorted to practical jokes to break up the monotony of hours spent at airports, on planes and in hotels. "The road trips could be quite gruelling and you didn't really see the cities that you were in," he recalls. "You could go to New York, sleep for a bit, play the match and then the next morning you're on a plane. Flights could take more than five hours between matches. That's like going from London to Moscow or from Stockholm to

Already on his way to six foot two, Jim's extra portions at school dinners help him stand out in his school team at Woodhall Primary in Lesmahagow.

With John Hannah and Mark Cowan, who went on to play for Airdrie, at high-flying youth side Fairholm.

Listening and learning at his first professional club West Brom under legendary Baggies boss Alan Ashman. When Jim was released, former Manchester United goalkeeper Harry Gregg moved in and took him to Gay Meadow, Shrewsbury (below).

SHREWSBURY TOWN
DIVISION THREE 1972-73

Back row (left to right): DAVE ROBERTS JIM HOLTON (now Manchester United) KEN MULHEARN
BOB TOOZE PETER DOLBY LAURIE CALLOWAY

Middle row (left to right): MAURICE EVANS (Manager) RICKY MOIR IAN ROBERTS
TONY GREGORY MICHAEL JONES NIGEL O'LOUGHLIN JOHN MOORE TERRY MATTHIAS
NORMAN HOBSON (Coach)

Front row (left to right): GERRY BRIDGWOOD TERRY HUGHES MIKE KEARNEY IAN MOIR
GEORGE ANDREWS PAUL BEVAN

Wedding day as Jim and Jan tie the knot on 17 June, 1972. The couple soon welcome son Neal into the world followed by daughter Sally.

Jim with Tommy Docherty shortly after his big move to Manchester United in January 1973. 'The Doc' described Jim as the best central defender in the league, but when injury struck his attitude towards his fellow Scot started to cool.

Saturday 7th December 1974 - Jim is carried from the Hillsborough pitch having broken his leg during a 4-4 draw with Sheffield Wednesday. Little did anyone realise at the time but this would be Jim's last competitive game for United after a meteoric career at Old Trafford.

Player of the Year - 1974

During his whirlwind Manchester United career, a fan club was formed in Jim's honour. He was also voted Player of the Year and met the Pope on United's trip to Rome. Yet he failed to get back in the team after injury and was soon deemed surplus to requirements.

Six foot Two, Eyes of Blue, big Jim Holton is after you.

Soon also a legend with Scotland, Jim made his international debut in 1973. His goal against Czechoslovakia helped take his country to their first World Cup since 1958 and by that summer he was soon a fixture in the team that starred at the 1974 World Cup finals as he lines up in Frankfurt to face Yugoslavia.

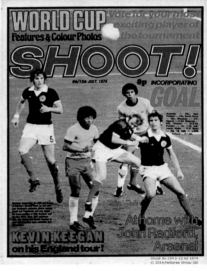

Jim makes front page news ahead of Scotland's crunch match against Yugoslavia at the World Cup. They were held to a draw, as they had been against Brazil, and Scotland's golden generation went out on goal difference.

A rare picture of Jim in the colours of Sunderland. His brief stay on Wearside saw him play under three different managers before a £40,000 move to Coventry City.

Jim and Jan settled into life pretty quickly in Coventry but Jim was soon thrust into a relegation battle with the Sky Blues ongoing survival fight against Sunderland and Bristol City. A controversial draw in the last game of the season saw both Coventry and Bristol survive and Sunderland relegated.

Jim became a mainstay of Coventry's defence as the club embarked upon a 34 year stay in the top flight. Paired with the likes of Terry Yorath and Gary Gillespie in defence, Jim became an influential figure in the dressing room as an elder statesman.

FRANZ BECKENBAUER'S FAREWELL GAME

WEDNESDAY, SEPTEMBER 24, 9:00 P.M.

COSMOS vs. **NASL**
WITH SPECIAL GUEST **SELECT TEAM**
PLAYER PELÉ COACHED BY
RINUS MICHELS

GIANTS STADIUM - THE MEADOWLANDS

NASL SELECT TEAM

Jack Brand   Francisco Marinho
Phil Parkes   Wolfgang Rausch
Laszlo Horsanyi   Jomo Sono
Jim Holton   Jan Van Der Veen
Rudi Krol   George Best
Peter Nogly   Roger Davies
Bjorn Nordqvist   Oscar Fabbiani
Wim Suurbier   Kurt-Heinz Granitza
Teofilo Cubillas   Keita
Leonardo Cuñar   Gerd Mueller
Jurgen Kristensen

Before Jim left the US for the final time he was invited to play in Franz Beckenbauer's final game. He had played against Der Kaiser for Scotland a few times and the former German captain was an admirer of Jim's.

After retirement Jim and Jan successfully ran pubs in Coventry that soon became a mecca for Coventry and United supporters as well as stars of pitch and screen such as Emlyn Hughes, then at the peak of his fame as a captain on Question of Sport.

Jim was as fit as a fiddle, as can be seen from this picture of him in his original Scotland jersey from the 1974 World Cup, which makes it all the more shocking that he died at the age of just 42 following a heart attack.

Rome. We travelled long distances and had a lot of flight time. We didn't do charter flights, we were just on commercial airlines, so it could be pretty exhausting."

Holton could have been forgiven for taking things easy in Miami, but he knew his stay would be temporary and that his future in the UK hinged on him being able to prove his fitness – if not to United, then to clubs who might be willing to sign him. With his career on the line, he was always a fierce competitor ready to give his all. Dr Myers recalls an incident against San Antonio Thunder, where another young Toros' goalkeeper – fresh out of college - ignored Holton's call of 'My Ball!' and tried to punch the ball, instead spilling the ball at the feet of an opponent, who rolled the ball into the unguarded goal. "That meant we lost 2-1, so when the game was over a fuming Holton told the keeper 'Some people consider me one of the best headers in the world. When I call for the ball, I'll get it. If you ever ignore me and come over my back again, I'll break your neck!'"

Myers also remembers an exchange with Rodney Marsh, who played for the Toros' arch–rivals Tampa Bay Rowdies. "We're about 15 minutes from the start and I'm on the pitch talking to Jim and he says 'Have you met Rodney Marsh?' I said no, so he called Marsh over and they talk a little bit and Jimmy says in a mildly threatening manner: 'Now Rodney, you know that the rules are the same over here as they are back home...'

"Jimmy, have I ever taken a dive on you before?"

"No, but if you do you'll be playing the rest of the game with one leg!"

Forever a fierce competitor, Jim was not afraid of imposing himself physically on opponents. Myers remembers him doing his best to stop Rochester Lancers forward Mike Stojanovic. "The Yugoslav guy was outstanding. He was having a field day and Jim was just working him, trying his best to slow him down," says Myers. "Finally the ball shifted down to the other end of the field, the linesman wasn't looking, the ref wasn't looking, so Jimmy cold conked this guy, knocked him out!

"The guy is clean out and I called Jimmy over. 'Jimmy, what

the hell are you doing? Look at him!' and he says 'Coach, he's killing us!' I said 'Jimmy, my God he's...' He just shrugged and said 'Nah, they didn't see it.' So anyway, the guy gets up, shakes it off, scores two more goals and after the game Jimmy goes 'let me tell you what, that is one tough cookie! I gave him my best shot and he came back and stuck it right up our butt. I respect that guy'."

As Holton's American adventure neared an end, *Sunday Express* sports writer James Mossop landed something of a scoop by catching up with Jim in Miami. Mossop had been on his way home from covering the 1976 Olympics in Montreal, and his detour to Florida paid dividends as Holton poured his heart out on being snubbed by Docherty at United.

After obligingly driving the journalist around some of the impressive sights in his Chevy, Holton opened up on the heartache he was feeling about facing such an uncertain future. "'It is worrying. I sit here and wonder just what is going to happen to me,' said an emotional Holton. 'I do not think United want me. I was shattered when Tommy Docherty said he wasn't taking me on tour because he did not think I was fit. I had played 15 matches in the reserves and surely going on tour would only have helped me get even fitter. The previous summer when I recovered from the first break and had not played in a solitary match, they took me on tour and I played in every game. Anyway, after a bit of argument with the manager, he has allowed me to come here. It has been a wonderful experience. I have been playing two matches a week all over the States and I have never felt fitter. I have taken whacks on the legs, smack on where the breaks were, and I have been playing well.'"

As much as he'd embraced the experience of the America dream, Holton insisted he was ready to return 'home'. "I know Britain is the only place I can live," he said. "It has been marvellous here. We have barbecues, we eat in the open air, the temperature is constantly in the 90s, oranges grow in the street and we take to the beach or I go sea-fishing every afternoon. But you still cannot beat your own folks!"

Holton had managed to come through an impressive 18

matches unscathed during his time with Toros, and while the team struggled against some of the bigger clubs, on a personal level the experiment had paid off handsomely. Holton, like any defender, hated nothing more than conceding a goal, but in his final match for the Toros, against New York Cosmos in Yankee Stadium, he would be the first to admit he had witnessed something of stunning beauty when Pele leapt in balletic fashion to thump home a bicycle kick he would say was one of the best goals of his magnificent career. At the end of an 8-2 rout – incidentally the worst score-line Holton suffered in his career – Pele said of his 1,254th career goal, "Goals like that don't come often."

That fixture was the last ever NASL match played at the old Yankee Stadium and Cosmos moved to Giants Stadium the following season. The Toros' days were numbered too – and when they moved to Fort Lauderdale in 1977, they were re-named the Strikers.

As Jim and his family packed their bags and prepared to return home in August 1976, Docherty was bluntly making it clear that the next time he pulled on his boots would probably not be with Manchester United. "If he wants to come to me and say that he wants away, I'll put his views before the directors. I would recommend we do it," said Docherty. "The ball is in Jim's court. He has to come back and show his fitness and that he is of the standard we need. Playing football in America and the English First Division is two entirely different things."

16: GOOD DOC, BAD DOC

"Tommy Docherty would say a lot of good words about you, but then he'd fall out with you. He used to tell porkies sometimes"

Mick Martin

WHEN I INTERVIEWED Tommy Docherty months before his 90th birthday, he was charming, helpful and had nothing but good words to say about Jim Holton. However, that wasn't the case back in the summer of 1976 when The Doc unceremoniously washed his hands of a player who had answered his every call.

There are already enough books and press cuttings examining the curiosities of Docherty's character, but the men who played under him seemed to love and loathe him in near equal measure. Blessed with razor-sharp wit and with a tongue to match, he still polarises opinion in a way few people can.

Docherty's football knowledge and what he achieved in five unforgettable years at Old Trafford is untouchable. The Doc, quite correctly, is remembered with great fondness as the man who brought the good times back to Manchester United and laid the foundations on which future glories were built. However, it is hard to argue with the view that he had his character flaws and suffered occasional errors of judgment – laid bare amid the tawdry circumstances surrounding his sensational sacking in 1977. A string of United players from that era saw the best and worst traits of Docherty's complex personality and Holton would fall firmly into that category.

The Doc shaped Holton from a raw, clumsy hopeful into a fast-maturing international footballer, and helped build his confidence to superhuman levels around the affirmation that he was one of the best central defenders in the world.

Talking to Docherty more than 40 years after he parted company with Holton, he states unequivocally: "He was one of my best ever signings as a manager."

Continuing the glowing tribute, Docherty explains, "With the greatest respect to them, people asked me what were a club like Manchester United doing signing someone from Shrewsbury? After a couple of games the fans just took him to their hearts. He was a revelation! It was only a matter of time before he was picked for Scotland. The way he played when he switched from Shrewsbury to Man United was tremendous.

"He was a no nonsense player, an out and out centre half, nothing else. He was great in the air because of his height, but he was quick for a big guy and centre forwards didn't like playing against him! Most importantly of all he was a winner. I can't speak highly enough of him, both as a great professional and as a player.

"You could praise him and he took it, and you could criticise him and he took it. He just got on with it. He was a model pro; he and Buchan together was a marvellous pairing. Martin was so quick and read the game fantastically well and, of course, anything that big Jim missed – which wasn't a lot – Martin swept it up."

Throughout 1973 and 1974, Docherty was saying much the same about Holton. Buoyed by such faith and encouragement, big Jim started to look up to Docherty in the same way he had his original mentor Harry Gregg. So when the United manager decided he no longer had any use for the big Scot, it must have hurt deeply.

Jan Holton confirms that her husband found the rejection from Docherty hard to take, particularly after such a positive start to their working relationship. "Jim saw the good and bad sides of Tommy Docherty," she says, "the good aspect was obviously that he chose Jim as his centre half, made him the mainstay of his defence, and played him game after game. As long as Jim was an asset, Tommy Docherty was great. But, when Jim broke his leg, The Doc's attitude towards him changed.

"The first time he broke it I don't think he was given sufficient time for that leg to heal, he was pushed and pushed. Jim, with his full leg in plaster, would be exercising hard in the gym. They used to come and collect him every day and take him to the gym to keep his muscle tone up because The Doc wanted him back. Then, when he broke his leg the second time in that reserve game, there didn't seem to be the same urgency to get him fit. I think The Doc felt that he had become a liability instead of an asset because by that time Brian Greenhoff had taken Jim's position, so he wasn't needed. Once the Doc realised that he didn't need him anymore he was out the door. Jim didn't have an agent so he had no-one really looking after his back. He was so easy-going that he was prime fodder for the likes of The Doc. Jim wasn't the first one he did that to, he did it to quite a few players – he could be ruthless when he wanted to be."

Docherty's own recollection of their parting is hazy, which is entirely understandable given the length of time that has elapsed since. "I forget what happened to be quite honest with you," says The Doc. "When he came back [from his broken leg] he was struggling a bit. For such a big lad, he was mobile with a bit of pace. When I had to switch Brian Greenhoff into centre half that worked even better because, without being disrespectful, I had two footballing centre halves instead of one sweeper like Buchan and a big stopper like big Jim. Jim couldn't get back into the team."

Willie Morgan would not be considered the most impartial judge of his former manager's character, given that the pair clashed in court during a failed libel case brought by Docherty against Morgan in 1979, but he is adamant that Holton deserved to be treated better than he was. "The Doc shafted Jim really badly, as he does, by spreading rumours and getting his pals in the press to write things about Jim Holton," says Morgan. "I had seen the way he got rid of guys like Denis [Law] and Jim McCalliog, and poor Jim never really saw it coming. Compared to Doc, Jim wasn't streetwise. He was just a big, happy, trusting guy."

David Meek of the *Manchester Evening News* was probably closer to United and Docherty than any other journalist, and while he found the wily Scot a breath of fresh air in terms of his forthright approach and punchy one-liners, he recalls putting their working relationship on the line to take him to task over his treatment of Holton, which he found unpalatable.

"I remember telling Docherty off," Meek recalls. "It was a bit patronising of me, but I didn't regret it because Jim was very popular with the fans, then he had a broken leg and he lost his way a little bit. I think the broken leg affected him more than was acknowledged at the time. Docherty then decided that he had to go, because he no longer figured in his plans.

"Docherty, being Docherty, said to me 'I've got to get rid of Jim'. After he'd referred to Jim in those terms a few times I said, 'Tom, can I just make a comment about your description of Jim Holton? You're being very foolish because he has a lot of admirers who won't want to hear his manager using a phrase 'getting rid of' as if he's some rodent or something that had to be got rid of'. Apart from that, I told him he was making a mistake and was letting down the United fans. I said 'It's no way to treat a player who has given you his all. I don't quibble with your decision to let him go, but why can't you talk about letting him go, or moving him somewhere else, and not getting rid of him, as if he was a pestilence?' Tommy found that a bit of a shock but I never regretted it because I liked Jim Holton, I admired him and I liked his wholeheartedness and that's why he was so popular with the fans. It distressed me to hear his manager, who he had served well, talking about getting rid of him; it was a terrible phrase."

Ironically, given the acrimonious way things ended between the pair, Willie Morgan was instrumental in getting Docherty appointed as Manchester United manager in the first place.

"Doc basically got the job at the golf club over there," says Morgan, pointing beyond his back garden towards Mere Golf Course. "I was playing golf with Matt [Busby], as I did every week. I was not long back from our tour to Brazil with Scotland and Matt asked casually: 'How was Tommy Docherty?' I said he was great, because he was. As manager of Scotland, he was brilliant. When you only got him in small doses he was great to work with. He knew the game and knew good players.

"I gave Matt his number on the Thursday and he got the job

on the Saturday. He came down to United, and at first he was great – the same way I had found him with Scotland. But at the end of that season he started to get rid of players – Denis was the first, and plenty of others followed. Then he brought in a little git as his assistant, Tommy Cavanagh, and it all changed.

"I didn't even see it coming. I had just signed a new contract and a testimonial was coming my way, but I fell out with him over Jim McCalliog. Jim was owed some money but was being paid in instalments and when I asked Doc to give him a break, he wouldn't budge. After that, I knew I had to watch my back. He could be an evil little bastard, but nevertheless he was a fantastic manager for Scotland and I think he could have won the World Cup with that team. But as a club manager, in terms of his man to man management, not so good."

George Graham, the first of Docherty's signings at Manchester United, had already played under him at Chelsea and for Scotland. Providing an insight into The Doc's management style, Graham – no shrinking violet himself – said at the time: "I wouldn't like to recall the number of times we've had words, but that's what I like about the man, he doesn't hold any grudges. The Doc is essentially an honest man. He is blunt, outspoken and he says what he thinks, sometimes irrespective of the cost. If you are playing well there's no-one like him in the game to build you up and fill you with confidence. But if you're playing badly watch out – he will drop you as quickly as look at you."

Martin Buchan, who became captain of United under Docherty, looks back on the era with fondness, and credits the manager with transforming the club's fortunes. "The arrival of Tommy Doc changed things. He realised the squad needed rebuilding. Frank O'Farrell had tried to do that, by bringing in myself and Ian Storey-Moore, but he didn't get the response he should have got from some of the players there. Tommy was a different character to Frank. I admired his honesty. Tom was very bullish and knew what he wanted. There was never a dull moment with The Doc. I had my moments with him – we had disagreements but he was larger than life."

Other United players who shared in the eventual success Docherty brought to the club are also quick to praise their former manager.

"Tommy went through a hell of a lot of players, but when he got what he wanted it was a great side and an enjoyable side to play in," says Sammy McIlroy. "When he put together the team that came back from the Second Division right through to winning the FA Cup in 1977, we were on the march. I think if we had added one or two players to that squad we could have pushed Liverpool a little bit more."

Goalkeeper Alex Stepney agrees: "It was tough for him at first, but getting relegated was the best thing that happened because we came out of the Second Division and got to the cup final and finished third. The following year we finished sixth and won the cup, stopping Liverpool doing the treble. So we all know and appreciate what Tommy Doc did."

Alex Forsyth outstayed Docherty at Old Trafford before he was sold to Rangers in 1978, but he had fallen out of favour by then and only made fleeting appearances in the 1976-77 season when he was usurped from the right-back spot by Jimmy Nicholl. Forsyth says he has no axe to grind with The Doc, who he found hard but fair, and he has good memories of those years – despite the odd brush with his boss over disciplinary matters. One particular clash is particularly amusing.

"The funniest time I got fined was after I played in a Monday night reserve game at Old Trafford. I owned a couple of greyhounds who would run at Belle Vue and White City, and my trainer said my dog was a certainty that night. The only problem for me was that it was running in the first race at quarter-to-eight, and the game I was playing in started at 7.30. There were no bookies shops in those days, and the only way to get decent money on was to be there in person at the track. White City dog track was only about 200 or 300 yards up the road from Old Trafford, so I thought to myself 'how am I going to get there and put the money down on it? Easy, I'll get myself sent off!'

"So the game kicked off, the ball got played to their left winger and boom, I went right through him. I did him hard, but I only got a yellow card. So, to make sure, I started effing away at the ref, and there it was – a red card. I was off in the first minute. I was rubbing my hands together as I ran up the tunnel. I changed as fast as I could, then ran as fast I could to get to the dog track. I made it with a minute to spare, and had a right few quid on it but – bloody hell - the dog got beat! The next morning when I turned up for training I was told 'the Gaffer wants to see you'.

"Docherty:'So, last night, sent off… what have you got to say about it?'

"Me: 'Aye, sorry about that, bad tackle Gaffer'

"Docherty:'Oh right…bad tackle.… I see …that will cost you a week's wages then. It's not been a good week for you eh because I heard your dog got beat last night and you lost a fortune!'

"What made it worse was that I had tipped it to all the boys. My dad also had a dog, and it was in a really good race and because it was 33-1 I told the boys not to bother backing it. Needless to say it won, without any of us having a penny on it, and they were all telling me I was bloody hopeless!"

Despite the way it ended for him at United, Jim McCalliog rates Docherty as one of the best managers he has worked with, and he too offers further insight into his attitude towards discipline. "The boys would go out as a team a lot, but you always had to be careful because Man United had a name and although Manchester is a big place, a lot of people know you. It's not like London, that's why George Best liked to go to London because he could disappear a bit.

"The rules were pretty strict though and Tommy Docherty wasn't stupid – he would have people out and about checking up on you. There were parameters and most players applied commonsense. You weren't allowed to go out after a Wednesday and you wouldn't see any of the boys in pubs or clubs. Three nights before the game was the deadline. The Doc also didn't like you going out at all if you were injured. If you were injured, he would also make sure you came in two or three times a day so he would know for sure you were injured! He took no nonsense. If you wanted to try and con him, he was one step ahead of you."

After a disagreement with Docherty, McCalliog left United for struggling Southampton midway through United's promotion-winning 1974-75 season. McCalliog had scored the winning goal for Scotland against then-world champions England at Wembley in 1967, but the move to Southampton gave him his greatest prize – an FA Cup winner's medal – after he set up the winning goal against United in the 1976 final.

Like Holton, McCalliog and Morgan, Mick Martin never featured again in a Docherty team beyond the Second Division season. "I had my ups and downs with Tommy Docherty, who didn't?" says the Irishman. "I was grateful that he took me over there and that I made so many great pals because of it. I was ungrateful because I thought he could have given me more of an opportunity than he did, before he got rid of me.

"The year we got relegated I played a fair amount, then the year we came back up I found my chances limited. Brian Greenhoff, Lord rest his soul, was basically a central defender but he played in midfield. He was good in that position as well, but so was I. Tommy Docherty seemed to fancy Brian in preference to me, and all of a sudden I wasn't in the team. But that was the way Tommy was, he could be a strange man.

"We all thought the way Jim left United was cruel, but everybody had a bone to pick with Tom at some stage. Willie Morgan, Ted MacDougall, Brian Kidd, Jimmy Rimmer, Jimmy McCalliog – over time, and for their own reasons, they were all unhappy with him, and he moved them on.

"He would say a lot of good words about you, but then he'd fall out with you. He used to tell porkies sometimes. I didn't like some of the stuff he said and did. A classic example was when we'd been relegated to the Second Division. We were top of the league, and he pulled me in and said to me, 'Mick, I can't make my mind up about you. I know you're a good player and you have your good points, but at times I see bad points. But I'm going to give you a chance, I'm going to play you four or five games on the bounce to help you find your form.' The first of those games was at home to

Hull. I made two, hit the crossbar and we won 2-0… and that was the last game I played 90 minutes for Manchester United! Tommy told the occasional lie but it wasn't something that really bothered me, it's just the way managers were. Life goes on."

Docherty could charm and offend in equal measure, and Holton's friend John Hillan recalls one excruciating example of the latter when he met the United manager following a game at Old Trafford.

"I took Jim's brother-in-law down to Manchester for a game after Jim had arranged a pass for us both. After the game, we were all standing in the players' lounge gabbing and the next thing Tommy Docherty appeared. I'd met him before and by way of introduction, Jim said: 'Boss, this is my brother-in-law' Now, Jim's brother-in-law had a bit of a big nose, so quick as a flash Docherty said to Jim: 'Aye, you werenae kidding about the size of his nose!' But that's what Tommy Docherty was like, he could be quite brash."

'Quite brash' is something an understatement, and Docherty was never far away from controversy. Indeed, his fall from grace at United was off the Richter scale in terms of scandal when he was sacked by United in 1977. After guiding the club to FA Cup glory, an affair with physio Laurie Brown's wife, Mary, emerged straight after the final. Docherty, who later married Mary Brown, protested he had been "sacked for falling in love" and they remain together to this day. The manner of his exit left a cloud lingering over his considerable achievements at United, but most fans who followed United during those exhilarating times remember him with the greatest of affection.

Docherty's managerial career was far from over, and although he had spells in charge of Derby, QPR, Preston, Wolves, a number of Australian teams and finally Altrincham, he was always left wondering what might have been if he had been allowed to stay at United.

Holton was left with much the same feeling, and when he was asked in 1980 about his departure from Old Trafford, he said: "The relationship between the Doc and I was never that good and we were not exactly the best of friends when I left, but I am a professional and I knew I had to go."

Jan Holton insists Jim did not take it personally and his relationship with Docherty improved after he had retired. "He never held grudges – it wasn't in his nature," says Jan. "Players didn't have agents to do their wheeling and dealing and that was just the nature of football at that time. He was hurt, no question, but Jim just said 'Oh well, it's on to the next club'."

17: SENT TO COVENTRY (VIA SUNDERLAND)

*"After the game you'd have thought we had won the cup or the league,
not just stayed up in the First Division. It was a strange sight"*

Ian Wallace

BETWEEN THE SUMMERS of 1976 and 1977, Jim
Holton literally didn't know whether he was coming or
going. He began the season as a Manchester United player
on loan to Miami Toros, returned from the States to be sent on
loan to Sunderland, signed 'permanently' for the Roker Park club
where he played under three managers in as many months before
he was dropped and sold and within two months of his departure
helped relegate them that same season with his new club Coventry
City!

As he and his family arrived back from Miami in August 1976,
Jim braced himself for a leap into the unknown. He had reached
the end of the road with Manchester United, he knew that much,
because Tommy Docherty had made that abundantly clear.

The Old Trafford manager briefed the press that he was eager
to offload Holton and the price tag was £100,000. Docherty's
public cold shoulder treatment gave football writers carte blanche
to indulge in some frenzied transfer speculation about the unsettled
defender and Stoke City and Bristol City were soon said to be
tracking developments. However, when Docherty got wind of
genuine interest from Sunderland, who were on the look-out for
a centre-half after the sale of Dave Watson to Manchester City,
dialogue was struck up with his opposite number Bob Stokoe.

When The Doc made his opening sales pitch, apparently the
negotiations went like this:

Docherty: "Jim Holton is a fine centre-half, strong, great in the
air, sledge-hammer tackle, fine passer of the ball. You have to be

talking good money for a stopper like him; one hundred thousand wouldn't buy him."

Stokoe: "I know, and I'm one of them!"

Whether Stokoe was trying to engage in some canny haggling, or indeed whether this exchange can be filed under urban myth, the upshot was that the Sunderland manager was persuaded to hand Holton a chance. Wary of the two broken legs Holton had suffered in as many years, Stokoe insisted that the arrangement would need to be on a loan basis initially, with a permanent deal to follow if the big Scot was able to satisfactorily prove his fitness.

"I would have preferred this to be a normal deal rather than a loan period," said Holton at the time. "Although I have never been fitter, I can understand Sunderland's point of view because I haven't played in the First Division for 18 months."

Stokoe despatched his assistant Peter Doherty to Old Trafford for preliminary talks with Docherty, then Holton headed to Roker Park to meet Stokoe and shake hands. With his Florida sun-tan and dressed in a stylish pale suit with dark open-necked shirt, Holton must have looked the coolest man in Sunderland!

Stokoe was delighted to get his man, and said: "He is the type of ready-made top flight player that I am seeking. It's no use kidding Jim that he's coming to the greatest club in the world, because he's probably just leaving it."

Sunderland, who had famously won the 1973 FA Cup under the legendary Stokoe, had arrived in the top-flight as Second Division champions, but had struggled to adapt to the First Division, winning only one of the six matches that preceded Holton's arrival. They had also been rocked further by a shock transfer request from their captain Tony Towers.

Ironically, as the talks with Holton reached their conclusion, Sunderland's next game was a League Cup tie against none other than Manchester United at Old Trafford. With the deal 24 hours from completion, Holton was in limbo between the two clubs, and as he resigned himself to taking a seat in the stand he joked: "I'll be there, but don't know yet who'll get my support. I'll wear a red scarf anyway!"

The unsettled Towers got on the scoresheet as Sunderland led 2-1, only for United to equalise two minutes from time when Jeff Clarke put through his own net.

Holton was registered with Sunderland the next day and, just as he had done for Manchester United in 1973, he made his debut in a draw against West Ham, this time at Upton Park. Also making his first appearance for Sunderland was striker Alan Foggon, who had followed Jim in making the move from Old Trafford.

In only his third game for Sunderland, Holton was pitched into battle against his former United team-mates in the League Cup replay. There was no room for divided loyalties and Holton gave his all, no doubt determined to prove a point to the man who had discarded him. Just as they had done in the first meeting at Old Trafford, Sunderland twice led and were twice pegged back in a 2-2 draw. Extra-time couldn't separate the sides, and a second replay was arranged for Old Trafford 48 hours later. The incentive became even greater when Sunderland's arch-rivals Newcastle were drawn out of the hat to face the winners in the last 16.

A near 50,000 crowd gave Holton a tremendous reception on his return to Old Trafford, and while he played well for his new club in a tense tie, he ended up on the losing side as United edged the game 1-0 – the winning goal coming from the man wearing the number 5 shirt Holton had once called his own, Brian Greenhoff.

Days later, a Monday night friendly up at Motherwell gave Holton the perfect opportunity to pay a flying visit to Lesmahagow, but that was the only highlight of the trip for him as the Scottish side ran out 3-1 winners.

Despite the arrival of Holton, Foggon, and several other new faces, morale was ebbing away in the Sunderland ranks, and the final straw for Stokoe came the following Saturday when a 1-0 home defeat to Aston Villa left them anchored to the bottom of the table. An honourable man, he did the honourable thing and tendered his resignation in the hope someone else could revive the team.

The local newspaper, the *Sunderland Echo*, commented: "Bob

Stokoe felt there was no alternative but to resign and allow someone new to step into his boots. Whoever that may be – and there will be no shortage of applicants – they will face a formidable task at a time when the fans have become intolerant of failure. Success will not necessarily come simply because there is a change of manager."

Ian MacFarlane who, like Holton, hailed from Lanarkshire, was placed in charge on a caretaker basis and kept faith with Jim and the majority of his team-mates for his first match in charge at QPR. It did little good as goals from Stan Bowles and Frank McLintock ensured Sunderland remained bottom.

However, a ray of hope was generated the following week, when a spirited Sunderland came away from Coventry with both points in a 2-1 win. Jim would never have believed it at that point, but he would finish the season back at Highfield Road as a Coventry player.

MacFarlane seemed to be instilling some battling qualities into the Sunderland ranks and there was no disgrace in losing 1-0 to runaway leaders Liverpool at Roker Park. The next match gave Holton another opportunity to return to Old Trafford, this time on league business, and the two sides shared six goals in a midweek humdinger where defences were certainly not on top. Buchan and Greenhoff were absent from the United ranks, and Docherty's central defensive pairing of Colin Waldron and young Scot Steve Paterson, looked shaky. Holton could have been forgiven for thinking to himself 'I should be playing in that United defence', although the Sunderland back four were hardly a model of solidity that day either. What was pleasing for MacFarlane was that Sunderland had battled back from 3-1 down.

The good run under MacFarlane continued with a come-from-behind win against Tottenham at Roker Park, but the Scot was only given two more games in charge.

His final match at the helm was a 1-0 defeat at Derby County, and despite the result, author and lifelong Sunderland fan Lance Hardy has many reasons to look back on the match with fondness.

"I was eight and this was my first game," says Hardy. "I was with my dad and I remember Derby used to have a big ram on their main stand. The Sunderland fans were just below us as we took our seats and over the PA system they started playing the song 'If You Leave Me Now' by Chicago which was number 1 at the time. But that was quickly drowned out by 'Six foot two, eyes of blue, big Jim Holton's after you!' Visually and audibly I have memories of Jim Holton and that day. We were wearing our yellow strip and he is the first player I remember watching in the flesh."

Sunderland's directors decided a permanent manager was needed to stabilise the club and turned to Jimmy Adamson, who had carved out a name for himself as manager of Burnley. He arrived with his own ideas and a determination to inject some youthful endeavour into the team. It was not a plan that would achieve immediate results, and MacFarlane's final game at Derby was the first of a desperate run of ten league games without a single goal.

Holton was involved in an incident which left him shaken and visibly upset when Sunderland hosted Norwich City the week before Christmas. With Sunderland trailing 1-0, Holton's tackle on Graham Paddon left the Norwich midfielder with a broken leg. There seemed to be no malice in the challenge, but City manager John Bond ran on the pitch in the heat of the moment to take issue with the Scot. When it became clear that no-one in the vicinity of the tackle was blaming Holton, who was in obvious distress, calm was restored, but Jim was left feeling low at Paddon's plight – having twice suffered the same injury himself. He would have at least have been pleased to read that after the game Bond, having had time to reflect, had cleared Holton of any blame.

Sunderland's next game, on 27 December, was the eagerly anticipated Tyne-Wear derby against Newcastle. With a crowd of more than 50,000 crammed into St James' Park, no quarter was asked or given in a bruising battle. The Magpies emerged victorious, and one of the Newcastle goalscorers Paul Cannell has dedicated a chapter of his autobiography to his physical encounter with Holton that day, entitled: 'Six foot two, eyes of blue, big Jim Holton's gonna kick the shit out of you!'

Cannell says Newcastle manager Gordon Lee pulled him aside

in the dressing room and told him. "Jim Holton is playing centre half for them today Paul. You know what he's like - put yourself about a bit, if you know what I mean, and I guarantee he'll get himself sent off."

Remembering his manager's advice, Cannell saw his big chance to rile Jim five minutes before the interval. "I had scored and we were winning 1-0, when our keeper Mike Mahoney booted the ball high downfield. Jim Holton and I rose to head the ball midway inside Sunderland's half and I 'accidentally' smashed him in the mouth with my elbow. He collapsed to the ground, there were teeth and claret all over the St James' Park turf. If it had happened nowadays with slow motion action replays I'd have done time! He was stretchered off just before the half-time whistle blew and we made our way back to the dressing room."

Lee was delighted with Cannell. "Great goal Paul and what a great result with Holton. Now we've got rid of him go out and get another one."

The teams prepared to head out for the second half and Cannell recalls: "I felt ten feet tall. I'd scored against the Mackems and got rid of Jim Holton. We took to the pitch first, then the Mackems emerged from the tunnel, one by one and shit, there he was, the third on the pitch – fucking Jim Holton! I nearly crapped myself. The second half saw me playing one touch football like never before. I played the second half like my life depended on it – it probably did! The papers the following day commented on our change of tactics 'with Cannell playing on the right wing.' Do you blame me?"

The derby defeat was a bitter blow and the games for Sunderland were not getting any easier – Leeds and Liverpool were up next. Sunderland lost both – Jim's pal Joe Jordan scoring the only goal of the game in the first match, then Liverpool beat them 2-0 at Anfield. Holton was absent as a miserable festive period concluded when Coventry scored a last-minute winner at Roker Park. In the grand scheme of things, that goal would come back to haunt Sunderland.

The FA Cup offered Sunderland a welcome distraction from

their woes in the league. The famous trophy had been on display in the Roker Park trophy room less than four years earlier, and the mere mention of the competition generated excitement among supporters. Wrexham at home looked like a favourable draw, particularly as the Welsh side had needed a replay to dispose of Goole Town in the previous round, but goals either side of half-time from the Dragons left the home side staring at an unthinkable defeat. Step forward Jim Holton, who hauled Adamson's team back into the tie with a goal 20 minutes from time, before Mel Holden salvaged a replay with a late equaliser.

It was only a brief reprieve for Sunderland. In the replay at the Racecourse Ground the following Wednesday Wrexham – belief coursing through their side – got ahead and stayed ahead, Billy Ashcroft scoring the only goal of the tie midway through the second half to complete the type of giant-killing for which the Welsh club soon became famous.

Adamson was left red-faced, like everyone connected with Sunderland, and he lost patience with the majority of the players he had inherited, making it his priority to bring in a crop of young players. Holton would be one of the casualties of his cull, which did not go down well with the Rokerites who had taken Jim to their hearts in much the same way fans of Shrewsbury and Manchester United had done. The feeling was mutual. Holton had not only proved that he still had what it took to play First Division football, he had been prepared to show his loyalty to the club by prolonging his stay, and had just started looking for homes in the area when Adamson swung the axe. "I just do not know why Adamson did not like me," Jim rued later, "but within two months of his appointment I was out of the first team."

"Jimmy Adamson made it his business to get rid of a lot of the old boys of the 1973 team," Lance Hardy recalls, "players like Jim Montgomery were shown the door at that time and Jim Holton was another player he chose to get rid of. It caused quite a reaction. A petition was organised by the Sunderland Supporters Association to keep Jim Holton at the club and that petition did manage to find its way to Jimmy Adamson's desk, then it found its way to his waste paper bin!"

While Holton was reluctantly placed on the transfer list along with five others, Adamson introduced a trio of young players – Shaun Elliot, Kevin Arnott and the prolific Gary Rowell. They were christened 'Charlie's Angels' because they had been discovered for the club by a scout called Charlie Ferguson. Ironically, he had also recruited Colin Waldron from Manchester United – the same player Tommy Docherty had brought in as cover for Brian Greenhoff and elevated ahead of Jim in the Old Trafford pecking order. Waldron had only played three games for The Doc at United, but he had worked with Adamson at Burnley, and was happy to be reunited with his former boss.

"Having gone ten league games without a goal, these young guys came into the team and suddenly they went on this incredible run," says Hardy. "In successive matches they beat Middlesbrough 4-0, West Brom 6-1 and West Ham 6-0."

Demoted to the reserves, Holton damaged ankle ligaments which forced him on to the sidelines and frustrated his hopes of finding a new club. Thankfully, when he returned to fitness, Coventry City, down near the bottom of the table and scrapping with Sunderland to survive, pounced when they learned they could have him for a bargain £40,000, half of what Stokoe had paid for him just months earlier.

The Sunderland fans were genuinely sorry to see Holton go, and had misgivings about the club selling to one of their relegation rivals. Lance Hardy says that despite the fact he had played only 19 times for the club, only playing in a winning side twice, Holton had made a lasting impression on the supporters. "The Six Foot Two song followed him wherever he went and he remained a popular player which was incredible given that he had been with us for a short amount of time."

While Jim was sad to break his bond with the Rokerites, Midlander Jan Holton was not so sorry to say goodbye to Wearside. "I was ecstatic," she says without the slightest hesitation. "We were staying at Seaburn, but I never saw the sea because the fog was always down. I also never understood a word that anyone was saying. I thought 'my goodness I'm going to have to live up here!' I must say, I breathed a sigh of relief when he got the chance to move to Coventry."

Having left a club battling relegation, Holton had jumped from the frying pan into the fire. Coventry were also labouring and had gone 11 games without a league win. Ominously, they had also just lost their goalkeeper Jim Blyth to a knee ligament injury. Future Manchester United keeper Les Sealey, then just 17, was thrust into the side as replacement.

Coventry had a good squad but then the same could be said about Manchester United when they succumbed to the drop in 1974, and Holton would have been quick to let his new teammates know that they should treat the threat of relegation very seriously.

Coventry manager Gordon Milne was surprised and delighted to lure Holton to the club at such a crucial stage of the season. Milne knew the big man's qualities well, not only from City's two meetings with Sunderland earlier in the season, but from four years earlier when he had tried to bring Holton to Coventry from Shrewsbury. Although he had been made to wait until 1977 to get his man, he was delighted when it quickly became apparent that Holton and Coventry would be a good fit.

"Jim had obvious leadership qualities, and off the pitch he was a really nice person," says Milne. "He brought experience and personality and he was an immediate hit with the fans. You can't win the public over on reputation alone, and in Jim's case it was down to what he did on the pitch. He carved that niche for himself very quickly he was worth every penny of our investment.

"The reputation he had could be unfair. Yes, he was a hard man, but he was a great example to everybody. He was a difficult guy not to like. Off the pitch you couldn't have anybody more amiable and pleasant to be with. He was a man's man, he knew his limitations and he gave you 110 per cent every time he went on the pitch."

Holton actually had to wait six weeks before he made his Coventry debut. An ankle ligament niggle had delayed his first match in a Sky Blue shirt, and after four outings for the reserves to tune up his fitness, he finally made his full Coventry debut in a Tuesday night fixture against West Brom at Highfield Road. Holton acquitted himself well in a 1-1 draw, but the ankle issue hadn't completely subsided and he was substituted towards the end of the game.

The defence was in need of stability, and Jim again did well in his second outing at Highbury, stifling his old adversary Malcolm Macdonald, but unable to prevent City from losing 2-0 after a late lapse.

Back-to-back wins against Derby and Stoke and a goalless draw against champions-to-be Liverpool showcased Coventry's fighting spirit during a fraught run-in, but a defeat in their penultimate game at home to Manchester City meant they had dropped into the relegation zone ahead of their final match, behind Bristol City on goal difference. They would play the Robins at Highfield Road in their last game of the season. Meanwhile Sunderland's incredible run had lifted them above Coventry and Bristol City, again on goal difference, but Jimmy Adamson's side faced a tough final fixture at Goodison Park. Tottenham and Stoke had already been relegated, so only one of three teams; Coventry, Sunderland or Bristol City would join them.

Due to a fixture pile-up, both games would be played on a Thursday night. There were plenty of potential permutations, but Sunderland knew that if they were able to avoid defeat at Goodison they would be safe. Even if they lost, they could still avoid relegation as long as Coventry and Bristol City didn't draw.

With every bus in Bristol booked to transport fans north for the match, and interest also at fever pitch in Coventry, the *Evening Telegraph* led its match preview with an interview with Big Jim. "I'm not interested in anyone else but Coventry," said Holton. "As far as we are concerned we just have to go out and win. It's up to us to do it. We have just got to go out there and play our hearts out."

The extraordinary drama that unfolded that night caused bitterness and consternation that has lived long in the memories of Sunderland supporters. The seeds of controversy were sown when the kick-off at Coventry was delayed by somewhere between 5 and 10 minutes. Highfield Road was close to capacity with almost 37,000 crammed into the ground and traffic congestion was the official reason given for the hold-up, although Sunderland fans are convinced that there was a conspiracy to delay the match, and pointed the finger of blame firmly at Coventry's managing director Jimmy Hill.

The delay didn't seem significant as Coventry raced into an early lead through Tommy Hutchison. News also filtered through from Merseyside that Sunderland were losing, Bob Latchford having given Everton the lead 10 minutes before half-time. As it stood, Bristol City were the unfortunate team heading down.

Bristol City seemed doomed when Tommy Hutchison doubled Coventry's lead seven minutes into the second half. However, rather than accept their fate, the Robins battled back knowing that their First Division lives depended on it. First Gerry Gow then Donnie Gillies scored, and it was Coventry who were left grimly hanging on.

Sunderland – having kicked off at the correct time – had conceded a second goal in the 90th minute, and when the full time whistle sounded at Goodison a stalemate ensued at Highfield Road as the score from Merseyside was broadcast with both teams aware they were safe if the score stayed 2-2.

Jim Brown, in his book 'Coventry – the Elite Era' describes the closing moments of the 1976/77 season. "The remaining five minutes saw the ball tapped this way and that, aimlessly from one side of the field to the other and back again. It was an extraordinary sight in competitive English football. The referee was probably as embarrassed as anyone. When he finally called a halt to the farce, both sets of supporters celebrated by embracing each other."

Sunderland were understandably fuming. It appeared they had been stitched up good and proper. "With the Sunderland game over the possibility of a totally unfair scenario arose where two teams could now play out a draw in the knowledge that they would both be safe," says Lance Hardy. "Jimmy Hill raced up to the Radio Sky Blue booth and demanded that the Sunderland result was broadcast. His request was carried out and the Sunderland result was also displayed on the electronic scoreboard, presumably just in case someone had failed to hear the radio announcement. Two former Leeds United players Norman Hunter for Bristol City and Terry Yorath for Coventry were on opposite sides that night and in his autobiography Yorath recalled hearing the radio announcement and calling out to Hunter 'Your lads can back off now'. Both sides played out time, passing the ball to ironic cheers from the crowd.

"To make matters worse for the Sunderland fans, the first announcement at Goodison Park gave the final score as 2-1 to Coventry! For a while Sunderland thought they were safe until then they learned it was actually 2-2."

Fans of both sides at Highfield Road celebrated, and the league table, before and after the game said it all:

BEFORE					AFTER				
POS	TEAM	Pld	Pts	GD	POS	TEAM	Pld	Pts	GD
18	SUNDERLAND	41	34	-6	18	BRISTOL CITY	42	35	-10
19	BRISTOL CITY	41	34	-10	19	COVENTRY	42	35	-11
20	COVENTRY	41	34	-11	20	SUNDERLAND	42	34	-8
21	STOKE	42	34	-23	21	STOKE	42	34	-23
22	TOTTENHAM	42	33	-24	22	TOTTENHAM	42	33	-24

Sky Blues striker Ian Wallace admits that he still looks back on the episode with a slight tinge of embarrassment. "After the game you'd have thought we won the cup or the league not just stayed up in the First Division," he says. "The fans invaded the pitch, it was a strange sight, although I suppose it was just sheer relief that we'd beaten the drop."

YouTube footage shows Coventry fans streaming on to the pitch to celebrate their survival, while players ran like greyhounds towards the dressing room to avoid the throng. As the two teams reached the sanctuary of the tunnel, Holton is seen hugging Peter Cormack of Bristol City – two Scots on opposing sides, sharing a moment of utter relief.

To add to the conspiracy theories, Bristol City were managed by Alan Dicks, a former assistant to Jimmy Hill when he had been Coventry manager. To rub salt into the wounds of Sunderland supporters, a beaming Dicks was pictured alongside Gordon Milne in his office after the match, the pair pouring champagne into their tea-cups. But one man, more than any other, bore the brunt of blame. "Jimmy Hill was hated for it. He was really, really disliked for his role that night and although we didn't play Coventry again for years it created years of bad feeling between the two clubs," explains Lance Hardy. "I was at Fulham v Sunderland in 2008 when they unveiled a statue to Johnny Haynes and when Jimmy Hill came out at half-time you've never heard booing like it."

Hill required a police escort from Craven Cottage to avoid the wrath of the Sunderland fans that day, more than 30 years had done nothing to ease their anger. In his own book, Jimmy Hill blamed the referee for delaying the match, and although the Football League investigated the circumstances surrounding the result, and dealt with sack loads of complaints from Sunderland supporters, both he and Coventry were officially cleared of any wrong-doing.

While Hill was the villain of the piece as far as Sunderland supporters were concerned, he remained a club legend at Coventry. As well as leading the club to Third and Second Division titles during his days as manager in the Sixties, his list of pioneering achievements at the club was phenomenal, from introducing the Sky Blue kit to instigating the redevelopment of Highfield Road. He didn't get everything right, far from it, but he was undoubtedly a visionary, and Gordon Milne found him a joy to work alongside.

"Jimmy was one of the finest chairmen and people I've ever worked with, he was an incredible man," he says. "Jimmy was always ahead of his time, in thinking of new ideas and showing innovation. Lots of his ideas didn't work — I used to occasionally say 'Jimmy that's daft, it will never bloody work' — but his attitude was, 'if you don't try something you'll never know'.

"We had a great set up for kids and signed a lot of good young players. We had to sell the better ones, but people accepted that. There were lots of pluses and the club had a lot of warmth to it. We had the first all-seater stadium, great training facilities and the club was always progressive. The boardroom was one of the best you could get in the country.

"The club knew its priorities - to stay in the First Division. Anything else was a bonus. I was proud that we were never relegated and on our day, we were more than a match for any team."

Having avoided the drop by the skin of their teeth, Coventry could look forward to starting afresh for the 1977-78 campaign, as could Jim Holton who dared to dream of a settled spell at a club which seemed well-equipped to give him and his family the security they craved.

His former love Manchester United weren't doing so badly either. Forty-eight hours after Coventry and Bristol City's escape double act, Tommy Docherty's side won the FA Cup in a blaze of glory against Liverpool. It was the pinnacle of The Doc's managerial career, but he would be gone before the new season started.

18: MR SKY BLUE

"Jim Holton had his limitations, but guys like him were men and the influence they had on the team was immense"

Gordon Milne

GIVEN THAT HE arrived at Coventry City slap-bang in the midst of a relegation scrap, it sounds a little strange to suggest that Jim Holton signed for the right club at the right time, but once safety was assured the big Scot must have been thanking his lucky stars for finding a team so compatible.

His wife Jan was happy to be back in the Midlands and Holton was happy to be playing for a manager who appreciated him, as well as team-mates he immediately bonded with. Just as had been the case when he signed on the dotted line at Manchester United, it was a bonus that he was surrounded by Scots.

Tommy Hutchison, Ian Wallace, Bobby McDonald and goalkeeper Jim Blyth were among Coventry's clan of proud Scotsmen in 1977. They were soon joined by an exciting young prospect by the name of Gary Gillespie and – despite an unmistakably Midlands accent – Andy Blair. "Yes, fortunately I'm Scottish," laughs Blair. "I was born in Kirkcaldy but I was brought up in England. Gordon Milne liked Scottish players. We've got a different mentality - a completely and utterly different mind-set to English people. Gordon probably recognised that hunger, that desire, the passion, the determination to be better than the rest. I honestly believe we are totally different animals, English and Scottish people!"

Milne was well served by the Scots contingent, but insists: "It was never planned, but Scots were often the backbone of the Coventry team. Shortly before Jim's time with us, the club had guys like Jim Brogan and Colin Stein, then later on we had

Gary Gillespie, Ian Wallace, Jim Blyth, Bobby McDonald, Tommy Hutchison - all, like Jim, made massive contributions on the pitch, and were also good characters off the pitch.

"John Rice was our chief scout at that time and was based in Glasgow. John was a first class scout and he concentrated on the Scottish scene, so he signed quite a lot of players from Scotland, as well as Scottish lads who were with other clubs.

"It is so sad that Jim's no longer around because I still see Hutchy and a few of the boys. When you see them, your mind goes back and it's just like you were working with them last week. I was a young manager when I was at Coventry and I had memories of playing myself at Liverpool with Scots like big Ron Yeats and Ian St John so it was just a carry over for me. I was in familiar territory working with those Scottish lads."

With so many broad Scottish accents flying around, subtitles would have come in handy for those born south of the Border. Welshman Don Nardiello laughs, "I've got to be honest, I struggled to understand them at times – the accent could be difficult, especially when they were talking quickly. The 'wee' word tended to come out a lot!

"There was a strong Scottish contingent at the club and there was a lot of good-natured stick and banter flying around. I was a young lad who been brought up very religious, and when I went into that merciless world of football, with plenty of swearing and mickey-taking going on, I thought 'what am I in for here?' It was quite lively and I had to learn very quickly, which has stood me in good stead in my life. You've got to learn to laugh at yourself; not take yourself too seriously, and go along with the jokes."

The camaraderie at Coventry came naturally but Jim found fitness was getting that little bit harder to maintain. The trauma of two broken legs, damaged knee and ankle ligaments, and countless other bumps and bruises, was slowly but surely catching up with him. At 26, he was far from over the hill, but he had never been known for being supple or flexible and he had to push himself harder than many of his team-mates.

"It is the first time in two years that I have been able to

complete a full pre-season training routine," said Holton after coming through the pain barrier with flying colours at the start of his first full season with the Sky Blues. "It has helped a great deal. I feel tremendous and fitter than I have ever done. My weight at 13st 4lbs is the lowest it has been for five years. I've got to be honest and admit that pre-season is a nightmare for me. Because of my size it is a real slog, but I am feeling the benefit."

Tommy Hutchison, who had played alongside Holton at the 1974 World Cup, already knew his team-mate would not be found wanting when it came to commitment, but would find Jim's obvious discomfort with some aspects of training quite amusing. "He trained hard and was a great professional but when it came to running he wasn't so keen," says Hutchison, an incredibly fit player who reaped the benefits of his dedication by amassing more than 1,000 career appearances and playing on well into his 40s. "We had a few lads at Coventry who could run and run, myself included, but big Jim hated it. Our coach Ron Wylie was a bit strict but training was good; everything had to be done to perfection. We'd come out and usually Ron would give us 15 minutes to get warmed up. But big Jim was so stiff that he used to look like a bed board when he came out, so by the time we were called in to start, Jim would be asking 'Ron, do you mind if I have another 10 minutes?' Ron was nobody's fool and he said 'Jim, if that's the case, you'll get out here at half past 9 to train at 10. Poor Jim usually had a stiff back, or his knees were playing up and it did take him longer to get warmed up."

Once Holton was finally warmed up, Hutchison was as impressed as ever with the big man's ability. He also noticed how Holton had intelligently re-adjusted his game since his Manchester United days.

"We used to do a drill in training. Jim would start on the goal line and we would be spread out to the halfway line and just be knocking balls into the box for him to come and attack. He would be heading them past the halfway line – he could head them further than I could kick it," says Hutchison. "He knew his strengths and although he wasn't particularly quick he very rarely got himself in a position where he got out-run. He was so clever tactically that he knew where to be and where not to be. He could actually sometimes be a bit timid in the training matches, which I found with most lads who were full pelt when they played in competitive games. He was probably just holding a bit back to make sure he was fit enough to play on a Saturday. But when it came to a game, it was a different story – oh yes, he would kick his Granny on the pitch!"

However, manager Milne disagrees and believes that Holton gave his all - whether it was in a bounce game or competitive match. "Jim trained the same way he played," says Milne. "They were playing 42 league games and training every day, so it was no surprise that players would pick up injuries. Jim could only play one way and there were no friendlies as far as he was concerned, and that included training. He'd clatter some of his team mates in training, but that's how he was. Nobody would accuse him of being overly-aggressive, that was just his style and personality, and he was respected for that."

Milne's message to the players throughout pre-season in 1977 was to forget about their close shave with relegation and get points on the board so the 'R word' needn't be mentioned again. They listened, and got off to the perfect start, beating Derby County 3-1.

Manchester United away gave Holton another chance to say hello to his friends at Old Trafford, and there must surely have been another flash of 'what might have been' in his mind when he saw his former team-mates parade the FA Cup at the stadium before what was their first home match since landing the trophy at Wembley. The man who had led them to glory, Tommy Docherty, had been sacked in wake of his affair with Mary Brown, and his replacement was Dave Sexton.

United were being tipped as title contenders, and had stormed to a 4-1 win at Birmingham on the opening day thanks to a Lou Macari hat-trick, but Coventry were arguably the better team on the day. A twice-taken penalty gave United a fortuitous lead, which was cancelled out by the lively Ian Wallace, and a late Dave McCreery winner was harsh on Milne's side, who won plaudits for an exhilarating display.

"Gordon Milne always set us out to express ourselves and play with a bit of style," says Wallace. "We were an entertaining side. We usually played a 4-2-4 formation with two wingers. Jim was the mainstay of the defence and at set-pieces he was excellent in the air; for and against. When we were defending corner kicks, we knew big Jim would always be there – you could rely on him. But any time he got the ball in the opposing half he used to panic because he was over the halfway line – unfamiliar territory for him!"

That said, before the opening month of the season was finished Holton did manage to get on the score-sheet for the first time as a Coventry player in a 2-0 League Cup win at Huddersfield. "Jim only scored a couple of goals for Coventry, but I do remember that one," says Tommy Hutchison. "Me and the other lads used to wind him up. When we got a corner or free-kick we would say 'Fuck it Jim, don't go up – it's waste of time! It will take you too long to get back'. Sometime he would actually agree! Because his knees weren't very good, you'd hear him grumbling 'Och, I can't go away up there!'"

Not long after the cup game at Leeds Road the close-knit club were rocked when their chairman Sir Jack Scamp, a fatherly figure greatly respected by fans, staff and players, fell ill and stood down as chairman. He passed away two months later, and Phil Mead took over as chairman, with Jimmy Hill in the role of managing director.

Coventry continued to perform well and by late November had only lost three times in the League Cup – at Old Trafford, Anfield, and a rare home blip against West Brom. Holton missed a big chunk of October and November with a knee injury and he was still absent when they suffered what could only be put down to an 'off-day' at Everton, losing 6-0. "We had a habit of going from the sublime to the ridiculous," says Don Nardiello. "We were a great team, but occasionally we would end on the wrong end of a thrashing."

Defenders at Coventry at that time included Mick Coop, Bobby McDonald and Brian 'Harry' Roberts, while Graham

Oakey had his career cut short by a knee injury and Keith Osgood arrived from Tottenham as defensive cover, while a crop of exciting youngsters were coming through the ranks.

Experienced Norweigan defender Jan Birkelund, who had faced Holton when he played against Scotland in 1974, also arrived on trial and played alongside Jim in a few training sessions. The pair were referred to as "Hulk and Bulk", and showed potential as a partnership. Part-timer Birkelund – whose day job was a newspaper typesetter - returned home, having failed to win a permanent deal, and was forced to retire from the game in 1979 when a heart defect was found. Tragically, he died in 1983 aged 32.

By now Jim's form had even led to talk of a Scotland recall, although when he was asked by football writers about his international chances, he played them down. "Obviously I'd love to get back into the squad, but then I look at Tommy Hutchison and how well he is playing and he can't get back. I can't fancy my chances too much."

It was a shame because under the enthusiastic leadership of Ally Macleod Scotland were on course to qualify for the World Cup finals in Argentina. A match against Wales, switched to Anfield to accommodate the Scottish masses, had fans scrambling for tickets – including big Jim, who pestered Coventry skipper Terry Yorath to find him a complimentary. The Welshman was heard groaning that he had about "50 tickets to find, all for Scottish team-mates."

Holton was one of the first names on Milne's team-sheet, but the Sky Blues manager quickly realised and accepted that the way the big man constantly put his body on the line meant there would be occasions that he would have to do without him. "Big lads could often be a bit more prone to injury, although much depended on their size and poise. My centre forward Mick Ferguson was 6 foot 2 but I think his boots were size 7. Jim wasn't the most elegant of players and sometimes the chemistry of their anatomy can make them susceptible to injury.

"Even though Jim was hard and frightened people, none of his injuries were self-inflicted. He would maybe pick something up on the training ground. He was a loss every time he was out. If you had to say there was any downside to him, it was his mileage per season, as he did have a few spells on the sidelines.

"I don't want to harp back to the past, but when you look around in the game today in two areas – centre half and centre forward – a lot has changed. It was a man's job and there used to be men in those positions, particularly at centre half. Jim was one of those. Colin Stein had his limitations, Terry Yorath had his limitations, Jim Holton had his limitations, but they were men and the influence they had on the team was immense. There seemed to be a lot more of those characters then than there is today. Players now get big fees and are blessed with a lot of skill and talent, but I'm not sure how many have real depth and substance to their character and have that manliness about them."

Holton epitomised manliness. It was around this time facial hair became all the rage among footballers, and Holton quickly developed a mean-looking mouser. The fact that he played minus any front teeth only added further to his intimidating presence. Holton used his false teeth as a prop in many a practical joke – much to the disgust of his wife Jan, and Coventry City's tea lady Joyce.

Writing in the Coventry programme Yorath revealed: "Jim dropped his false teeth into a bowl of trifle at the training ground and had to fish them out. He then told our cook Joyce that they had fallen into another bowl of trifle and when an angry Joyce threw that into the dustbin, believing his teeth were still in there, Jim produced his dental plate from his behind his back. Joyce was not amused, but I was, until I finished my cup of tea and found his teeth at the bottom. To cap it all, Gordon Milne found Joyce's resignation on his desk the following morning, written by – you've guessed it – Jim Holton!"

Ian Wallace adds: "Big Jim always used to like a laugh and a joke. A group of us would go to the pub together now and again for a beer and if you left your pint while you went to the toilet, people would sometimes mess about with your drink. Jim had his own way of getting round that – he used to take his false teeth out and leave them floating in his pint so nobody would touch it! You ought to have seen the faces of the rest of the customers, it was brilliant."

Wife Jan winces at the mention of Jim's teeth. "You'd be amazed at the number of football players back then that didn't have a full set of teeth," she says. "They just used to chuck them all into a sink before a game or training. How disgusting! I would ask him, 'what happens if you pick up the wrong dentures?'

"Even when I met him he had already lost two of his front teeth. We were out for dinner this one night and Jim couldn't resist gnawing off whatever little ounces of meat might have still been on his T-bone steak. The next thing, one of his false teeth fell out onto the plate. It had come off the wiring. When I got home I super-glued it back on for him, without realising that the Bostik I had used was actually toxic. I think he thought I was trying to poison him!"

Much like the glue that held together Jim's dental plate, there were plenty of strong characters at Coventry who kept the squad bound tightly together. "We had a really strong group of players and the whole club had a good feel about it," says Tommy Hutchison. "We just went from strength to strength when guys like Jim, Terry Yorath, Ian Wallace and Barry Powell joined. We would go and have a game of golf up in Kenilworth, usually on our day off and have a game of snooker and a few beers. It was good times. Big Jim was bonkers! We all knew the song 6 foot 2, eyes of blue, big Jim Holton's after you but off the pitch he was so gentle and easy going. He was very funny and a real good laugh."

Wallace agrees: "We had a close bond at Coventry, especially the Scots and if ever we had a free weekend or our game was postponed we would head up to Scotland together. With so many Scots in the squad, you certainly felt at home.

"There was a group of us that used to go for a couple of beers and Sunday lunch near where Jim stayed – myself, Terry Yorath, who arrived from Leeds the same day that I signed, Barry Powell, and Tommy Hutchinson. I was five years younger than them, but the camaraderie at Coventry was second to none and I always felt part of it. Coventry was a lovely family club, and I remember Jim as a family man. We did quite a few things together like fishing, golf and drinking.

"On the pitch, we won games and lost games together. We used to have friendly arguments at half time or full time between the defenders and forwards. Mick Ferguson, Hutchie and myself used to blame the defence if we lost, and they blamed us for not scoring enough goals. It was all good banter though.

"The experienced players really helped develop the younger ones. They looked after the younger kids and kept their feet on the ground. At the training ground, there were about five different dressing rooms. Eight or nine of the senior professionals were in one dressing room and we used to make the young apprentices chap the door before they came in – it was all good natured. In those days apprentices were cleaning your boots and learning good discipline, which you don't get so much of nowadays. It was all part of their upbringing, from the apprenticeship to first team and it created a good atmosphere of respect at Coventry.

"Gordon Milne was an excellent manager and a lovely man. He was quiet, but knew his stuff. We would usually finish mid-table or above, but we often beat Man United and Liverpool, or at least gave them a hell of a game. We always scored goals and although we were known as an attacking side, we could defend as well with guys like Jim and Mick Coop at the back. We always believed that we'd score more than we'd lose and we were exciting to watch."

Three days after suffering a 6-0 drubbing at Goodison, Coventry headed back to Merseyside to face Liverpool at Anfield in the last 16 of the League Cup. With Holton fit again and restored to the team, the teams fought out a thrilling 2-2 draw. But his injury woes resurfaced following a defeat at Nottingham Forest ahead of the replay, and goals from Kenny Dalglish and Jimmy Case ended the Sky Blues' interest in the competition.

Between mid-December and March, the injured Holton was left frustrated on the sidelines, missing out on an emphatic 3-0 win over Manchester United at Highfield Road on the last day of 1977, and memorable home wins against Chelsea (5-1) and reigning champions Liverpool (1-0). He also missed a quite incredible game of football against Norwich City, which Coventry won 5-4, Jim Blyth saving a penalty in the dying seconds to secure the victory.

Milne gave his players freedom to attack and express themselves, and although they lacked the consistency to challenge at the very top of the table, where Forest, Liverpool and Everton were slugging it out for the title, they found themselves deservedly in contention for a place in Europe.

Holton finally returned to the side in March and the Sky Blues showed their well-being with a brilliant 4-0 win at home to Birmingham, inspired by a Mick Ferguson hat-trick. Three more victories followed that month, and with eight games to play they sat slap bang in contention for a place in Europe.

However, an April Fool's Day defeat signalled the start of a sticky spell, and Coventry would win only once more that season, missing out on Europe by a wafer-thin margin. Like the previous year, Highfield Road was once again the scene of wild end-of-season celebrations – but this time it was Brian Clough's Nottingham Forest who were doing all the rejoicing, as a 0-0 draw allowed them to clinch the championship with two games to spare.

As they had done 12 months earlier, Coventry once again wrapped up their season with a draw against Bristol City – this time thankfully without the controversy. The Sky Blues had missed out on a European place by a mere two points, and would still have qualified if Arsenal had beaten Ipswich in the FA Cup final, but they could be immensely proud of their seventh place finish.

There was no time for Jim to put his feet up however, Jan was nine months pregnant and he was about to become a dad for the second time. He still managed to squeeze in a trip to Glasgow, before Jan got a hold of him to say she was going into labour and he needed to get himself back down to Coventry pronto.

Anyone that has been in a delivery room or watched Channel 4's 'One Born Every Minute' knows that relations can become more than a little strained between couples during labour, and big Jim was proving more than of a hindrance than help to Jan.

"He arrived at the hospital about 8 o'clock in the morning while I was still in labour," she says. "He never did hospitals very well; he always looked worse than the patients! He walked in and promptly went very pale. With every contraction he was getting on my nerves so I told him to go and get a newspaper. Every time I would stop talking, he would peer over the top of his newspaper to see if anything was happening. I got very tetchy and told him 'you're about as much use as a chocolate teapot, so go away!'

"So off he went, and I gave birth to Sally just before 1pm on 8 May, 1978. He sauntered back about 1.30 and even though I was feeling like Twiggy compared to the beached whale I had felt like before I gave birth, his first words to me were: 'Well... have you had it?' Luckily there was a nurse walking past or I would have killed him. She stepped in and said to him 'Would you like to come and see your daughter, she's in the nursery?' She whisked him off down to the nursery before I could throttle him. Overall, he was a good dad though and Sally was definitely a daddy's girl."

19: OLD DOG, NEW TRICKS

"Off the pitch Jim Holton was one of the nicest, gentlest men ever, but if you riled him you were going to get it!"

Garry Thompson

GARRY THOMPSON admits he saw his life flash before his eyes the day he asked Jim Holton outside for a fight at Coventry City's training ground. Eight years younger than the giant Scot, Thompson had a reputation as an aggressive centre forward always determined to stand up for himself. So when several senior Coventry players took issue with the striker's challenge on keeper Jim Blyth during a training ground match, the adrenaline was still pumping as he sat down for lunch in the club canteen.

"I'd accidentally stood on Jim Blyth's hand, and during the verbals that followed, big Jim Holton had said to me 'I'll have you for that'," recalls Thompson, who broke into the Coventry team towards the end of the 1977-78 season. "So later, when we were having our food, I was sitting with Tom English, Mark Hateley, Danny Thomas and a few of the other young pros, and they started winding me up. They were saying 'Big bad Garry Thompson, he's the scourge of the First Division, people saying how rough and tough he is, then big Jim Holton threatens him a little bit, and all of a sudden the big man's backing down.'

"Danny kept it going, saying 'The Garry Thompson I know wouldn't stand for that, he'd be saying to Holton "come on then!"'. This went on for the whole of lunch and finally I put my glass down, got up and walked over to Jim's table. 'Come on then!' I said. 'You called me out, let's go do it.' It was at that moment I knew I had fucked up. Everything just seemed to stop around me and I thought 'My God, what have you said? I've let me mouth run away with itself again.' I wanted to take the words back, but it was too late. Jim just stroked his moustache, calmly got up from his seat, and started walking out… and I had to follow him.

"As we got downstairs Mick Coop got in between me and Jim and basically saved my life because he would have pummelled me. I was only 17 or 18 and even though I'd called him out, I was bricking it. I've never been so grateful in all my born days. To be fair to Jim, he just broke into a broad smile and we all went back in. After that, they took the mickey out of me something rotten, but at least I hadn't been beaten to a pulp!

"I was a hot head and the irony was that it was Jim and Terry Yorath who had taught me to stand up for myself in the first place. And I got on great with Jim too. On the pitch he was aggressive as hell. Off the pitch he was one of the nicest, gentlest men ever, but if you riled him you were going to get it. It was just one of those heat of the moment things, and I'm so glad it never got to the stage of a punch being thrown because that big man would have killed me!"

Coventry had established a well-balanced mix of experience and youth in their squad by the start of the 1978-79 season. Having turned 27, Holton fell into the category of senior professional, while at the other end of the spectrum Gary Gillespie had just celebrated his 18th birthday when Gordon Milne told him he would be partnering big Jim in the centre of defence for their season-opener at Middlesbrough. "If you were good enough you were old enough and Gordon gave everybody a real good chance and a good opportunity," says Gillespie. "It was the perfect environment to learn in. There were many seasoned professional players that had been around a bit and most of them were, or had been, international class players. It was a good time to be there as a youngster. They were hard guys, but they guided you through games and we looked up to them.

"As a boy I had seen Jim play for Scotland and the song had stuck in my mind - 6 foot 2, eyes of blue, big Jim Holton's after you – so to get the pleasure to play alongside him was just fantastic. I always remember my debut alongside Jim at Middlesbrough. Terry Yorath was our captain and I'll never forget the two of them clashing that day. I made a mistake and put it out for a corner, but Terry went a bit ape and started ranting and raving at big Jim for some reason. Terry was one of these guys actually that no matter how badly or how well he was playing, he always tried to get the best out of all the team mates around him. The two of them squared up to each other. The ball had gone out for a corner to Middlesbrough and the two of them were chest to chest, saying 'I'll see you after the game in the dressing room!' I was just a kid and I was thinking to myself 'what the hell is going on here?' I was a bit shell shocked. Nothing came of it, it was just two guys wanting to do as well as they could for the team. Both were winners in their own right and obviously wanted the best for everybody. Thankfully we won the game 2-1, and after the game everybody was best of pals again."

Expectations were high at the club following their seventh-place finish the previous campaign, and the win at Middlesbrough paved the way for further victories against Norwich, Derby and Coventry. After five games, the only point dropped came in a goalless draw at Highfield Road against champions Nottingham Forest.

So far so good? Not quite, a shock League Cup defeat at Chester City indicated that Coventry were far from the finished article, and a 1-0 defeat at Anfield then triggered a run of six league games without a win, the last of them a devastating 7-1 defeat against West Brom. This was the worst domestic defeat of Holton's career, albeit at the hands of a supremely gifted Albion team. He and Gillespie had simply found Cyrille Regis and Laurie Cunningham too hot to handle at the Hawthorns, and both scored two apiece, while Holton's old pal Len Cantello also got on a crowded scoresheet.

As you would expect after such a humiliation, strong words and opinions were exchanged in the dressing room afterwards, and whether or not it was directly down to something said in the aftermath of the seven-goal caning, skipper Yorath did not feature again until the turn of the year.

If the defeat against West Brom wasn't humiliating enough, Coventry City risked embarrassment every time they pulled on their new away kit — a shocking chocolate brown strip, complete with Admiral's trademark braces. The unique kit was not to everyone's liking, although it has gained cult status down the years. "Everywhere I go, I still get a hard time about that chocolate strip, especially because I live near West Bromwich," laughs Don Nardiello. "Living there, I have been used to plenty of stick over the years. I have friends who support West Bromwich and they still mention the time they thrashed us 7-1 - the only good thing I can say about that is I didn't actually play in that game. But there's no escaping the ribbing I get for wearing that strip."

Coventry responded well to the Hawthorns humbling, winning four, drawing two and losing only one of the seven league games that followed. However, despite the introduction of young Garry Thompson to the side, they were struggling to find the net in the same way they had done the previous season. Ian Wallace found himself marked more closely, while injuries disrupted Mick Ferguson's involvement.

Another bad day on the road occurred when Coventry were soundly beaten 4-0 at Southampton, although Wallace revealed in his weekly newspaper column that there had been extenuating circumstances – namely that half the team, including Holton, had been stuck in a lift for nearly an hour after their pre-match lunch and team talk at their hotel.

"We had been up on the ninth floor for a team meeting and used two lifts to return to the ground floor," said Wallace. "The lift I was in made it without trouble but the other dropped a couple of feet too low and stuck. From then on it was like the Keystone Kops! It would have been hilarious had it not been so serious. There was the boss, jacket off and shirt sleeves rolled up, trying to force open the lift doors with a crowbar. Then big Jim Holton tried to kick the doors down, which considering they were sliding doors, didn't make a lot of sense! We've nicknamed Jim 'The Incredible Hulk' and I think he was just trying to live up to that."

Milne and his coach Ron Wylie continued to work the players hard on the training ground, and players like Holton led by example. Youngsters in the Coventry ranks looked up to the big Scot, and respected and admired that he could be such a warrior on the pitch, then flick a switch and become such a gentle, caring

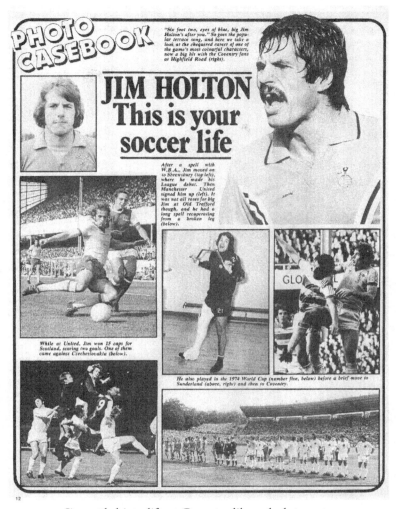

*Jim settled into life at Coventry like a duck to water
and became a huge hit with the Sky Blues' fans*

figure the moment he took his boots off.

"He was fearsome," says Thompson. "When I broke into the first team you'd be looking at the opposing centre forward thinking 'if only you knew what you are going to get today!' Jim's reputation went before him, although I think people were surprised to see what a good footballer he was. He read the game well and for such a big, powerful guy he was very quick.

"Someone texted me recently and asked who were the toughest people I'd played against. I mentioned guys like John Wile and Ally Robertson of West Brom, but then I remembered that in the two years before I made my debut, every Tuesday the first team would play the reserves and Jim Holton basically brutalised me!

"By the time it came to me playing for the first team he had toughened me up for it. I hadn't won a free kick in two years. At training, I used to complain to the gaffer 'Any chance of a free kick?' but after a while I'd know just to play on, and there would be big Jim in my ear saying 'you're learning big man, you're learning'. It was tough, but it was a good grounding. Even the training sessions where he kicked lumps out of me, he would just laugh after the game and say 'come here, give me a hug! Come on, let's go and get a drink!'

"Jim may have been booting the hell out of me every week, but he was doing me a favour. He was preparing me for what was ahead, because you never know how players will react when they get into the first team; whether they can cope with the abuse from fans, and abuse from other players. Guys like Jim Holton, Jim Blyth, Tommy Hutchison, Barry Powell and Terry Yorath schooled me in a way that made me a decent pro in the end. Your club is only as good as the senior pros and at Coventry I was brought up with some of the best. I didn't realise until I went to bad clubs with bad pros how lucky I had been to be brought up in a proper environment at Coventry."

Holton, in particular, would go out of his way to encourage and educate the younger players – as long as you didn't ask him outside for a fight like Thompson had! "Out of all the senior professionals at the club at that time, Jim treated me the best. He was fantastic," says midfielder Andy Blair. "On the pitch and around the training ground, Jim was a larger than life, inspirational character who gelled the group together. He was a real man in what I'd describe as a fantasy world.

"I was on the fringes of making it into the first team, but there were no cliques. He was a big influence on my career. He treated me with such respect that it held me in good stead. When I got older, I wanted to show the same attitude towards young professionals as they started their careers. He was a great role model and someone that you could look up to."

Although Blair was born in Fife and won five caps for Scotland Under-21s, he spent most of his life in the Warwickshire area and his accent reflected that. Despite some good-natured ribbing, Jim and the other Anglos accepted Blair as the fully-fledged Scot he considers himself to be. "I had paid to get in to watch him play for Scotland and when Coventry City signed him it was a marquee statement at the time. He was a massive signing and he embraced it. It was a dream for me to be in the same team as him."

Thompson agrees: "You could see he was a legend – he'd been at Man United and was a big name signing. I joined Coventry as a kid with Paul Dyson. We'd come in at 15, played in reserves, then all of a sudden you had guys like Tommy Hutchison, Barry Powell and Jim signing. As young kids it was exciting to be around them."

Nardiello was forcing his way into the Coventry team around the time Holton signed, and had already played against him when Holton was trying to prove his fitness in Manchester United reserves. He says Holton left a lasting impression, "I have nothing but fond memories of him," says Nardiello, who would also play alongside Holton at Detroit Express in 1980 prior to a long post-football career with West Midlands Police. "He used to have a saying: 'it's nice to be nice'. I hadn't heard it before, but it stuck with me. It conjured up other thoughts – it costs nothing to be nice, it costs nothing to smile and I put it altogether and thought it's a positive outlook to adopt.

"There was a six year gap between him and I. He mixed with the older group of lads and I was mixing with the younger group of lads, but because he was a great bloke he had a way of bringing the two groups together. He was easy to get along with, without making you feel like you were younger or inferior. He was approachable, encouraging and very helpful. He had a soft manner about him, but he was tough when he needed to be.

"He was probably the first name on the team-sheet if he was fit. When I think of Coventry I think of the strong characters we had at that time and the influence they had. Terry Yorath, our captain, could be having a bad game – and he didn't have many to be honest - but he would still be giving people a rollocking and geeing everybody up. I didn't see Jim as a leader in the same way as Terry, but you saw him as a solid, dependable figure that had an immense impact on our team. He'd win the balls in the air and he'd get his tackles in.

"Being young you were in awe of the bigger players around you, as I was of Jim. He had all the necessary qualities to make an excellent defender. In the dressing room he was a very likable chap, very amenable, very friendly. You can always have one or two people who were too big for their boots and big headed, but Jim was never that type of person. He was always approachable to all the young lads."

The development of Gary Gillespie perhaps best exemplified the influence of Holton. The old dog was teaching his young defensive pupil new tricks, and the classy Gillespie was a quick learner.

"I learned a great deal from him," says Gillespie, who would go on to become a Scotland international and win an array of honours with Liverpool later in his career. "We complemented each other well and formed a good partnership. Jim was a big, rugged, old-fashioned centre half. He was always one of these guys that wanted to dominate the centre forward in the air. He loved the aerial challenges and he felt he probably hadn't done his job unless he won his fair share of headers against the centre forwards. If you watched him he was fantastic – he didn't necessarily have to out-jump opponents. He was cleverer than that. He used to subtly barge the centre forward just before the ball was coming, and knock him slightly off balance. Big Jim would just stand there and win headers all day long.

"Playing alongside big Jim was certainly a great experience for me. Jim was that special kind of guy and, up close, you could see the power that he had on the pitch. He had massive big thighs but really slim calves. He would always say, 'That's where my speed is Gary, in my calves!' He wasn't the quickest to be honest, but he at least convinced himself he was the quickest!"

Gillespie prospered in the family atmosphere that prevailed at Coventry, and thanks Holton for helping him make the transition so comfortably. "It was great for me because I was just a raw laddie coming from a small village called Brightons just outside Falkirk. It was nice to have so many Scottish players there at the time. Jim and Jan, his wife, really made it quite easy for me to settle in. I remember going to their house a couple of times and they always looked after me, as did other guys like Ian Wallace and Hutchie.

"The seasoned pros looked after the younger ones well and Jim would be a big part of that. It was the time when you could have fun off the field without too much intrusion. We used to go and have games nights on a Wednesday or something like that. We'd go to the local pubs and play darts and pool and skittles and dominoes and things like that. It was just a good club and a good time to be there."

Garry Thompson agrees that Coventry was the ideal environment for young players to listen, learn and prosper. Milne was a forward-thinking manager, and he recognised the need for young players to be given first team outings to accelerate their development. It was no place for the faint-hearted though, and the only way for the youngsters to win the respect of their elders, was to show they had the heart and thick-skin that was required to survive in the late 1970s First Division.

"It could be a tough school," says Thompson. "In those days the dressing room banter was cutting. Jim and Hutchie were amongst it and although they'd take the mickey out of you, they'd make you feel part of it. We also got bollockings on a regular basis, because as young lads there were obviously times that we got too big for our boots."

One such occasion was when Thompson had an impact in both penalty boxes when Coventry faced Aston Villa at Villa Park. "We had a fierce to desire to win in our team, which I think was especially true of the Scottish players – they had a tribe mentality," says Thompson. "I'm a Villa fan, so my dad had 20 tickets when we played them at Villa Park, and I was so wound up for the game I made a mistake in the first half and cost us a goal by not picking my man up at a corner. When I walked into the dressing room at half-time I thought I'd make my apologies as soon as I got through the door. I didn't even get as far as 'I'm sorry' before Jim had me by the throat, screaming: 'You fucking...' I looked to Gordon Milne for help, but he just said 'he's right.'

"In the second half I equalised, and after the game - me being the shy, retiring person I am – I said to them 'Well there you go, I put food on your table again lads'. All I got back was 'fuck off you little twat, if it hadn't been for you we'd have won the game 1-0!' They absolutely hammered me and cut me right down to size. Lessons like that kept me grounded. It's only when you get older yourself you realise what a good school it was."

Milne's up-and-coming players had talent to burn, but he sometimes needed to hold them back for their own good, and with so many youngsters in the team, consistency suffered. Heavy defeats at Southampton, Bristol City, and again at West Brom – in an FA Cup replay - preceded the much-needed return of Yorath, and while his guile and experience steadied the ship, a run of eight draws out of 10 league matches curtailed hopes of a surge up the table.

The most exciting league match of the season was against Manchester United at Highfield Road. Holton's old club were also struggling for consistency under Dave Sexton, but few expected Coventry to race into a 3-1 half-time lead. Bobby McDonald made it four, two minutes after the restart, and while goals from McIlroy and Coppell set up a grandstand finish, the Sky Blues held on for a 4-3 memorable victory. Jim savoured another win over his old team, although he still had many pals in the United line-up – Joe Jordan, Gordon McQueen and Martin Buchan to name but three.

Jim was once again being asked about the possibility of forcing his way back into the Scotland team, with new manager Jock Stein scheduled to come and watch Coventry – especially their flame-haired forward Ian Wallace. "I'm desperate to play for Scotland, there's no way I'd let the side down," said Holton. "I've heard Jock Stein is coming down to take a look at my team-mate Ian Wallace. My hope is he'll take more than a passing interest in me as well."

Stein already knew how well Jim was playing – Holton had been conspicuously effective in a goalless draw against Leeds earlier that season, which happened to be Stein's final match as Leeds manager.

Holton was still fondly remembered by Scotland fans and although he had endured a five year hiatus from international duty, he wasn't ready to give up on a 16th cap. The man blocking his way back to the dark blue No 5 shirt was his good friend Gordon McQueen.

McQueen insists that the 'rivalry' was no more than newspaper talk. "Me and Jim were very good pals – always were," insists the giant blond defender known by Jim as 'Go-Go'. "We used to go up to a pub in Glasgow and meet before the Celtic-Rangers games and we would have a pint and a laugh. Me and Joe (Jordan) also used to go over and see him in Manchester when he was there and we were at Leeds. Big Jim was always very supportive of me, probably more so than I was of him. I remember trying to take his position, but he wasn't for budging until he got his injury."

Talk of a Scotland recall was just a mild distraction for Holton, who continued to give his all for Coventry. Following the exciting win over Manchester United, Holton was missing for the midweek defeat at Forest that followed, but he was back in the fold as Coventry lost only one of their remaining nine league fixtures and played out of his skin to keep Manchester United at bay in a 0-0 draw in the reverse fixture at Old Trafford on Easter Monday. They did suffer a cruel blow towards the end of the season when Garry Thompson broke his leg in training two days after scoring at Villa Park. Before you ask, it had nothing to do with Jim!

With Thompson recuperating, Milne was able to hand a debut to emerging young striker Mark Hateley in the final match of the season, a 3-0 victory at home to Wolves, which confirmed their place in 10th – another highly respectable top-half finish.

Hateley, who went on to win 32 caps for England, believes he wouldn't have done so without the opportunities and footballing education that came his way at his first club Coventry. "I was lucky enough to have great managers during my time there," says Hateley. "Gordon Milne, who signed Jim, was my first manager, and his knowledge of the game was fantastic.

"When I started my career at Coventry Jim was an established centre half with big Paul Dyson and Gary Gillespie coming through. We had some really decent young guys, then a group of mature players – guys like Jim and Tommy Hutchison - that bound us all together. It was a really good outfit. Jim was a great guy to be around and had bags of experience. He was a gentle giant and a bit of a father figure to the younger players. Not a person to be messed with mind you! He had words in training with certain people now and again, but once Jim spoke, people tended to listen because of his manner and his presence."

Whether he liked it or not, with so many young players coming through, Jim was fast becoming something of an elder statesman at the club. Would he be able to hold on to his place though?

20: PUT YOUR HANDS UP FOR DETROIT

"The game and the stadiums in the NASL were completely different to what we were used to at home"

Mark Hateley

ON A PERSONAL LEVEL, season 1978-79 had been a good one for Jim Holton. He had managed 37 first team appearances for Coventry City – his best rate of involvement since his Manchester United days, and he had established himself as a hugely influential figure who the club's crop of emerging youngster all looked up to.

Jim had every right to be proud of his contribution during the 1978-79 campaign, and this was reflected in him being awarded the club's Chrysler Fair Play Award (which raised a few eyebrows, given his reputation) and a runner-up spot in the Player of the Year award, with his fellow Scot Bobby McDonald narrowly pipping him to that prize.

Holton had shown the intelligence to change his game, choosing not to lunge needlessly into tackles he had little chance of winning – not that had ever stopped him in the past! He had spent a large enough percentage of his career on the treatment table to know that any hopes he had of prolonging his career depended on a more considered approach.

Having played alongside players like Martin Buchan at Manchester United and Tommy Hutchison and Terry Yorath at Coventry, Jim had watched, learned, and emerged a far more rounded-player.

Coventry had benefitted from having a relatively settled squad, boosted by shrewd additions, since Holton's arrival in Spring 1977, but that was about to change as the 1979 season neared.

In came Dave Jones from Everton for a fee of £250,000

and Gary Collier, another centre half, joined from Bristol City – making history as the first out of contract player to negotiate his own transfer, a fee of £325,000 was later agreed by a tribunal.

A bigger shock was the sudden departure of skipper Terry Yorath to Tottenham, just three days before the season was about to start. The Wales international had been a stabilising influence at Coventry since joining from Leeds in 1976, and had led the Sky Blues (or Chocolate Browns as they were in that infamous kit) to victory in a four-team pre-season tournament in Edinburgh following victories over Manchester City and Hearts and a draw with Hibernian.

But as Coventry prepared for their season-opener at Stoke, Gordon Milne called Yorath into his office and asked him if he would be interested in a move to White Hart Lane. "When you get told something like that, there's no point in hanging around – you get out," said Yorath. "I was really disappointed because I had enjoyed my spell at Highfield Road. I had prepared hard during pre-season to play for Coventry and then suddenly this had come out the blue."

Whether Yorath's abrupt exit had an unsettling effect on the team is anyone's guess, but they looked at sixes and sevens against Stoke – new boys Jones and Collier looking particularly rusty in a 3-2 defeat. Holton missed his sparring partner Yorath but could at least console himself with the new choice of captain, Tommy Hutchison.

Another source of encouragement for Jim was the education of young Gary Gillespie, the elegant Scot who was mature beyond his years and would soon take over the armband from club legend Hutch. Gillespie, an absentee at Stoke, was back in the side alongside Holton, for a midweek victory over Bristol City, but the pair could do nothing to stave off a heavy defeat at Nottingham Forest, which was incidentally the last of just three league appearances Jim's old pal Asa Hartford made for the European Cup winners before Brian Clough sold him to Everton.

Holton and Gillespie looked an effective pairing, but occasionally Milne would experiment with three central defenders, and with Collier thrown into the mix alongside the Scots duo the tinkering back-fired at Anfield as Liverpool rampaged to a 4-0 win, which seriously flattered the bedraggled looking Sky Blues.

West Brom were a bogey team for Coventry, especially when they travelled to the Hawthorns, and true to form the Sky Blues were edged out of the League Cup 2-1, then comprehensively beaten 4-1 on league business.

Inconsistency was dogging Coventry, but it was not all doom and gloom, and there were solid early-season wins against Norwich, Bolton and Everton, who of course had the nomadic Hartford in their side following his brief 'holiday' at Nottingham Forest.

Holton was continuing to look after himself, and some of the form he was showing was as good as any time in his career, especially during a purple patch in November. While Mick Ferguson and Ian Wallace were terrorising opposition defences, Holton and Gillespie were watertight at the back for Coventry. Three-goal wins against Leeds and Wolves were followed by a disciplined 0-0 draw at Crystal Palace and a stunning 4-1 win against Ipswich, in which Ferguson scored all four of Coventry's goals.

Since leaving Old Trafford, Holton boasted an impressive record against his beloved Manchester United, but he suffered a rare defeat against the Red Devils shortly before Christmas, and it was his opposite number Gordon McQueen who scored the winner.

With Britain in the grip of a deep freeze, and games abandoned up and down the country, Highfield Road's new undersoil heating allowed Coventry's New Year's Day match with Middlesbrough to go ahead, and in the team's 27th match of the season, Holton was one of the few ever-presents. A happy new year was assured as the Sky Blues beat Boro 2-0. However, a booking tipped Jim over the 20-point disciplinary threshold and ended his run of consecutive games. In terms of his Coventry future, it would ultimately prove to be a costly suspension.

Waiting in the wings was young Paul Dyson, another excellent centre-half, for whom a bright future was predicted. Alongside Gillespie he looked comfortable and assured, and he did enough to convince Gordon Milne that the number 5 shirt should be his for keeps. His case was strengthened further when he scored the winning goal in a 1-0 win against champions-to-be Liverpool.

As Holton played out the remainder of the season in the reserves, the pattern of good, bad and indifferent continued for Coventry's first team. Dyson and Gillespie continued to impress as a partnership, but the goals had dried up and Milne's side had to settle for an unremarkable finishing spot of 15th in the First Division.

Life was never dull at Coventry, however, and managing director and club legend Jimmy Hill remained a man with his finger in many pies. He was responsible for opening the impressive 'Sky Blue Connexion' at the club's training base in Ryton-on-Dunsmore and even persuaded the Duke of Edinburgh to come along to perform the official opening. "Philip being Philip did his usual and headed for a group of young ladies – which we were at that time – and he turned on the charm!" laughs Jan Holton. "It was a nice experience and from that day I could say that I had met a member of the Royal family."

Jimmy Hill's next venture was a foray into the North American Soccer League with the Detroit Express franchise. Hill had money to re-invest following a successful project developing the game in Saudi Arabia, and together with co-owner Roger Faukner, an English broadcaster and promoter, they launched the Express in 1978, and cajoled George Best into playing a couple of games for the team on a publicity-raising European Tour.

Coventry and Detroit already had much in common, and Hill tried to use the new football team to strengthen the cities' links. In the 1950s, Coventry drew comparisons with 'Motor City' Detroit, due to its burgeoning car industry. But bust followed boom in both cities, and as the car-makers fell into difficult times, so did Detroit and Coventry. By 1980 – with Margaret Thatcher one year into her reign as Prime Minister – both cities were in the grip of rampant unemployment and urban decay. Sport at least provided an outlet for people to forget about the tough challenges they were facing in their lives.

The irrepressible Hill set about the Detroit project with his usual gusto and dug deep into his network of contacts to lure some big British names across the Pond. He succeeded in securing Trevor Francis from Birmingham and Alan Brazil from Ipswich on short-term contracts in 1978 and the Express duly made the play-offs, reaching the semi-finals. Francis – who then joined Nottingham Forest to become Britain's first £1 million player - returned to Detroit in 1979, along with Ted MacDougall, and while the Express again made the play-offs, they fell at the first hurdle.

Hill cleverly used his connections with Coventry City to breathe some fresh life into the squad for the 1980 outdoor season. As he had done in the previous seasons, Hill hand-picked a select number of Sky Blues players to cross the Atlantic and spend the NASL season with Detroit. Hill was unable to better his earlier coups when assembling the Class of 1980, but his list of recruits from Coventry included Holton, Don Nardiello, Gary Bannister, Mark Hateley and Jim Hagan. Hill had the backing of Gordon Milne, who felt the American experience could only benefit his players "Jimmy ploughed a lot of personal money into Detroit Express and he was careful to take reliable people with him," says Milne. "He didn't take players who he wouldn't have faith in, and taking Jim Holton confirmed what Jimmy Hill thought about his character."

Also in an Express squad dominated by Britons and managed by Englishman Ken Furphy, were Graham Oates from Newcastle United, and former Scotland internationals Eddie Colquhoun and goalkeeper Jim Brown, who had principally made their names at Sheffield United.

While Detroit Express were in the midst of a struggle, due to dwindling interest and crowds and an outbreak of boardroom turmoil, the NASL was still very much in its heyday, and the league was awash with superstars from all over the world. Holton had already had a taste of the razzmatazz four years earlier during his enjoyable spell playing for the Miami Toros, but for others the experience was new, exciting and very different to what they were used to in the English First Division.

"I went to the NASL purely for the experience and my first taste was playing against the New York Cosmos, who had Pele and Franz Beckenbauer in their team – how good is that for a young player?" Mark Hateley recalls, "It really whet my appetite and I resolved to make the most of my time there. The relationship Coventry had with Detroit Express was a working partnership to develop Coventry's young players, but big Jim went out there to keep himself ticking over. It was great experience playing against these players – George Best was playing for San Jose at the time; Rodney Marsh was playing for Tampa Bay – all the big characters of the game.

"The game and the stadiums were completely different to what we were used to at home – sometimes we played on some baseball surfaces with a diamond across the pitch, which was interesting! It was a bit like throwing a school game together on a made-up pitch, but it was all part of the experience and it forced you to adapt. We shared the Pontiac Silverdome with the Detroit Lions American football team, and it was massive. It was a good place and a really valuable learning experience for the younger players."

Don Nardiello agrees that it was a culture shock. "We had come from First Division football with Coventry and I must admit I thought it was like second division football. The big difference was that you had all these great players coming to play, but at the end of their careers - the likes of Beckenbauer, Pele and Cruyff. The other big difference was that we played on Astroturf – my first experience of that surface – and the ball would be bouncing around everywhere."

The synthetic surfaces were not to everyone's liking and could be tough on the body. It would be 1981 before QPR became the first club to introduce an artificial pitch to England, but many of the games Jim played with Detroit were on concrete-like 'carpets'. "I knew plastic would be difficult for Jim, it wouldn't suit his game," says Gordon Milne.

Holton's friend John Hillan recalls: "I remember asking Jim how football was taking off in America and he said 'It's no' for me!' He was a big strong centre half who liked the ball just to be tossed up so it was there to be won. But the pitches in America were synthetic, and they didn't agree with him. Even though he had grown up in the west of Scotland playing on ash surfaces in Larkhall, the American surfaces were tough on him. You could rip your skin, especially if you were into slide tackles. Jim said the side of his arse would be stinging by the time he got in the shower!"

Jim wasn't in Detroit for a holiday, and rarely held back. In a 3-2 defeat against Tampa Bay Rowdies, rival forward Neill Roberts felt the full force of a trademark Holton tackle and although he had to leave the pitch with a dislocated shoulder, Rowdies player Jan Van der Veen was quick to exonerate the Scot. "I don't think he was trying to put Neill out the game," said the Dutchman. "It was bad luck for Neill that he fell on his shoulder. It was a tackle you see a thousand times during a game."

Detroit's home ground was the space-age Pontiac Silverdome – an 82,000 capacity state-of-the-art stadium featuring a fibreglass roof held up by air pressure. While it would be packed to capacity when the Detroit Lions played there, average crowds were nearer 10,000 for Express matches in 1980 – less than half what they had been the previous season when golden boy Trevor Francis was the main attraction. The one exception was for the visit of the star-studded New York Cosmos. More than 27,000 turned out to watch a 0-0 draw (a scoreline which must have baffled your average American), followed by a shoot-out win for Detroit. "The atmosphere itself was excellent," says Don Nardiello, "and we gelled really well with the American contingent - I liked them. They were warm, welcoming guys.

"Apart from the home-based players, the rest of us all lived close together in apartments on an estate, and the wives and families all got on well. We played all over the country but the outdoor seasons were short. If you wanted, you could stay for the indoor season, which I did, although Jim went home. Then, the following year, Jimmy Hill moved his franchise and we became the Washington Diplomats, and I had another six months out there. It wasn't for everyone, but I really enjoyed the experience of mixing up my football at home and in the United States.

"What impressed me most though were the fans. They really wanted to engage with you and we were forever signing autographs and having gatherings and get-togethers. The club encouraged a lot more contact with the public and I think the British were way behind the Americans on that score."

The hardcore of Express fans were certainly loyal and loud and made the players feel at home. This was reflected in the team's form at the Silverdome, where defeats were rare. It was a different story on the gruelling road trips, where the Express didn't tend to fare well. Tommy Hutchison – who played for Seattle Sounders that season – suggests Detroit's lack of away-day success may not have been helped by their budget travel arrangements.

"Everything about Seattle was first class - travel and accommodation – but from what big Jim told me, Detroit could be a nightmare. He told me that their team used to go on standby, and there were occasions where half the team would be on one plane, half would be on another. He wasn't the type to complain though, and I'm sure he just got on with it. I think he really enjoyed his time in America."

Jan Holton agrees: "Jim thoroughly enjoyed his time out there, he was well liked. We lived in Rochester, about an hour outside Detroit, and it was a nice way of life. Because I had two babies, I never went to any of the games, but I did go to some training sessions and we socialised a lot with the other families. The kids and I returned to the UK just before him, because he was contracted to play another couple of games. He did lose a lot of weight playing out there because they played in arenas where temperatures down on the pitch could soar to ridiculous levels. He was the thinnest I'd ever seen him when he came back from Detroit because he had lost so much weight playing in the heat."

American sports fans love stats, and the facts and figures around Holton's spell with Express show that he played 21 matches, 1,821 minutes and scored three goals. The number of opponents he booted into the air is unavailable!

Detroit narrowly missed out on the play-offs, but Holton's American adventure was not quite over... he was about to be invited into the court of football royalty.

The Express finished their season with a 3-2 win over Philadelphia Fury at the end of August, but before he could think about heading home Holton received an invitation he couldn't refuse, when he was named in an NASL Select side to face New York Cosmos in the Franz Beckenbauer Farewell Match at Giants Stadium.

One of the greatest and most-admired players on the planet 'Der Kaiser' – who had captained Germany to World Cup glory in 1974 and Bayern Munich to three successive European Cups – had been a revelation since joining the Cosmos in 1977. Alongside stars such as Pele and Giorgio Chinaglia, Cosmos were simply on another level to their rivals, and they swept all before them to win the Soccer Bowl in 1977 and 1978.

In 1980, they tasted Soccer Bowl glory again, brushing aside the Fort Lauderdale Strikers 3-0 in the final, three days before Beckenbauer's grand farewell. The German great was heading back to his homeland to sign for Hamburger SV, but would be afforded one last chance to take the acclaim of the Cosmos fans.

It was a real feather in the cap of Holton to be selected, as Beckenbauer had hand-picked the players who would make up the 21-strong squad of the NASL Select. It is not known whether the Kaiser had memories of being bulldozed to the turf by Holton when Scotland played West Germany at Hampden seven years earlier, but whatever his reasons, he picked Jim - a genuine honour. From an original list drawn up by Beckenbauer, Cosmos fans were then given the chance to choose the final squad in a ballot.

The squad represented 16 of the NASL's 24 clubs and included George Best, Gerd Muller, Oscar Fabbiani, Phil Parkes, Karl-Heinz Granitza and Teofilo Cubillas, although Best and Muller were unavailable and didn't play. Rinus Michels, who had been coach of the Netherlands when they lost the 1974 final to West Germany, was named coach of the All-Stars team. For Cosmos, Pele came out of retirement to join his fellow luminary on the pitch.

Glitz and glamour was the order of the day, and in front of a bumper crowd of 71,413, each player was announced individually as they ran from the locker rooms on to the pitch through the obligatory guard of dancing cheerleaders. When Holton's turn came, he emerged grinning from ear to ear to take his place alongside his NASL Select team-mates.

The match was broadcast nationwide on the USA Cable Network, and while the scoreline was of secondary importance to Beckenbauer's final bow, the NASL select came out on top. South African Jomo Sono, Cubillas (the Peru veteran who had been the hammer of Scotland at the 1978 World Cup) and Karl-Heinz Granitza scored for the All-Stars, while Pele marked his cameo comeback with a goal, and Paraguayan Roberto Cabanas scored the other Cosmos goal.

Players were presented with personalised, engraved mementoes to take away after the game, and Holton was proud to round off his American adventure with such a gala occasion.

The adventure wasn't quite over for Jimmy Hill. The following year, following a bitter court battle, he relocated the franchise from Detroit to Washington, where they were re-named the Diplomats. It was an unmitigated disaster, financially and in a sporting sense, and they folded within a year.

Local businessman 'Sonny' Van Wernem, meanwhile, retained the Detroit Express name and built a new team in the second-tier American Soccer League, and they won the title in 1982. However, with superstars like Pele and Beckenbauer no longer around to prop up its popularity, the bubble had burst for soccer in America. The ASL folded in 1983, and the NASL collapsed in 1984. The American Dream was fun while it lasted and Holton was proud that he had enjoyed two bites at the cherry.

21: LAST ORDERS

"Jim frequented lots of pubs, even when he was playing, and the idea of running one himself appealed to him"

Jan Holton

WHEN JIM HOLTON returned from the United States, Gary Gillespie and Paul Dyson were immovable as Coventry's City's first choice pairing in central defence, and he spent a frustrating season in the reserves, fretting about his future as his 30th birthday neared.

Dyson and Gillespie were eight and nine years younger respectively than Holton, and they became the cornerstone of the new, young team Gordon Milne was building. They also had a knack of staying fit and free of suspension and big Jim had been around long enough to know that his chances of returning to regular first team football at Highfield Road were severely limited.

Holton had experienced these emotions before at Manchester United, and was left feeling a spare part as Coventry embarked on an exhilarating run to the semi-finals of the League Cup. In the first leg against West Ham they produced a barnstorming performance to come from 2-0 down to win 3-2, only to lose the second leg 2-0 at Upton Park.

By that stage, Jim was seriously pondering his future, and when the end of the season arrived he was a granted a free transfer – choosing to join Second Division Sheffield Wednesday, managed by Jack Charlton. The World Cup winner was in his second job as a manager after a successful spell in charge of Middlesbrough and had secured promotion from the Third Division for Wednesday in 1979, and then led them to a tenth-placed finish in their first season back in the Second Division. Holton was among a number of new faces arriving at Wednesday, lifting confidence of a strong promotion push.

Holton, Gary Bannister – who had also made the move from Coventry – and Gary Megson featured on the front cover of Wednesday's first home programme of the season, for the match against Crystal Palace, standing alongside a proud Charlton at a sun-drenched Hillsborough. Holton, with socks rolled to his ankles, appears fit, slim and ready for action, but before the ink had time to dry on the programme, he was injured.

Charlton had wooed Jim to Hillsborough with the incentive of first team football, but when Holton picked up a hamstring injury during pre-season, the number 5 shirt was filled instead by Peter Shirtliff and the Scot was back kicking his heels on the sidelines.

Relations between Holton and Charlton quickly soured and Jim was surprisingly told he could leave. "I really thought this was the ideal chance to resurrect my career," rued a sad Holton.

There was immediate interest in Holton and he turned down a potential move to Newcastle United because they were only offering a one-year contract. The truth is Jan wouldn't have been best pleased about moving the family to the North-East, having failed to take to Sunderland four years earlier.

Then, like a bolt from the blue, he heard that Tommy Docherty was ready to offer him a two-year deal with Preston North End, who were then struggling in the Third Division. The Doc hadn't covered himself with glory when he manoeuvred Jim out the door at Old Trafford, but with his career on the line, Holton was prepared to let bygones be bygones and go back to work under his former manager.

Holton met Docherty in his office, along with Preston assistant Ken Shellito, and after a brief, upbeat discussion terms were agreed. Everything changed the moment the phone rang. It was the Preston chairman, calling in a panic after some bad news from the bank. The club was in a dire financial predicament, and with every penny needed to stave off the bailiffs, he instructed Docherty to call the deal off immediately. A flummoxed Holton said afterwards: "I am beginning to think there is a jinx on me. It was a shattering blow."

Holton remained on Wednesday's pay-roll, but his relationship with Charlton was damaged beyond repair, and he left the club without playing a single competitive game.

With his body starting to grumble, and no agreeable deals on the table, Holton decided enough was enough and took the difficult decision to retire from professional football at the age of 31. He didn't spend too much time scratching his head, agonising over what to do next. An idea that had long been on his mind quickly came to pass.

"He just arrived home one day and said 'By the way, we're going into the pub trade'," says Jan. "Jim frequented lots of pubs, even when he was playing, and the idea of running one himself appealed to him. A friend put him in touch with a guy from the pub chain Mitchells & Butlers, who was in charge of tenancies, and when they hit it off and a plan was hatched for us to go into the pub trade. I'd never been behind a bar before in my life!"

Like pre-season training for publicans, Holton was first given some prep work, pulling pints behind the bar at the Burnt Post in Kenpas Highway. "I have always fancied a pub since my father had one in Scotland," Jim told the local newspaper.

When word got out he was planning to go into the pub game, offers came in from Manchester and Glasgow, but with two young children and a wide circle of friends in Coventry, Jim set his sights on securing a local lease.

"Jim did a training course and then for six weeks we were put into one of the busiest pubs in Coventry – the Town Wall Tavern in Bond Street - which had a massive reputation for food and was mainly frequented by a rugby crowd and police officers. It was a very popular pub and the thinking that the brewery had was: we'll throw him in at the deep end and he'll either sink or swim. As luck would have it, he swam and swam very well in actual fact.

"With Jim pulling the pints, I got thrown into the kitchen. Our children were 3 and 6 at the time, so it was all a bit of a challenge, juggling all those balls in the air. Once we'd finished our six weeks at the Town Wall, we got offered the tenancy of a pub called the Rising Sun on Spon Street, which had been declining and was on its uppers. We were given 12 months to turn it round, which we did, with a promise that the brewery would totally refurbish after 12 months, which they did. From there, it really took off and we were in there 10 happy years!"

The Rising Sun refurbishment was marked with a grand re-opening, and some big names from the world of football were invited to sprinkle some star dust on proceedings, including Martin Buchan and master of the one-liner Tommy Docherty. "I decided to drive down and when I got there, Tommy Doc made a speech and wished Jim and Jan well. Then, spotting me, he said it was nice to see one of Jim's team-mates here, before adding – to everyone's amusement – 'Only an Aberdonian would drive 100 miles for a free pint of lager!'"

Sharing the bill with Docherty was former Liverpool skipper Emlyn Hughes, whose celebrity status was sky-high as a captain on BBC's flagship quiz show, A Question of Sport. The ebullient Hughes had always been pally with Holton despite playing against him for club and country, and he was only too happy to come along and lend his support to Jim. Hughes died of a brain tumour, aged 57 in 2004, and Jan reflects: "It's so sad when I look at the picture from that night of Jim and Emlyn, so happy, and both of them no longer with us."

As Jan mentions, many of the Holtons' regulars were Coventry police officers, and the pub soon became known for its atmosphere – much of that down to the engaging personalities of the couple working hard to make it a success. "For a city centre pub it was a really nice, friendly atmosphere," says Jan. "For all the time that we were in the trade I think I only ever witnessed two scuffles – not even full blown fights. We never had any problems."

The Rising Sun was located around a mile-and-a-half away from Highfield Road, and while many Coventry City fans were already among the regulars, there would be a pilgrimage of buses calling in to pay their respects to big Jim whenever Manchester United came to town.

While the vast majority supporters were well behaved at Jim's pub, football-related violence was still rife in the Eighties, and one notorious Manchester United hooligan recalls a city centre battle which took place on the doorstep of the Rising Sun. In an interview with Cass Pennant for his book 'Top Boys: True Stories of Football's Hardest Men' United fan Eddie Beef describes how he was saved from taking a beating at the hands of rival fans by a fellow member of his firm. "It was outside Jim Holton's pub in Coventry," says Beef. "They used to sing Six Foot Two, Eyes of Blue, big Jim Holton's after you. I remember looking at him before it went down and his eyes were fucking brown! Jim Holton was a top fellow."

Scottish journalist Kenny Farquharson was a regular in the Rising Sun when he worked in Coventry, and he waxed lyrical about his memories of Holton in a recent column in *The Times*. "He was one of the most formidable men I have ever met," said Farquharson. "The way he ruled that bar with an iron will was awe-inspiring. Any tomfoolery by customers could be dispelled by a hardening of Big Jim's stare.

"On one occasion when I was propping up the bar, a regular complained that the fag machine wasn't working. Big Jim walked over to the machine, started at it for a moment, then gave it a sledgehammer thump with his mighty fist. The sound of the blow echoed around the room. There was a pause. Then a packet of Embassy Regal fell helplessly into the tray. Jim was a lovely man. Scary, but lovely nonetheless."

Taking pride of place within the Rising Sun was a large class cabinet displaying many of Jim's football keepsakes, including pennants, photos and international shirts he had collected during his appearances for Scotland.

It fast became a hub in the community and dominoes, darts and pool teams were soon representing the Rising Sun in local leagues. The competitive animal in Jim also came out, and he was even talked in to dusting off his boots and occasionally representing a couple of Sunday league teams in the late 1980s, Finham Park Rangers and Talbot. When Coventry fans recently shared their memories of Holton on an online forum, one member – Irish Sky Blue – recalled: "I remember playing for the Supporters' Club against Jim and his team on Cardinal Wiseman School playing field.

I played at full-back and I remember overlapping down the wing and being absolutely wiped out by Jim who completely scythed my legs from under me. No malice though as he had a big toothless grin on his face when he picked me up!" Old habits did indeed die hard!

The Holtons' pub was also the perfect excuse for friends and family from far and wide to stop by, and the hosts were always ready to lay out the welcome mat. Gary Campbell, Jim's friend since they were boys growing up together in Lesmahagow, recalls coming back home for a short break from his new life in Canada, and being talked into a sojourn to see Jim by their mutual friend John Hillan. "We decided on the spur of the moment that we should go down and see Jim in Coventry," says Campbell. "We hadn't told him we were coming, and when we got to the Rising Sun I casually walked up to the bar and asked him for a pint of lager. He did a double-take, grinned and said 'Oh dear, it's going to be a long night tonight!' And it was! We were drinking till 5 in the morning. It was a lock-in and not strictly legal, but there were even a couple of detectives who popped in to join us!

"My brother in law came with us too and it was the first time he had ever been out of Scotland, but Jan and Jim looked after us all. That was Jim and Jan - hearts of gold – they would always put themselves out for you and nothing was ever too much trouble."

It wasn't the only time John Hillan paid a surprise visit to Jim and he did the same when their other pal John Hannah was back in the UK from South Africa. "I asked Jan to get someone to cover Jim's shift and we would come down and surprise him," he says. "I went in the lounge door on his blind side, thumped my fist on the bar a couple of times and shouted in my best Lesmahagow accent: 'Two pints of heavy!' He jumped out his skin, but he was delighted to see us. We ended up in the Tam O'Shanter Burns Club in Coventry and it ended up quite a night."

Len Cantello and Asa Hartford, apprentices with Holton when they were teenagers at West Brom, also remember swinging by to see Jim. "I was doing some scouting and was heading down with Len to watch a game in Coventry," says Hartford. "It was just a spur of the moment thing, but we said to each other 'shall we call in and see Jim?' Neither of us had a clue where the pub was, so when we saw a guy standing at a bus stop we pulled up and asked if he happened to know where it was. He ended up showing us where it was, and then we went into Jim's pub. Needless to say we never got to the game!"

Jim proved a natural as a pub landlord. It was an environment where he felt completely at ease and the good humour and sense of fun he had long possessed in football dressing rooms easily transferred to banter in the bar. Plenty of footballers from that generation went down the same route of running a pub, and many found the temptation of having drink literally on tap too great to resist. Before long, years of conditioning could give way to a tell-tale paunch and a double chin. Holton was far more disciplined than that. While he was a social drinker, and enjoyed a pint or two, he stuck to a rigorous fitness regime and kept himself in good shape.

As if to prove the point, one family picture shows him proudly wearing the all-white Scotland shirt he wore against Yugoslavia at the 1974 World Cup. He perhaps wasn't at the same fighting weight he had been during that memorable summer in West Germany, but he appears very much a man who had looked after himself.

Jan Holton reveals that the big, hard, rugged player could also be prone to amusing bouts of vanity. "He would spend a lot of time in front of the mirror," she laughs. "You should have seen the ritual he had every time he washed his hair. No-one was allowed to touch his hair while it was wet. We used to wind him up something dreadful. Sally in particular would go up and ruffle his hair while it was wet and he used to go absolutely ape. He did have a thing about his hair.

"He was fashion conscious too, but I'm taking the credit for that. I was the one who found him his own tailor in Coventry, a little Italian guy called Gino. He didn't follow trends he just knew what he liked. He'd always take me along as a second opinion and if I didn't like it, he didn't get it! He had some lovely clothes."

Jim did have his limits, however, and trying to get down with the kids and keep up with their taste in music exposed them. "He really had no clue who was who," says Jan. "I can always remember that Moving On Up was one of his favourite songs not long before he died and when Sally asked him who sung it, he said ABC People! It was M People of course, so at least he knew it had something to do with the alphabet! I can't say he was a music connoisseur unlike his son and his Grandson. Jay and Neal have very eclectic taste in music and films and can spend hours talking about it together. It goes right over my head, and it certainly would go right over Jim's. No, he was very much more into his horse racing and his football and his sport and his golf rather than the arts. Let's just say he was far more physical than cerebral!"

Holton was known as a very sociable person, and was particularly good at keeping in touch with his close friends, and vice versa. If the opportunity to go back to Scotland arose, he would take it, usually when tickets became available for Celtic matches. When his old Manchester United team-mate Mick Martin became Liam Brady's assistant manager at Parkhead in 1991, Jim wasn't backwards at coming forwards!

"When he had his pub in Coventry and I was first team coach at Glasgow Celtic at the time and I used to get him tickets," recalls Martin. "He used to ring me up and here's how the conversation usually went...

"'Hiya Mick, it's Jim here.'

"'All right Jim? Okay, before we go any further how many do you want?'

"'What do you mean? I'm not ringing you up for tickets.'

"'Well what the fuck are you ringing me up for?'

"'I just wanted a chat with you, to see how you're getting on mate.'

"So we would have our chat, and at the end of the call – 5, 10, 20 minutes later - sure enough he would hit me with it... Oh, by the way, can you get me two tickets for the Celtic v Rangers match on Saturday?' And, obviously, I did."

On one such trip up to Glasgow to watch an Old Firm game at Celtic Park, he spent the day in the company of Taggart actor

Mark McManus. There wasn't quite a murder, but there could have been!

On this occasion, Holton and his friend John Hillan had been invited to hospitality for the game by Celtic Lisbon Lions legend Bobby Murdoch, along with TV detective McManus, then one of Britain's most recognisable stars of the small screen. The guests arranged to convene at McManus's local – the Queen's Park Café in Victoria Road - and paid him a visit in the morning ahead of the game.

Hillan takes up the story: "So we knocked on the door and there's Taggart answering the door in a string vest. I couldn't believe my eyes. We had a few in his local pub then got a taxi to the game. As we headed towards Parkhead, we got stopped at traffic lights and a 20-seater minibus pulled alongside us, full of Rangers punters going wild. We didn't have any colours on because we were suited and booted for the match, all of us wearing a collar and tie. But then Mark McManus started winding them up by crossing himself at the window! They were all snarling and going crazy. We drove away from them, but when we got to the next set of traffic lights, we got stopped again and who rolls up alongside us? The same bus! There were a few words exchanged, but then Taggart started crossing himself again. It was like a red rag to a busload of bulls! Wee Taggart could have got us all into bother. It ended on a funny note though. As he was crossing himself, some big Rangers fella stuck his head out the bus window and shouted: 'I hope you die in the next series ya wee shite!'"

One of the most memorable weekends in the Rising Sun – and, the whole of Coventry to be honest – was in May 1987 when, against all odds, unfancied Coventry City won the FA Cup after a thrilling 3-2 victory against Tottenham. "We were thrilled to bits with the result for Cov which had been a long time coming and, of course, it was amazing for our trade!" says Jan. "When Coventry won the FA Cup our pub was rammed for the whole weekend to the point where we had to close the doors as we couldn't let any more people in because of safety concerns. We actually took more over the bar that weekend than we had during the course of the whole of the previous Christmas and New Year! It was crazy. Sometimes customers were 10 deep at the bar and we ended up serving beer in bottles because we couldn't get out to collect glasses. Mad times but so good. It's a lovely memory."

After a decade of memories at the Rising Sun, the Brewery decided they wanted to do something different with the pub, and Jim and Jan were left searching for a new tenancy. They quickly took a lease out on The Stag in Bishop Street and made a seamless transition, helped by the fact that most of the Rising Sun regulars faithfully decamped to the Holtons' new base. "It was right opposite the Royal Mail sorting office, and we had a great clientele," says Jan, "we were happy there, and doing well, and that's where we stayed until Jim died..."

22: GONE BUT NEVER FORGOTTEN

"It was heart disease, which they said could have taken Jim at any time. He could have been 6, 16 or 60 when it struck"

Jan Holton

SUNDAY, 3RD OCTOBER 1993 was a proud day for the Holton family. Jim and Jan had just dropped off their 18-year-old son Neal up to Leeds University, where he was about to start studying for a degree in Electronic and Electrical Engineering, and had returned to Coventry to meet their daughter Sally, 15, and Jan's sister to celebrate.

As they sat together in the window at TGI Friday's, Jim noticed a young woman pull up outside in her car, clearly having difficulty with the vehicle. Her anxiety increased when smoke started billowing out of the engine. Before the others had time to react, he had sprung out his seat and rushed to her aid.

It turned out she was a student, also on her way to university, and most of her possessions were packed into the smouldering car. "Without a thought, he helped the girl to take all her stuff out the car before it exploded. It was a knight in shining armour act, but it was so typical of Jim," says Jan Holton. "He would always go out of his way to help people, and this was yet another example of his good nature. His favourite phrase was 'It's nice to be nice'. It was advice that we both lived by: to treat people the same as you like to be treated and never belittle anyone because you might meet them on the way down as well as on the way up. The phrase fitted Jim very well."

After his selfless act of kindness, the heroic Holton returned to his meal and the inevitable good-natured ribbing from Jan, who asked him where his cape was.

It rounded off a good weekend, and while Jan often invited

her sister Pauline up from Plymouth to come and stay over the weekend, the pair decided to extend her stay into the Monday and go on a shopping trip to Birmingham. It was the day that the family's world fell apart.

Jan Holton describes how the darkest day of her life unfolded, "It's been 25 years now so it's not quite as raw as it used to be, but I can remember every single minute of it. That morning we got up and Pauline and I prepared to head into Birmingham. First of all, I needed to go down to the pub to see our bar manager Colin, who had asked me if he could borrow an electric typewriter. Jim was standing in the doorway of the house, already changed into his running gear, and I was in the driveway, about to put the typewriter into the car. After asking me what I was doing standing there with a typewriter, his very last words to me were 'I love you'. We always said it to one another. We had a kiss and off I went down to the pub to give Colin the typewriter. When I got back to pick up Pauline, she said Jim had gone off on his run and been away for around an hour. This was about 10 o'clock, but I said 'Don't worry, he'll be gassing to someone somewhere'. So we got in the car, drove off into Birmingham for a tootle around the shops, had lunch then drove back.

"I remember driving into Jacklin Drive, Finham, where we lived and seeing Colin's car parked outside the house, which was odd because he should have been at the pub. As we pulled into the drive, Colin immediately came running up to me and started trying to usher me in through the door. He'd got his hand on my back and was sort of pushing me up the drive. Something wasn't right. 'Colin, why are you here?' I said, followed by 'Where's Jim? Is there something wrong with Jim? Where is he?' Colin just wouldn't answer me, he was lost for words. Then, bless her, Sally came flying out, and just came out with it: 'Mum, DAD'S DEAD!'

"That's when I lost it. I just collapsed on the spot. They hauled me into the hall and I remember screaming 'WHY?' Then all hell broke loose. Half of Coventry CID seemed to descend on the house, many of them friends of ours. I remember Pauline walking me round the back garden. I was just pacing about, gibbering nonsense. I was completely in shock.

"We had a good friend, big Keith Edgar, who had been in the police, and came round the moment he heard the news. He was about 6 foot 5, and when he came out to see me in the garden, I grabbed him by his tie and dragged him down to face to face level with me, then shouted: 'Why Jim? Why not some of the bastards that you deal with – the rapists and scum that you lock up? Why mine?' These were questions that would never get a logical answer. He just hugged me and said 'I can't answer that pal. I'm so sorry'.

"The day and night all seemed to merge into one. I sat up all night, completely awake, trying to take it all in. The next morning the paperboy arrived, then the milkman arrived, and I remember thinking to myself how strange it was that life goes on. They are just turning up to deliver the paper, deliver the milk, and they don't know that I'm inside feeling that my life has come to an end."

Numb with shock, Jan somehow found the strength to piece together the circumstances surrounding Jim's sudden death.

"When he went out for a run he always used to take the car, because his favourite spot to go running was the local airfield at Baginton. It was only a little airport, where light planes used to land, and like he had done umpteen times before, he had taken the car, parked up, and gone for his run.

"To get from Baginton back to the house, he used drive through Mill Hill, and it was halfway down that road where it happened. The coroner's officer explained to me that he would have either felt light-headed or he would have started to have palpitations. He stopped the car, put his hazards on, but then almost immediately collapsed onto the wheel. Coincidentally, right behind him was one of our pub regulars who was also a first aider. This lad knew that there was something badly wrong immediately. He stopped his car, dragged Jim out onto the road and started CPR, but Jim was already gone. The coroner's officer told me that he'd have been dead before his head hit the wheel.

"They had to do two post mortems, because when they performed the first one they thought they would discover evidence of massive heart damage. When they didn't, they asked my permission to do a more in-depth post mortem. I was in complete agreement, because I needed to know what had caused his death. I needed to know why he'd died at 42. I don't think I could have ever have lived with not knowing. When they came back to me, they explained it had been ischaemic heart disease and coronary atheroma, which they said could have taken him at any time. He could have been 6, 16 or 60 when it struck."

Ischaemic heart disease is now more commonly known as coronary heart disease (CHD), and occurs when coronary arteries become narrowed by the gradual build-up within their walls, affecting the supply of oxygen-rich blood to the heart muscle. Jan has been told by experts that Jim's underlying problem could, in all probability, be traced back to his childhood diet. Coronary atheroma is the name for the fatty deposits on the walls of the arteries around the heart.

While lifestyle is so often a contributory factor to CHD, the reasons behind Jim's heart attack are much for more of a mystery. He didn't smoke, drank in moderation, ate healthily and kept himself fit. He also had the benefit of years of conditioning as professional athlete.

Jan continues: "I asked why the heart problems hadn't been picked up in any of the football club medicals that he had undergone during his career. However, it was basically a hidden problem. It wouldn't have been something that showed up, unless you were specifically looking for it. Medical staff at the football clubs would just been concentrating on anything to do with his sporting side; they wouldn't have thought to check for ischaemic heart disease."

Laurie Brown, Holton's physio at Manchester United, confirms that medical checks were fairly rudimentary in the Seventies, particularly in the lower divisions. While ligaments, muscles and bones were checked as a matter of course, the medical examinations did not have the depth – or technology available – to detect deeper-rooted problems.

"Jim's death was a complete shock to everyone," says Brown. "No-one, including Jim, had been aware that there was anything wrong. It's correct to say that medicals back then were nowhere near as rigorous as they are now. The advances that have been made in technology and sports science has obviously played a big part in that. When we signed players back then from other teams, you could phone up and ask the player's medical history, only to be told 'Oh, we don't keep medical histories!' so you didn't know what was what.

"Players weren't always completely honest either. Everybody wanted to come and play for Manchester United and they wouldn't say anything that might jeopardise that happening. For example, if you knew of a player who had had a little bit of trouble with their ankle in the past, you would be sure to X-ray it. When you asked them about the ankle, they would insist it was all right, but you could sometimes see the sweat pouring off a player while they waited for the results for their X-rays coming back, because they didn't want anything to get in the way of moving to Manchester United. Jim obviously had his injury problems while he was at United, particularly the two leg breaks, but he always appeared fit, healthy and incredibly strong."

The Holtons' family doctor was also dumbfounded by the sudden death. He hurried round to the house within hours of Jim's death, absolutely distraught, and Jan had great sympathy for him. "The GP came to me with Jim's records in his pocket, saying 'I had no idea. There had been no clues. No indication.' Jim had never once complained about his heart or brought it to the doctor's attention. The biggest problem he had raised was breathing problems, but the doctor – bless him – had put it down to the fact that Jim had hay fever and he thought that the breathing problems were possibly down to a sign that Jim was becoming asthmatic. I didn't blame the doctor in the slightest, it wasn't his fault, and I told him that. How could he have known? The GP had taken the death really badly, and was agonising over whether he might have missed something. It was so hard on him and I really felt for him. The GP actually said Jim was the last person he thought it could happen to, because he appeared such a fit and strong man, and rarely even had cause to go and go and see a doctor.

"The doctor must have been asking himself 'Why didn't I pick up on this, why didn't I do this, why didn't I do that, why didn't we run these tests?' But it's easy after the event and you can't go around blaming yourself. You can go around forever saying 'What if?' But what's the point? It doesn't resolve anything. The fact of the matter was that Jim had died at 42; and the only crumb of comfort for me was that he had died very quickly. He would have felt no pain. That was the one thing that I insisted that the coroner's officer told me because I would never have been able to live with the idea that he had died on his own and in pain. The coroner's officer told me all the evidence showed that it would have been very, very quick. It would literally have been like flicking off a light switch."

Helped by friends and her sister, Jan also had the incredibly difficult task of letting people know about the tragedy. Jim's oldest pal, John Hillan, will never forget the moment he heard the news.

"I had been off work for a week and it was my first day back on the Monday when I heard. A guy that worked beside me had a brother in Coventry who ran a pub, just as Jim did. The week before he told me he was going down to see his brother, so I phoned Jim to fix up a couple of seats for him to go along and watch Coventry City. He had gone into Jim's pub, had a couple of beers with him, got the tickets and enjoyed the match. That was the Saturday, and on the Monday when I saw him at work I asked 'everything alright with the tickets?' He said 'Aye, the big man looked as fit as fiddle, he looks like he could still be playing!' About two hours later I got a phone call and it was Jan telling me that Jim had gone. They sent me home, I was in shock. As I came out the office I saw my work-mate, and I said 'That big guy you said who looked fit enough to still be playing... he's away. He's dead'.

"It was strange that he had died in a car, the same as his dad. It was one of these odd coincidences. I just couldn't understand it, it didn't seem real. Jim kept himself so fit. He didn't smoke and didn't really bother too much with the beer. He had just been away having his regular run, like he had done hundreds of times before. He would go to the bottom of this hill, like a ski slope, and run up to the old airport at Baginton. He got in the motor after his run

*The legend 'Jim Holton' and MUFC adorn a bridge
on the Leeds/Liverpool canal to this day.*

and, just like that, he was gone."

News of Jim's death shocked the close-knit community of Coventry. Not only had Holton been a hugely popular figure wearing the sky blue of the city's football team, he had added further to his reputation as a local celebrity by showing a great work ethic and good nature behind the bar of his pubs. He may have been raised in Scotland and made his name at Manchester United, but the city of Coventry had truly accepted him as one of their own. Jan was overwhelmed by the response and love shown towards her late husband. "It just became a whirl, trying to organise his funeral, which was something else," says Jan. "There were just so many messages, cards and flowers. I had to order an extra hearse simply for flowers. He was taken into St Thomas More Church on the Sunday and he lay there overnight before the funeral. The church was full that night as people went to pay their respects. That church holds 800 people and it was full. At the funeral itself, it was standing room only at the crematorium. There wasn't enough room to get everybody in so they had to put speakers outside. I have vivid memories of coming out of the car from St Thomas More to the crematorium, and looking back down the A45. All I could see was a massive line of cars, as far as the eye could see, behind the funeral cortège.

"I couldn't get over the number of people that were there. Then we had the wake at a social club that he'd regularly been a patron of and they told us afterwards that mourners had drank the place dry. Jim would have approved! My sister Pauline and I only stayed at the wake for about an hour. What was so ironic was that Colin, our bar manager and his wife Louise, had their second child on the day of Jim's funeral. Pauline and I immediately went to see the baby. One in one out, as they say."

Many team-mates, managers, supporters and friends were among the 1,000-strong attendance at the funeral - Tommy Docherty, Joe Jordan, Mick Martin, Gordon McQueen and Ian Wallace to name but a few. To lose somebody so well respected so suddenly led to a lot of introspection and soul-searching, and nobody could quiet believe that a man of the stature of Jim Holton had been taken at the age of 42.

"I was shattered when I heard about it," says Mick Martin. "I was up at Glasgow Celtic when I heard about it. Me and my wife went to his funeral. I couldn't have missed it for anything in the world."

Joe Jordan says: "It's not nice when you look at the photographs of Scotland's World Cup side in 1974 and there's a few of them gone; Sandy Jardine, Eric Schaedler, wee Billy (Bremner), Jimmy Johnstone and big Jim. When you're a sportsman, you don't really think about anyone dying. You think you're a wee bit immortal, things will just go on and on, but unfortunately they don't. You're just as normal as everyone else. You look at the percentage of people gone from that squad and a lot of them are no longer with us. It does make you stop and think and make you enormously grateful for the memories and times that you shared together. Jim was a great character in the dressing room, and he was loved by the Scotland punters. I was there alongside him - you could hear it and you could feel it — they loved his presence in a Scottish jersey. When he did pass away it was such a sad day and such a big loss, it was a blow to us all. It emerged that it had been a heart problem. It could have happened at any time."

Martin Buchan agrees: "I was abroad when we heard that he'd

passed away. Jim Blyth told me. Apparently he had a heart defect that had gone unnoticed and he could have quite have easily died at 21, never mind 42, so I'm just grateful for the time I had with him."

Goalkeeper Jimmy Rimmer, Holton's good friend from his early days at Manchester United, was among those left in disbelief. Rimmer himself suffered a heart attack later in life, in 2006, when he was a coach in Canada, and knows how fine the line can be between life and death in such circumstances. "I had just come off the football field. I was off to the bank to meet the woman who cleaned my house, who just happened to be an ex-nurse, and if she hadn't been there I would have been dead, there's no two ways about that," Rimmer explains. "I had a heart attack and they only gave me two days to live. That was 12 years ago, and I count myself incredibly lucky. What happened to Jim was tragic. I couldn't believe it, but sometimes you never know what is inside of you. If you saw how he trained, played and looked after his body – never smoked, rarely drank – you would just never believe it could have happened to an athlete like Jim Holton. We all miss him."

News also quickly travelled across the Atlantic, where Holton's former Miami Toros goalkeeper Bill Nuttall was devastated to hear of his passing. "I was the General Manager for the US World Cup team in 1994 and we had several American players playing in Europe. Roy Wegerle was playing for Coventry and John Harkes was at Derby County, so I planned to look up Jim while I was over. I asked an English football reporter to get a hold of him and tell him I was coming. But a week before I was supposed to arrive in England, the reporter called me to say big Jim had died of a heart attack. No way, I thought. He was fit as a fiddle and I couldn't believe he'd gone."

Several newspapers carried obituaries of Holton the day after the funeral. The tribute to Jim printed in the *Independent*, said: "Traditionally, Manchester United's footballing idols tend towards the glamorous and spectacular; where once Best, Law and Charlton captivated audiences at the Old Trafford 'Theatre of Dreams' now Cantona and Giggs hold centre stage. But in between, during a period when the Red Devils' fortunes were at a low ebb, Jim Holton emerged as a cult hero with a difference."

Holton's playing days at Manchester United, which in turn led to his international caps, made him a well-known figure in British football, and for Ian Wallace – who would become his team-mate at Coventry – it meant playing alongside on of his teenage heroes. "I was five years younger than Jim and we used so sing the 6 foot 2 eyes of blue song, which Man U made up for him, at the Scotland games. To hear that as a young boy used to make you shiver to your boots! When he joined us at Coventry I was delighted. When I thought of some of the great players he had played alongside, it as a thrill to be in the same team as him. He brought that reputation with him and the Coventry fans loved him. I think it was just the stature of the man.

"Then, to find out, he had been taken from us so suddenly was hard for everyone to take. He always kept himself fit, he was always conscious of his weight. It was such a blow, because you think that because you play football and you're fit that you'll live longer than anybody else, but that's not the case. It was a massive shock to the system. Our goalkeeper Les Sealey was another one who died suddenly as a young man. It makes you sit down and think how lucky you are even to kick a ball, never mind anything else. I just couldn't believe it. I thought 'No, it can't be. Why?' Especially for it to happen after he had been out jogging and keeping himself fit. It is a true saying that only the good die young because big Jim was a big gentleman, he definitely was."

Wallace is an active member of the Coventry City Former Players Association, alongside players like Andy Blair, Jim Blyth, Gary Gillespie, Tommy Hutchison, Barry Powell, Garry Thompson and Terry Yorath. At any gatherings, former team-mates who are no longer with us are fondly remembered: Holton and Les Sealey, now sadly joined by the great Cyrille Regis, who made a huge impact at the club after Jim had hung up his boots.

Gillespie, who had moved to Celtic to work alongside Mick Martin at the time of Jim's death, recalls: "I was gutted when I heard. I found it unbelievable because he was such a fit fella. Sometimes, especially when you go into the pub game, you can let yourself go and put loads of weight on, maybe lose control a little bit. But Jim was never like that, he was as fit as a fiddle, he never looked any different from the day that he packed in playing. It was just a major surprise and a shock to us all. The good die young don't they?"

Fans and friends will occasionally call by to pay their respects at Jim's final resting place in Canley Garden Cemetery, Coventry. The well-tended marble headstone reads: James Holton (Big Jim) 1951–1993. Always loved, never forgotten.

In the years immediately after Jim's death, an annual golf day and auction was staged in Coventry in Holton's memory, with proceeds donated to the British Heart Foundation. There have also been many events in Manchester over the years in Holton's honour, while a placard displayed on a wall underneath the Stretford End stand at Old Trafford recognises his memorable contribution in a United shirt.

In Scotland, Holton remains a folk hero, and in 2014, Clydesdale Sports Council admitted him posthumously to their Hall of Fame, with his nephew David Coats accepting the award on the family's behalf. David – the son of Jim's sister Annie – grew up in Lesmahagow and still lives in Lanarkshire. "I can remember going down to Manchester and Coventry for my holidays. We would stay with Jan and Jim and, when I was wee, he would take me to go and see him play at Old Trafford," says David. "He was brilliant as an uncle and a person – just a lovely person with a great sense of fun, and a great role model. I always looked up to him. Everyone in The Gow (Lesmahagow) saw him as a hero and I was so proud to be his nephew."

As for Jan, Neal and Sally, they had to set about rebuilding their lives, which wasn't easy.

"After the funeral, the reality sinks in and it was incredibly tough for us all," says Jan. "I kept asking myself why… why did this happen? It took me about 12 months to get my head around why, why mine and not somebody else? I was very bitter and twisted for a long time. But my sister got me out of that. It took me a while to accept it, but I did eventually."

Jan decided that she was in need of a fresh start and her sister Pauline encouraged her to go and live close to her in Plymouth. The pace of Devon life suited her, and soon her and the kids had put down new roots and settled in the area. Jan worked as a PA for 12 years and has been in her current job as a senior administrator for six years.

"With regards to the effect it had on Neal and Sally they both reacted in totally different ways," Jan explains. "Neal didn't go back to university for two years after we lost Jim as he believed that as he was now the man of the house I would need him to be available. It took me almost the whole of that time to eventually convince him that I would be fine and that he could go back to continue his course. He went back but dropped out after the first year. He then took another year out when he went travelling and returned to start a Computer Studies degree but, again, he dropped out. He has since deeply regretted not graduating but obtained his current IT skills via an alternative route and he is now a highly qualified technician working with a globally renowned company.

"Sally, on the other hand, as you can imagine took Jim's death very badly and rebelled against everyone and everything over the course of the next few years which culminated in her becoming a single parent at 18 years old. However, during the course of quite a difficult pregnancy she and I became very close and have remained so ever since sharing the raising of Jay between us.

"I often say that Jay is in this world today in order to compensate for us losing Jim who I know would have been very proud of his grandson. Jim would also have been very proud of his daughter who has worked her way up from being a Teaching Assistant to become an Assistant Head of Year and someone who has a very close rapport with pupils of all ages at her school."

There isn't a day that goes by where Jan doesn't miss Jim. He left a hole in her life, which has been part-filled by the arrival of her grand-children – first Sally's son Jay, and now Neal's baby boy Harrison who has James (to give Jim his Sunday name) as one of his middle names.

He's also got genuine eyes of blue!

APPENDIX - CAREER STATISTICS

Season	Club	L	FA Cup	L Cup	Other	Total
1968-71	West Bromwich Albion	-	-	-	-	-
1971-72	Shrewsbury Town	44 (3)	3	2	-	49 (3)
1972-73	Shrewsbury Town	23 (1)	3	1	-	27 (1)
1972-73	Manchester United	15 (3)	0	0	4 (1)*	19 (4)
1973-74	Manchester United	34 (2)	2	1	-	37 (2)
1974-75	Manchester United	14	0	3	0	17
1975-76	Miami Toros	16 (1)		-	-	-16 (1)
1976-77	Sunderland	15	2	2	-	19
1976-77	Coventry City	8	-	-	-	8
1977-78	Coventry City	25	-	3 (1)	-	28 (1)
1978-79	Coventry City	34	2	1	-	37
1979-80	Coventry City	24	-	3	-	27
1980-81	Detroit Express	21 (3)	-	-	-	21 (3)
1981-82	Sheffield Wednesday	0	0	0	0	0
TOTAL						305 (15)

*Anglo Italian Cup

INTERNATIONAL CAREER

(HI= Home Internationals; WCQ= World Cup qualifying; WC =World Cup finals; F = Friendly)

Year		HI	WCQ	WC	F	Total
1973	SCOTLAND	3	1 (1)	-	3 (1)	7 (2)
1974	SCOTLAND	3	-	3	2	8
	TOTAL	6	1 (1)	3	5 (1)	15 (2)

INDEX